The Best on Quality, Vol. 10

Also available from ASQ Quality Press

The Best on Quality, Volume 5
International Academy for Quality,
John D. Hromi, editor

The Best on Quality, Volume 6
International Academy for Quality,
John D. Hromi, editor

The Best on Quality, Volume 7
International Academy for Quality,
John D. Hromi, editor

The Best on Quality, Volume 8
International Academy for Quality,
John D. Hromi, editor

The Best on Quality, Volume 9
International Academy for Quality,
Madhav N. Sinha, editor

To request a complimentary catalog of ASQ publications, call 800-248-1946.

THE BEST ON QUALITY

Edited by Madhav N. Sinha

Book Series of
International Academy for Quality

Vol. 10

ASQ Quality Press
Milwaukee, Wisconsin

The Best on Quality, Volume 10
Madhav N. Sinha, editor

Library of Congress Cataloging-in-Publication Data

The best on quality : targets, improvements, systems / edited by Madhav
   N. Sinha.
      p.   cm.
      "Book series of International Academy for Quality vol. 10."
      Includes bibliographical references and index.
      ISBN 0-87389-456-1 (alk. paper)
      1. Quality control. 2. Total quality management. 3. ISO 9000
Series Standards.   I. Sinha, Madhav N.
TS156.B468 1999
658.5'62—dc21   99-18242
                                                              CIP

10 9 8 7 6 5 4 3 2 1

ISBN 0-87389-456-1

Acquisitions Editor: Ken Zielske
Project Editor: Annemieke Koudstaal
Production Coordinator: Shawn Dohogne

ASQ Mission: The American Society for Quality advances individual and organizational
performance excellence worldwide by providing opportunities for learning, quality
improvement, and knowledge exchange.

Attention: Bookstores, Wholesalers, Schools and Corporations:
ASQ Quality Press books, audiotapes, videotapes, and software are available at quantity
discounts with bulk purchases for business, educational, or instructional use. For information,
please contact ASQ Quality Press at 800-248-1946, or write to ASQ Quality Press, P.O. Box 3005,
Milwaukee, WI 53201-3005

To place orders or to request a free copy of the ASQ Quality Press Publications Catalog, including
ASQ membership information, call 800-248-1946. Visit our web site at http://www.asq.org.

 Printed on acid-free paper

American Society for Quality

ASQ™

Quality Press
611 East Wisconsin Avenue
Milwaukee, Wisconsin 53202
Call toll free 800-248-1946
http://www.asq.org
http://standardsgroup.asq.org

Contents

SECTION I: Exploring Models and Systems of Total Quality

Chapter 1: The Development of a Generic Quality Management System

Chapter 2: Quality Systems in Higher Educational Institutions

Chapter 3: A TQM Model for Value-Based Customer-Supplier Relationships

Chapter 4: Integration: The Key Word for Quality-Based Organizational Transformations

Chapter 5: Quality Certification Scheme for Integrated Safety Management Systems in Shipping Industries

Chapter 6: Insights on Quality Process from the Perspective of Sociology

Preface

Only the International Academy for Quality (IAQ) has under its umbrella an unmatched class of quality professionals, authoritative writers, world-renowned quality leaders, much sought-after consultants, and respected speakers who can share their expertise and experiences together through the medium of an unmatched calibre of a book series like *The Best on Quality*.

For over 30 years, the IAQ has been a leader in developing, disseminating, and transferring quality knowledge and maintaining an international communication link between the leading quality professionals around the world. Its shared values include the best use of world resources, development of a spirit of mutual comprehension and cooperation at both the national and international levels, and promoting research into the philosophy, theory, and practice of all activities involved in achieving quality of both products and services.

Presented to you is the tenth volume of the series. Volume 10 is once again a compendium of new thoughts put together as stand-alone chapters. Each author has defined his and her own subject area in as different and compelling styles as their own record of success (see the "About the Contributors" section). Some chapters are concerned with new ideas or conclusions that have not been recognized before. Others involve rethinking the old ones in a brand new relationship. Still others require unlearning and ask us to go back to basics. It is this kind of quest for the right answers in the field of quality management that the members of the Academy have been searching in every volume. An index of all articles published so far in the book series appears at the end of the book.

This volume has four sections and 22 chapters.

- Section I, titled, "Exploring Models and Systems of Total Quality," has seven chapters. The chapters in this section address one of the most powerful but difficult activities in the field of quality: namely, the development of workable models and the designing of systems. These are years of change. The dynamics of change and their impact on competition are working their way into every sector of our economy. We see this happening in all sectors, from manufacturing to service industries, computers, to public sector government organizations. The mechanics of addressing the change through generating correct workable models and systems of total quality are putting a high premium on all kinds of organizations. If there is a lack of focus on "how do we manage quality" or "how robust our system of total quality is," then that certainly reflects a poor foundation of the organization's quality capacity. The chapters in this section highlight the significant importance of building a strong quality foundation through proper linkages in models and systems of total quality for committing the whole organization to a common goal.

- Section II has five chapters. Getting the quality systems ready and having designed a correct model usually sets the stage to begin to select the proper tools, techniques, and application methodologies. The chapters in this section on "Tools, Techniques, Technology, and TQM" emphasise the power of such management tools and statistical techniques and provide a mechanism for aligning these and making their integration possible across all functions and disciplines in the organization to achieve flawless quality.

- Section III has three chapters. The authors have undertaken a critical examination of the most popular and widely used series of quality standards; that is, the ISO 9000 standards. Their thought-provoking analyses give essence of many of its central aspects of success, and show the ways in which a more powerful quality leadership can emerge through better understanding of the roles of ISO 9000 standards.

- Section IV, entitled "Quality's Worldwide Trends and Projections," has seven chapters. These chapters further explore how companies and organizations both in public and private sectors around the world are succeeding by identifying quality leadership criteria and using various tools and techniques in their own distinctive styles step-by-step: in Denmark, Europe, India, Japan, the Asia Pacific region, and in developing countries in the Asian subcontinent.

The editor invites you to open up to the new ideas. Take the best from each and apply what you have learned. This is your, our readers, challenge. We have been doing our best to provide you with the latest thinking from many of the world's best minds. If we have successfully done that, then our purpose has been served. Happy reading!

Madhav N. Sinha
Academician, IAQ
Editor, *The Best on Quality*

About the Editor

Madhav N. Sinha, Ph.D, P. Eng, is a well-recognized educator, practitioner, and author in the field of total quality management. In a career of professional engineering spanning over three decades, Dr. Sinha has pursued varied assignments as research scientist, quality manager, university professor, and government administrator. A long-time quality activist in Canada, he is an elected Fellow of ASQ, a Certified Quality Auditor, and has received more than a dozen awards and honors, including ASQ's E. L. Grant Award, a Testimonial Award, and its Inspection Division's Regional Councilor of the Year Award.

Acknowledgments

To each Academician and coauthor who has contributed to this volume, the editor can only say, *Thank you.* I know how busy everyone is and I can, therefore, only appreciate everyone's time and continued dedication.

I would like to thank Academicians who submitted articles that were not included in this volume. These will be valuable additions to the future volumes in the series. Academician Ken Stephens of the Southern Polytechnic State University, Marietta, Georgia, provided valuable help in tracking down and communicating with potential contributors of this volume. He is very good in electronic means of communication. I thank him for his help and look forward to working with him on future volumes. Academician Ken Case of Oklahoma State University, the Academy's editor of the IAQ newsletter, *Contact,* always informed all colleagues about the progress and updates on the book series.

My research associates never refused and said they were busy doing something else whenever I approached them for their assistance in finding a research article in a journal or to verify a fact or two from the library. Roger Holloway, Manager of ASQ Quality Press, earned special appreciation. He has been very friendly and courteous in answering all of my questions so timely that very few can match. My wife, Sharda, once again kept me regularly informed about the papers and manuscripts piled up on my desk at my home office and provided traffic control for all IAQ letters, E-mail, faxes, and most importantly, the deadlines. I sincerely thank everyone.

Madhav N. Sinha
Academician, IAQ

Executive Summaries

Chapter 1: The Development of a Generic Quality Management System

The chapter discusses a methodology for analyzing and developing a company's overall quality framework as an integral part of the company's strategic quality management. A key aspect of the methodology is a generic TQM model consisting of three generic dimensions: the total amount of company's activities, the employees behavior toward quality, and the results of the company's quality efforts. It outlines and discusses the contents of the three generic dimensions and the tools necessary for analyzing and developing the three generic dimensions.

Chapter 2: Quality Systems in Higher Educational Institutions

Similar to businesses striving for excellence, there are nine critical success factors that have been identified in this chapter for higher educational institutions. The highest ranked and indicated critical success factor is *leadership*. The research compiled proves that TQM is suitable for all higher educational institutions, regardless of age, size, and type of control, or whether public or private. A model is developed by the authors to complement the theoretical discussions.

Chapter 3: A TQM Model for Value-Based Customer-Supplier Relationships

Regardless of whether the company is a customer or supplier, the relationship issue must be addressed for competitiveness in the future. A new tool is described in this chapter to provide a comprehensive perspective and dialogue toward continuous improvement strategy throughout the customer–supplier chain.

Chapter 4: Integration: The Key Word for Quality-Based Organizational Transformation

By Tito Conti 55

Quality is no longer a product or service's expected attribute, but an attribute of the organization itself reflected in its *system*. Success in quality requires that quality "disappears" as a separate entity in the organization and becomes absorbed and metabolized by the already accepted management and organization concepts. The dichotomy between quality objectives and business objectives must disappear. This is possible only when quality is *integrated* into every aspect of business substantives.

Chapter 5: Quality Certification Scheme for Integrated Safety Management Systems in Shipping Industries

By Alain-Michel Chauvel 71

A mere possession of a uniform set of statutory certificates for shipping industries is no longer sufficient. Companies have to comply with new mandatory international requirements, culminating in certification of provisions for safety on board ships and prevention of pollution risks. The author of this chapter outlines the key items of new requirements and offers a new view of certification in order to help simplify the shipping industry's integrated quality systems.

Chapter 6: Insights on Quality Process from the Perspective of Sociology

By Timothy E. Weddle and William A. Golomski 85

The assumption in global companies usually is that one approach to quality equally applies at all corporate locations and with all customers. If it did, then one set of rules and methods would have universal applicability. Why not use the Malcolm Baldrige National Quality Award criteria, or the ISO 9000 series, or QS 9000? The authors offer unique insights from the field of sociology to explain the variation of successful practice in different settings.

Chapter 7: TQM as Winning Strategy in Public Sectors

By Madhav N. Sinha and Geoffrey H. Bawden 113

Never before in history has TQM been so challenged, and never before in history has TQM been found to be so critical in achieving organizational successes in its utilization as in today's biggest service business; namely, in the public sector (government) organizations. While TQM is not a simple substitute for the old bureaucratic model, managers of public sector organizations are indeed achieving tremendous successes. The authors analyze the critical success factors for maturity in TQM and build a powerful argument to find the right kind of leadership based on the "fusion" of old and new models for public sector management.

Chapter 8: Transferring Quality Using Technology

An organization's ability to apply its knowledge is a well-known competitive advantage. Only those organizations that can flawlessly execute its routine operations while also building its competitive knowledge will reap the benefits of sustained success. One lesson business has learned over the past decades, however, is that technology alone is not the panacea for growth or productivity. Recently, the ASQ Future Team sought to identify the potential influences from the eminent convergence of information, telecommunications, and data management technologies to determine its impact on quality profession. This chapter provides a summary of the futuristic investigations of the quality profession.

Chapter 9: A Quality Management Assessment Grid

A TQM implementation *grid* containing seven different characteristics of TQM adoption is discussed in this chapter, with its application in four different organizations. It is concluded that its use can help the decision makers to understand what exists now, what is going well, and what is not going well, and pinpoint the root causes of problems to help decide what needs to be done to improve to achieve the goal.

Chapter 10: New Quality Cost Model Used as a Management Tool

This chapter presents a new poor-quality cost model that is based on customer focus and process control ideas. The input to the model is customer requirements and the output is expected poor-quality costs estimated through the Taguchi loss function. Quality function deployment (QFD) is used to translate the voice of the customer to key process parameters; that is, the process parameters having a direct influence on the fulfillment of customer requirements. The intended use of the model is explained as a top management decision-making tool that is able to link quality improvement to customer satisfaction and loyalty.

Chapter 11: Statistical Tools and Techniques: Development of a Framework for Quality Improvement Strategies

The importance of statistical methodologies to quality improvement is well known. However, the development of knowledge for a more comprehensive approach from strategic perspectives in the uses and applications of these methodologies is lacking. This chapter aims to bring about an appreciation of various practical approaches at both the organizational level and personal level. The potential and limitations of some of the most popular procedures are highlighted and their respective roles in quality improvement initiatives discussed.

Chapter 12: Tools and Techniques: An Examination of Their Use

A methodology based on a *recognition and use grid* and an *application grid* is used in this chapter for assessing the utilization of tools and techniques in an organization. Three separate case studies are described to demonstrate the applicability of the tool in a wide variety of situations. Reasons are explored with suggested actions for improvement.

Chapter 13: ISO 9000 and Total Quality

With all the hype going on these days concerning ISO 9000, the author of this chapter goes through a deep soul-searching on quality assurance fundamentals and asserts that the national and international communities of quality professionals have a serious responsibility to see that the ISO 9000 series is "properly used" and "rightfully promoted" to create the correct and beneficial awareness for real improvement of quality in its broadest terms.

Chapter 14: Effective Use of ISO 9000 in Quality Management

The system for certifying supplier's quality systems to ISO 9000 is halfway from both the purchaser and supplier standpoint to achieve total quality.

However, this very incompleteness allows the purchaser and supplier flexibility in the way they use the system. The author discusses the manner in which to utilize ISO 9000 and certification systems for realizing the maximum benefits.

Chapter 15: Quality Systems: The Evolution from ISO 9000 to TQM

World-class companies today are in a "post-ISO" era in search of business excellence to meet the challenges of market globalization. Only the *total integration* of quality system elements into business management will bring the breakthrough that is needed. The author asserts that we are on the way from a quality management system to a total quality-related *integrative management system.*

Chapter 16: Some Experiences of Implementing TQM in Higher Education in Denmark

This chapter discusses the possibilities for improving the quality at educational institutions. The European Model for Business Excellence is used as a framework to show how a successful implementation was achieved at the School of Business in Denmark. Part of the discussion focuses on how to transform the European Foundation for Quality Management model into a tool for teachers' self-assessment of quality in the classroom.

Chapter 17: Managing the Quality of Management Training: An Overview of European Experience

A recently conducted study in the Czech Republic on experiences with quality assessment and assurance of management training (QAMT) has yielded some interesting findings about the situation in different European countries. This chapter describes the most significant results of the investigation and makes proposals for a generalized QAMT model on the level of individual training institutions and on a national level.

Chapter 18: Case Studies of Quality Engineering Applications in India

BY BASANTA K. PAL   319

The author describes different quality engineering concepts and the method developed by Dr. Genichi Taguchi of Japan as applied in Indian industries. A quality engineering journey that began with the application of orthogonal arrays experimentation for speedy and reliable decisions has progressed to discovery of new process/products and is tackling problems of reproducibility, reliability, and cost. All case studies described have proved beyond a doubt the power of these concepts and tools that affect quality improvement and cost reduction.

Chapter 19: TQM in the Twenty-First Century: The Japanese Approach

BY KENZO SASAOKA   345

A new approach to integrating quality management into business management responding to the name change from total quality control (TQC) to total quality management (TQM) in Japan is described in this chapter.

Chapter 20: Quality in Developing Countries

BY LENNART SANDHOLM   353

An increasing number of developing countries are liberalizing their economies and adopting export-oriented policies. These changes are leading to an increased awareness of the importance of quality. While developing countries face many problems en route to industrialization, the author of this chapter discusses how such countries are meeting the challenges of quality and competition in their own extraordinary way.

Chapter 21: Stages of Quality Practice in Developing Countries of the Asia Pacific Region

BY MIFLORA M. GATCHALIAN   367

Based on her more than two decades of quality promotions, training, work, and consulting experiences, the author of this chapter concludes that there are five distinct stages of quality practices identifiable in countries of the Asia Pacific region. She describes each of these stages, and examines the details of respective levels of quality attainment by companies of different size, background, and organizational culture.

Chapter 22: New Roles of a Manager in the Twenty-First Century

By H. James Harrington 379

Management used to be defined by the people who always accomplished tasks through others. For the twenty-first century, management needs to be redefined as people who accomplish tasks through their effective use of processes and enablers. The author of this chapter discusses what the new manager should be like in the twenty-first century.

Exploring Models and Systems of Total Quality

Chapter 1

The Development of a Generic Quality Management System

OVE HARTZ

Introduction

Total quality management (TQM) has become an important part of the overall management function in many industrial companies. This is partly because of the lessons learned in many upwardly mobile companies that the appropriate implementation of quality management results in both increased sales and reduced costs. In general terms, TQM is an accepted means of improving a company's ability to handle increasingly dynamic market conditions.

During the last decade many companies have implemented comprehensive quality management systems. Numerous companies have chosen to base their quality management systems on one of the quality assurance models depicted in the ISO 9000 series standards, namely the ISO 9001/9002/9003. Many companies have also undergone a third-party certification/registration in order to provide confidence in the quality management system's conformance to the requirements in the quality assurance model. In some situations, the company's basic needs are met by its quality management system, which is narrowly based on fulfilling the minimum requirements in one of these standards. In most situations, it is insufficient for a company to have just a minimum quality management system. Often the company's potential competitive advantages are not optimally utilized. There are many reasons why companies have implemented quality management systems that do not suit their specific situation, ranging from lack of knowledge about quality management to moderate understanding of the purpose of the ISO 9000 standards, and to the inadequacy of the ISO 9000 quality assurance models forming the basis for designing an overall quality management framework.

The use of the ISO 9000 quality assurance models varies considerably as an important milestone in the process of developing an overall quality management framework. It is of great importance, however, that the development does not stop by fulfilling the minimum requirements as dictated in one of the ISO 9000 standards. The aim of this chapter is to outline and describe a methodology for analysis and development of generic quality management systems at an optimal level for any specific company. The term *optimal* is used in a broad sense, meaning the most favorable situation for the company when all factors are taken into consideration, both quantitatively and nonquantitatively.

The process toward optimization of a company's overall quality management framework is like pursuing a moving target.[1] The development should be considered as an ongoing process of realigning the company's quality activities and employee behavior toward requirements of its surroundings. Optimization is, therefore, a dynamic process based on continuous improvements.

The development of appropriate quality activities and employee behavior often implies solving interdepartmental problems which present great challenges to many companies. With reference to solving these interdepartmental problems it is important that the development is based on a valid and reliable decision basis. Therefore, focus should be on systematic analysis of the company's existing quality management framework and the use of the results of the analysis as the essential input to the future development. It is also important that the development is focused on achieving a set of well-defined and agreed upon strategic goals with a high degree of involvement from top management.

Much of the existing literature in this area is general in contents and appears to focus on final outcomes rather than on generic processes and means that may be used to realize such goals. The literature does not take the particular characteristics of the specific company into consideration. The methodology for analysis and development of quality management in industrial companies as presented in this chapter focuses on issues that relate to the development of appropriate quality activities and employee behavior with the aim of attaining an optimal design of the overall quality management framework. The results presented in this chapter are part of the current research activities at the Department of Industrial Management and Engineering, Technical University of Denmark.[2] In 1990, the Department won the European Foundation for Quality Management European Award for Best Doctoral Thesis on quality management.[3] The award-winning thesis was based on some of the basic principles outlined in this chapter, which is the result of the ongoing quality management research at the department and includes case study–type research conducted at several industrial companies.

A TQM Model

Analyzing and developing a company's quality management framework is a complex and unique task because of the number of interrelated parameters involved in the consideration. The overall objective of the TQM model presented herein is to provide a suitable structure that can be used for the analysis and development of a company's quality management framework. The model embraces a broad TQM philosophy and is easy to apply, being consistent with its purpose in mind.

Three generic dimensions have been identified in the model to form the main structure.

- The dimension related to quality results

- The dimension related to quality activities

- The dimension related to employee behavior

The *quality results dimension* covers all results that are correlated with the overall quality management effort. Quality-related results are discussed elsewhere in the existing literature.[1,4,5,6] Focusing on quality awards has obviously increased the consideration and the integration of quality results in the companies' quality management framework. The rationale for this has been to provide a measurement of the results of the quality management effort, and thereby provide a basis for putting the overall quality management tasks as first priority. Integrating the quality results in a company's quality management framework, however, counteracts the "religious" doctrine of TQM—putting the blind faith in results.

A fundamental principle in the methodology adopted by the author is the consideration of inadequate results as the basis for the further development of a specific company's quality management framework, including results that do not meet the company's objectives or results that do not ensure the company's future competitive position.

The *quality activities dimension* covers the total amount of activities in a company to determine and implement the quality policy. The dimension embraces the processes, procedures, organization, resources, interrelations of input and output, information need, etc. related to the quality activities. This dimension is the subject of the majority of the basic literature on quality management.[7,8,9] The quality activities dimension represents mainly the formal part of the quality management system.

The *employee behavior dimension* covers terms such as *quality culture*, *quality awareness, motivation for quality*, etc. The positive commitment to quality is emphasized as one of the key aspects of successful TQM.

Much of the literature on this subject tends to focus on "what was done" instead of "why it was done" in order to achieve employee commitment. Only a small amount of literature deals with a systematic structuring of employee behavior toward quality. The generic TQM model and the methodology presented in this chapter intend to outline a way that can assist companies in the structuring of this intangible but vital part of TQM.

A key thesis of the proposed generic TQM model is that the cause of inadequate quality results in a company is found in the quality activities dimension and/or the employee behavior dimension. Thus, a positive development of the company's quality results must be obtained through a development of the quality activities and/or the employees' behavior toward quality goals.

Three Generic Dimensions

For most practical applications of the TQM model some normative paradigms have to be outlined to describe the concepts, parameters, and criteria against which a company can analyze and develop its particular quality management framework. The paradigms can be characterized by incorporating and structuring contemporary thinking through activities on TQM to embrace experiences of both the industry and academia useful for a company-wide implementation of TQM philosophy.

For developing the methodology of analyzing and developing a company's quality management framework, a paradigm has to be outlined for each of the three dimensions in the proposed TQM model. Such a paradigm can be structured in two parts: one covering the structure of the paradigm (that is, containing a set of parameters constituting the paradigm itself), and the other part identifying the reference level (that is, the optimal level) for each parameter.

The Quality Results Dimension

The development of a paradigm for the quality results dimension begins with the identification of parameters which are correlated with the quality management effort, and then with setting of a reference level for those parameters. Literature as mentioned in connection with the presentation of the quality results dimension deals with the first part of the paradigm. In the model for the European Quality Award[4] the following categories are addressed in evaluating the results: customer satisfaction, business results, people satisfaction, and impact on society.

In our methodology, the aspects of people satisfaction are further divided into two areas: as an *enabler* in the paradigm related to employee behavior and as internal customer satisfaction parameter for quality results. The placement of the general employee satisfaction as an enabler reflects the consideration of the general employee satisfaction as means to obtain the results. The parameter based on internal customer satisfaction provides a measure of the quality of internal products/services as a measure of the performance of processes and employees. Therefore, the internal customer satisfaction and external customer satisfaction parameters are included in the paradigm for the quality results dimension.

The quality results dimension has the following structure:

- Customer satisfaction

- Potential customers' perception of the company and its products

- Internal customer satisfaction

- Business results

- Relation to society, environment, and public bodies

For application of methodology, it is necessary successively to decompose each of the above five parameters. Each decomposition represents a stepwise particularization resulting in a set of parameters at a company-specific level. For example, an appropriate decomposition of the main parameter of customer satisfaction results in the following five segments:

- Primary product

- Secondary product (manuals, packaging, etc.)

- Service before sale

- Service after sale

- Contacts to company employees

For the proposed TQM model, the quality results dimension requires a company-specific adaptation of the paradigm. Type of product, market conditions, generic strategy, external system requirements, dependence on suppliers, size, structure, and company culture are all examples of such factors that influence the adaptation of the paradigm. It is a top management task to identify the company-specific structure of the paradigm. The question to be answered by top management is: Which parameters are of strategic importance and how are they correlated with the overall quality management effort?

The above parameters constitute the first part of the paradigm for the quality results dimension. The second part of the paradigm involves identifying a reference level for each of the parameters. The principles of benchmarking[10] are utilized here in identifying a reference level for the parameters' determination.

The Quality Activities Dimension

The identification of a paradigm for quality activities embraces the identification of types of activities to sustain the total quality philosophy along with a description of each of the activities. Various literature describes activities relating to the company's quality management area. Parts of models for quality awards[4,5] can be applied, describing enablers as a normative paradigm. Another possibility is to use a generic guideline as described in the ISO 9004-1.[9] In small and medium-sized enterprises (SMEs), the ISO 9004-1 may be found useful as a description of a part of the quality activities dimension. Quality award models and ISO 9001-4 contain both the identification and description of the quality activities. For a number of medium-sized companies, however, our experience shows that parts of a quality award model (for example, the European Quality Award (EQA) model[4]) can be combined with ISO 9004-1 and then tailored to the specific characteristics of each company.

The Employee Behavior toward Quality Dimension

The purpose of a paradigm for employee behavior is to identify the parameters that influence the employee behavior toward quality and describe these parameters. Literature discussing quality culture and organizational behavior is available that can be applied in outlining a paradigm for this dimension.[7,11,12,13]

Table 1.1 outlines structures relating to the employee behavior for the purpose of analysis and development of the behavior model.

The rationale of the outlined behavior model is that any employee behavior can be explained by the four direct determinants and any sustained development in the employee's attitude, motivation, knowledge, and skills in relation to quality can be achieved by creating a change in the employee's perception of the basic determinants of behavior. Key points of the basic determinants of behavior are mentioned in the fourth column of Table 1.1.

The determinants in the behavior model constitute parameters for the behavior dimension and the objective is for all employees to perceive the parameters and possess the corresponding personal characteristics in a way that would promote a positive behavior toward quality. In our research, each parameter has been described for each quality activity.

A Methodology for Analysis and Development

Based on the behavioral model, a generic TQM methodology is outlined in the following sections for analysis and development of quality management for

Dimension	Direct determinants of behavior (individual level)	Basic determinants of behavior (company level)	Key points in basic determinants		
Behavior		Leadership	Visible management Actions corresponding to proclamations	Inspiring Focus on facts	Coaching the improvement process
	Attitude	Interdepartmental relationship	Interdepartmental cooperation	Perception of overall positive behavior	No sub-optimization
		Procedures related to quality	Understanding of purpose	Connection with quality policy	Documented procedures perceived as an aid
	Motivation	Training	Sufficient and satisfactory		

Behavior				
Knowledge	Reward system	Knowledge of goals	Compliance between performance and reward	Equal to other rewards Continuous feedback on performance
	Resource allocation	Sufficient and satisfactory		
	Organization	Knowledge of responsibility and authority	Knowledge of the connection between individual work and quality	Right information available Accessible managers
Skills	Symbols and stories	Symbols, stories and language not in conflict with quality policy	Marketing and advertising not in conflict with quality policy	
	External relations	Willingness to "listen" to external relations		

Table 1.1. Key points in basic determinants outlined in the behavior model.

application at a strategic level. The methodology is structured in the following five phases:

1. Analysis of the three generic dimensions of TQM

2. Identification of potential developments for the quality results dimension

3. Identification of the need for developing the quality activities dimension and/or the employee behavior dimension

4. Elaboration of a development plan

5. Implementation of the development plan

Each of the five phases are briefly outlined as follows.

Phase 1: Analysis of the Three Generic Dimensions of TQM

The purpose of this phase is to form a picture of the overall quality management framework and the results thereof. The results of the analysis will provide the company with the valid and reliable decision making needed to determine an optimal design of the company's overall quality management systems framework.

The analysis of each generic dimension involves two tasks.

• Analysis at the present level of the parameters in the paradigm

• Determination of the parameters at the reference level

The analysis of the quality results dimension starts with the top management's acceptance and agreement of a normative paradigm. In the section "Analyzing the Three Generic Dimensions" some of the tools are outlined that have been found applicable for analyzing the present level and determining it at the reference level of the parameters.

Each paradigm can be conceptually illustrated in this fashion in a system of coordinates where the two parts in the paradigm constitute the axes. This enables a presentation of the present level of each parameter in the paradigm indexed according to the reference level showing the gap. The lessons learned during the research confirm the importance of conducting this type of analysis based on interdepartmental representation in order to increase the validity and reliability of the results. The results of the analysis must be aggregated stepwise in order to create a clearer picture of the possibility for identification of the most important areas to develop. Intensive analyses of all three paradigms can be said to be significant as a basis for the quality of the development plan.

Phase 2: Identification of Potential Developments for the Quality Results Dimension

The purpose of this phase is to identify a set of potential developments for the quality results dimension in the company. The basis is the result of the analysis of (quality) results and the company's quality policy. Based upon these the top management has to decide on an optimal level of the adapted parameters for the normative paradigm, reflecting the top management's position on the reference level, at the present level, the quality policy level, and for overall vision. As the result of this, the set of potential developments for this dimension are found as being the difference (gap) between the optimal level and the present level.

The identification of potential developments can be conducted by applying the principles of policy deployment[14] to increase the validity and reliability. Finally, the potential developments can be ranked in order of priority. Relevant points to address in this ranking are:

- The expected economic benefit

- The possibility of synergy between the identified developments

- The expected rate of success

- The importance according to the overall policy and strategic developments

Phase 3: Identification of the Need for Developing the Quality Activities Dimension and/or the Employee Behavior Dimension

The purpose of this phase is to identify the specific areas of development relating to the quality activities dimension and the employee behavior dimension to achieve the preceding identified potential developments for the quality results dimension. The task of this phase encompasses identifying the cause-and-effect relations between the potential results and means. This implies an identification of the relations between the parameters in the quality results dimension and parameters in the quality activity and employee behavior dimensions.

The outcome of this phase is the identification of a set of areas that needs to be developed. According to our experience in the case study research, this phase of the methodology provides the company with a very good basis for elaborating a plan for the development of the company's overall quality management framework aimed at an optimal situation.

Phase 4: Elaboration of a Development Plan

The purpose of this phase is to elaborate a plan for the identified areas of development that relate to the quality activities dimension and the employee behavior dimension. The development plan should outline a proposal for developing each of the identified areas and a schedule for the implementation of these. In order to maintain the general view of the plan, structuring the contents under a few pointed themes is recommended. Sources that could be utilized in outlining the solutions are internal know-how, knowledge of quality management literature, lessons learned from other companies, conferences and courses, and consultants' seminars.

Phase 5: Implementation of the Development Plan

This phase completes the implementation of the development plan. It is recommended that the development plan be implemented through a project-by-project approach with an extensive interdepartmental involvement. A project-by-project approach should be utilized in order to ensure that the resources are dedicated to specific assignments and selected areas are developed.

In this phase it is important to focus on obtaining sustaining solutions and not just solutions that would give the company a short-term economic benefit.

Analyzing the Three Generic Dimensions

A set of tools for the analysis of the three generic dimensions in the TQM model is important when applying the methodology, particularly at the phase 1 level. As stressed earlier, the decisions about areas to be developed should be based on quantitative details as much as possible. The issues of identifying parameters and tools to be applied in study projects in industrial companies are discussed in the following sections.

Analyzing Quality Results

The structure of the paradigm for quality results is also used as a structure for a set of tools for analyzing the quality results dimension. Analyzing customer satisfaction is a well-known area. The most applied tools are questionnaires and interviews. The choice between questionnaires and interviews is determined by conditions such as:

- Number of customers or products sold
- Familiarity of the customers, and the extent of contact with these

- Consumer or professional market

- Customer satisfaction, to be measured continuously

In analyzing customer satisfaction it is important to focus on two tasks: (1) identifying the parameters that customers perceive as correlated to overall satisfaction, and (2) the level of the parameters. For the analysis of potential customers' perception of the company and its products and for analysis of internal customer satisfaction the tools to be used are similar to those used to analyze customer satisfaction. Analyzing business results should focus both on analyzing and aggregating exiting data registered in the company and on conducting specific quality-related studies on an ad hoc basis. Additional studies could apply the principles of quality-related costs to measure the performance of a company's quality management framework.[15,16] Other parameters to be analyzed within the scope of business results are:

- Financial results

- Turnover and market share

- Asset turnover and return on investments

- Quality-related measures such as development time, number of design changes, supplier performance, production yields, product reliability, complaints and returns, etc.

The analysis of relation to society, environment, and public bodies should also be based on analyzing and aggregating exiting data registered in the company-specific studies, conducted on an ad hoc basis for the analysis of business results. The analysis should focus on parameters that are related to:

- Internal environment (for example, labor turnover, work conditions, and accidents)

- External environment (for example, consumption of raw material, level of recycling, use of ecological technology, and discharge of toxic chemicals)

- Products (for example, safety, level of recycling, energy consumption, and packaging)

- Local community and public image (for example, number of employees, relation to neighbors, sponsorship, and charity)

- Public bodies (for example, number of remarks and prohibitions from authorities like the FDA, etc.)

Examples of Danish companies that worked on analyzing results of their quality management effort include Danfoss[17] and Rank Xerox, Denmark.[18] Determining the reference level of the quality results dimension can benefit from the principles of benchmarking[10] by identifying superior companies whose quality results may constitute the reference level.

Analyzing Quality Activities

Two issues should be addressed when analyzing a company's quality activities: (1) the existence of specific quality activities, and (2) the effectiveness and efficiency of the quality activities. An analysis of the first issue provides a sound basis for assessing the second issue. Only the first issue will be discussed.

To analyze a company's quality activities it has been useful to structure the overall quality activities according to three primary characteristics:

• Planned quality activities

• Documented quality activities

• Implemented quality activities

For the analysis of quality activities a systematic approach consisting of the following steps can be developed and applied.

1. Obtaining a comprehensive knowledge about generic quality activities

2. Review of the company's quality-related documentation

3. Interviews with heads of functions/persons responsible for quality coordination/key persons in the organization

4. Review of quality assessment/audit reports

5. Performing additional quality assessments/audits

The purpose of step 1 is to ensure that the person responsible for conducting the analysis has the knowledge of generic quality activities as outlined in the paradigm (for example, based on quality award model of ISO 9004-1). The purpose of step 2 is to identify the extent to which the activities described in the paradigm are documented. The analysis can be done by considering each of the activities in the paradigm and by determining to what extent they are covered by the company's documentation. In our case study research, a number of categories have been defined to describe the degree of conformity; for example, high conformity, some conformity, low conformity, and no conformity.

The tasks in steps 3, 4, and 5 are to identify and obtain more detailed information about the extent to which quality activities are planned, but not for quality-related documentation or for the documentation that is not implemented.

The conclusion of the overall analysis of the dimension is thus related to quality activities and the categories where the greatest potentials are present should be emphasized. These are often:

- Quality activities described in the paradigm but neither planned nor implemented in the company

- Quality activities planned but not implemented in the company

- Quality activities described in the company's quality-related documentation but not implemented satisfactorily

In the analysis of a company's quality activities other issues may also be addressed in order to obtain more detailed information about inadequacies of the quality activities. These may include information requirements, responsibility and authority related to the activities, resources allocated to the activities, and the degree of formalization and documentation.

Analyzing Employee Behavior

The primary tools to be used in the analysis of employee behavior are questionnaires or focus groups with employees. The aim of the analysis is to examine the employees' perception of the basic determinants of behavior and to examine the employee's direct determinants of behavior. This provides a basis for the identification of areas to be developed. Thus, the design of written questionnaires or of interview guides should start from the structure of the paradigm for employee behavior.

Conclusion

Quality management has become an important part of the overall management function. It embraces all of the administrative, human, and technical issues. Therefore, in developing a company's quality management framework based on TQM principles, the paradigm has become a complex process which still must be conducted by the company's top management using a systematic approach. A valid and reliable decision base should be established through systematic analyses of the company's overall quality management framework. The ideas of this chapter outline results from research projects and case study research used in several industries in Denmark based on a methodology for analysis and development of quality management principles.

A generic TQM model which contributes to the systematization of analyzing and developing quality management has been developed. The model consists of three generic dimensions. Two dimensions are related to the overall quality management system and employee behavior, and the third dimension is related to the results of the quality effort. A fundamental principle in the methodology presented is the consideration of inadequate results as the basis for further development of a company's quality management framework.

The process of analyzing and developing a company's quality management framework may seem intangible to many companies. But, the structure for analyzing the quality management framework to identify areas as developed in this chapter outlines the complete paradigm and covers the three generic dimensions in the TQM model: quality results, quality activities, and employee behavior.

To carry out systematic analysis and development, a systematic methodology has been put forward. The methodology is in five phases and covers the analysis of the three generic dimensions of quality management, identification of the need for developing the quality management framework, and the elaboration and implementation of appropriate solutions based on continuous improvements.

Acknowledgments

The author would like to thank Jens Holmegaard, Jens Hoegsted and Soeren Nielsen for their assistance and contributions to the quality management research conducted at the Department of Industrial Management and Engineering, Technical University of Denmark.

References

1. Conti, T. 1993. *Building Total Quality*. London: Chapman & Hall.

2. Hartz, O. J. Hoegsted, and S. Nielsen. 1995. *Optimization of Industrial Quality Management Systems*. Department of Industrial Management and Engineering, Technical University of Denmark, Lyngby.

3. Holmegaard, J., 1989. *Analytical Principles and Design Strategies in Industrial Quality Management* (Danish language only). Ph.D. diss., Department of Industrial Management and Engineering, Technical University of Denmark, Lyngby.

4. *The European Quality Award 1998, Application Brochure.* 1997. Brussels: European Foundation for Quality Management.

5. *1998 Criteria for Performance Excellence: Malcolm Baldrige National Quality Award.* 1997. Gaithersburg, MD: U.S. Department of Commerce, National Institute of Standards and Technology.

6. Zairi, M. 1994. *Measuring Performance for Business Results.* London: Chapman & Hall.

7. Feigenbaum, A. V. 1991. *Total Quality Control.* 3d ed. New York: McGraw-Hill.

8. Hartz, O. 1989. *Quality Management Implies Cross-Functional Commitment.* International Academy for Quality, IAQ Book Series, The Best on Quality, vol. 2. Munich: Hanser Publishers.

9. ISO. 1994. *ISO 9004-1, Quality Management and Quality System Elements—Part 1: Guidelines.* 1st ed. Geneva: International Organization for Standardization.

10. Camp, R. C. 1989. *Benchmarking—The Search for Industrial Best Practices that Lead to Superior Performance.* Milwaukee: ASQC Quality Press.

11. Luthans, F. 1995. *Organizational Behavior.* 7th ed. New York: McGraw-Hill.

12. Robbins, S. P. 1991. *Organizational Behavior—Concepts, Controversies, and Applications.* 5th ed. London: Prentice-Hall.

13. Pike, J., and R. Barnes. 1994. *TQM in Action.* London: Chapman & Hall.

14. Akao, Y. 1991. *Hoshin Kanri—Policy Deployment for Successful TQM.* Cambridge, MA: Productivity Press.

15. Dale, B. G., and J. J. Plunkett, 1995. *Quality Costing.* 2d ed. London: Chapman & Hall.

16. Campanella, J. ed. 1990. *Principles of Quality Costs: Principles, Implementation, and Use.* 2d. ed. Milwaukee: ASQC Quality Press.

17. Danfoss. 1993. *Metrics* (In Danish: *Metrikker*). Publ. no. TC.11.P1.01. Danfoss Corporate Quality, Nordborg.

18. Rank Xerox, Denmark. 1995. *Example of Self-Assessment/Winning Application* (In Danish: *Eksempel på selvevaluering/vinderansøgning*). Aarhus: Danish Quality Award Association.

Chapter 2

Quality Systems in Higher Educational Institutions

ABDUL MALEK BIN A. TAMBI

GOPAL K. KANJI

Introduction

Total quality management (TQM) has been adopted by many higher education institutions in many parts of the world, including the United States, the United Kingdom, Australia, and New Zealand. Examples can be obtained from descriptive reports on cases in the United States[1,2] (Fox Valley Technical College, Oregon State University), the United Kingdom[3,4] (Wolverhampton University, Aston University), Australia[5] (University of Central Queensland), and New Zealand[5] (Otago Polytechnique). Because of the good international reputation of higher education in these countries, they attract large numbers of students from the Asian region. While providing quality higher education to foreign students, these countries also reap substantial revenues. For example, Great Britain reported an average revenue of £100 million from Malaysian students alone.[6] Similarly, Australia reported A\$3 billion foreign education market with students from Asia contributing A\$2.5 billion,[7] or 85 percent of the market.

The history of TQM application in U.S. higher education institutions is influenced by its success in the country's industry in the 1980s. During that time, TQM companies such as Texas Instruments, Xerox, IBM, and Motorola were able to improve their business positions by overcoming threats from global competition and other changes in the business environment.[8] These companies were recipients of the coveted Malcolm Baldrige Quality Award (MBA), established by the U.S. Department of Commerce to give recognition to organizations that exhibit high standards of product and service quality. In the field of education, Lozier and Teeter[8] report that U.S. higher education had faced its own crisis during the same decade. The reports by education authorities such as the National Institute of Education and Education Commission of the United States indicate the unfavorable state of U.S. education and consequently the realization of the need for greater involvement in learning. The authorities also acknowledge the complaints received from various sectors of the economy, including business, industry, and the government over the decline in quality of baccalaureate graduates. Other writers, such as Burkhalter,[9] report the continuing public concern for accountability and responsibility on higher education institutions, spiraling tuition, and decline in student performance in standardized and professional licensing examinations. Lozier and Teeter add that signals of a higher education dilemma are received from various facets of the environment within which higher education institutions operate (for example, demographic, technological, economic, legal, and public facets, and competing institutions and accrediting bodies).

Sherr and Lozier[10] say that there are many business management techniques that have made their way into higher education and have failed. According to

Kells,[11] the reasons for failure of new management concepts being applied in higher education are due to unclear goals, complexity of processes and delegation of authority in the university, the variety of ways by which decisions are made, resistance by the faculty, and lack of relevant and timely information. However, Kells and many other quality exponents believe that TQM has a good chance of success in higher education because its principles and concepts are compatible to the education process.[9,10,12-17]

Narasimhan[18] suggested that the first TQM adaptation in U.S. higher education was at Fox Valley Technical College (FVTC). As a result of TQM, FVTC has become more efficient in areas such as placement of graduates, employer satisfaction with contracted training programs, acceptance of college credits at receiving institutions, and improvement in its learning environment. Many other institutions followed suit, including the University of Wisconsin-Madison, the North Dakota University System, Delaware Community College, and Oregon State University.[13] Burkhalter[9] reported that within the United States, there are 160 universities that are involved in applying quality improvement principles, and approximately 50 percent of the universities have established an organizational structure for quality.

In the United States and elsewhere, various TQM models for higher education institutions have been developed for planning, implementing, and measuring the TQM process. These models are derived from a combination of quality methods proposed by various people. An example is the HETQMEX Model developed at DeMonfort University.[19] In this model, Ho and Wearn combined several quality methods, including 5-S by Osada, QCC by Ishikawa, Total Preventive Maintenance by Senju, and TQM. Despite the variations in model designs, however, Hackman and Wageman[20] concluded from their research on contemporary TQM practices that the application models describe the same core concepts. In our research, we have conducted an empirical study on U.S. higher education institutions to determine the TQM factors that influence success of institutions. This knowledge can be used to develop a measuring instrument to measure progress of the TQM process and to develop a holistic TQM model for showing interrelationships among the factors.

The Problem

The purpose of this research is to develop a suitable TQM model for use in higher education institutions by incorporating factors that are crucial for the institutions' success. These factors are called *critical success factors*, a term coined by Daniel.[21] Hofer and Schendel[22] define critical success factors as those variables that management can influence through its decisions, affecting significantly the overall competitive positions of the various firms in the industry. In order to determine the critical success factors for higher education institutions, a survey is carried out to examine how TQM is being implemented in the institutions. Some crucial aspects examined in the survey are the extent of TQM implementation, how resources are utilized, the barriers faced, causal factors and critical success factors, and the relationships between critical success factors and organizational performance.

Initially, Daniel[21] carried out research on critical factors that influence information technology managers.[23] Then, more research on critical success factors were conducted by other researchers in areas such as information systems,[23,24] education,[25] planning,[26] new product development,[27] new service development,[28] flexible manufacturing systems,[29] and advanced manufacturing systems.[30] There are reports of critical success factors in higher education institutions, particularly on information systems. They are represented by applications at Indiana University,[31] the University of Virginia,[32] and the University of Sheffield.[33] Higher education institution TQM models that incorporate critical success factors are given by the Aston University model,[4] and the University of Pareaus in Greece.[34] However, the latter two models are not generic models and do not emphasize TQM principles and concepts.

A Survey of Existing Models

The authors have performed an exhaustive literature survey of TQM models for higher education institutions. The following observations are made on the models surveyed.

- Almost all models surveyed are special-purpose models, such as FVTC and the Oregon State University model.

- All models do not incorporate critical success factors and therefore model measurement is very subjective.

- Most models do not emphasize TQM principles within their structure. However, they are a combination of methods proposed by quality authorities such as Deming, Juran, and Ishikawa (see HETQMEX model by Ho and Wearn[19]).

- Models have not been validated by suitable statistical methods.

From the survey, it was found that only one model seems to satisfy a holistic approach, Kanji's modified pyramid model.[17] The model consists of a prime, four principles, and two core concepts that are attached to each principle, as shown in Figure 2.1. Kanji has shown that his model has an overwhelming similarity to the European Quality Award (EQA) model. The authors believe, however, that the importance given to weightings on the quality element of the EQA model for the purpose of measuring need to be more accurate. For example, the model gives a low weighting of 10 percent on leadership, which the authors believe should be higher because previous research has shown that leadership is the most important factor in driving the organization toward its goals. In addition,

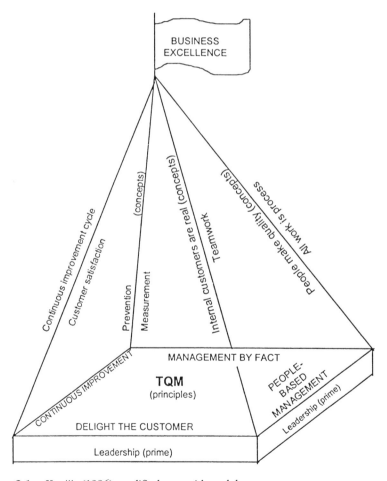

Figure 2.1.   Kanji's (1996) modified pyramid model.

Adapted from: Kanji, G. K. and M. Asher. 1993. *Total Quality Management Process: A Systematic Approach*. Carfax: Abingdon.

the authors believe that a latent structure model among the principles and concepts in the pyramid model can be established.

The authors explore the importance given to the principles and core concepts underlying the pyramid model in higher education institutions. This information can be used to develop a suitable TQM model for higher education institutions that incorporates critical success factors. A survey was conducted of quality directors of higher education institutions in the United States. In this research, the principles and concepts in the pyramid model were conjecturally labeled as the critical success factors on which respondents could give their rankings. They were also allowed to provide an additional factor.

The study also makes use of Kanji's other related work on quality culture. Kanji and Asher[35] refer to quality culture as a unified approach through which everybody in the organization thinks, acts, and feels in a quality sense for most of the time. With respect to culture, Kanji and Yui[36] define TQM as the culture of an organization committed to customer satisfaction through continuous improvement. The authors say that this culture varies from one country to another and between industries, but has certain essential principles which can be implemented to secure greater market share, increased profits, and reduced costs. Kanji and Yui introduced a universal total quality culture model, where the TQM process is described as a never-ending improvement of all people and management systems, as shown in Figure 2.2. In this context, quality culture has been described by the authors in Figure 2.3, which can be easily customized for individual organizations.

The authors continue that the culture can be manipulated by management to influence organizational performance. It can also help managers to believe in profitability through customer satisfaction, provide the employees with the understanding of the value of being close to the customer, and invite both managers and employees to share the challenge of business excellence. This research looks at some cultural aspects of U.S. higher education institutions, such as determining whether quality culture exists in the institutions and that suitable initiatives are taken to make the transformation to quality culture.

The Empirical Study

As described earlier, the problem addressed by this research is to study the extent of TQM practice in U.S. higher education institutions, TQM barriers, the reasons for TQM implementation, and factors that influence its success as well as relationships between TQM and an organization's quality and institutional

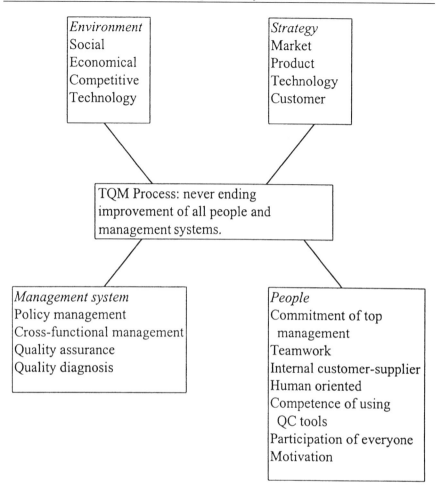

Figure 2.2. A model of quality culture.

performance. The researchers use this information to build a suitable TQM model that incorporates critical success factors for use by higher education institutions. Aspects of the research problem are described in the following sections.

The Extent of TQM Implementation

Descriptions of the TQM implementation process have been given by many prominent quality gurus. Deming is remembered for his P-D-C-A cycle; Juran

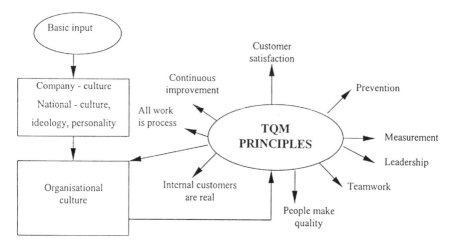

Figure 2.3.   Creating quality culture.

suggested the six steps of problem solving, the use of Pareto principle in quality improvement, and quality council; Crosby introduced the zero-defects performance standards; Ishikawa developed the fishbone diagram, quality control circles, and classified the statistical quality tools; and Feigenbaum introduced the concept of hidden plant and total quality control.[37] Interestingly, Ho and Wearn[19] developed the HETQMEX model to combine methods introduced by various quality proponents. Many other TQM models in higher education institutions have used similar approaches for their TQM processes. The present research involves an empirical study on how TQM is being implemented in U.S. higher education institutions. This covers the following areas: time since the inception of TQM, organizational coverage of TQM implementation, and role of leadership, organization for quality, level of TQM knowledge, provision for training, and types of reward given to staff who contribute to quality.

TQM Barriers

TQM practices do not operate without experiencing implementation barriers.[11,13] The researchers have made a thorough review of the literature to explore the potential barriers faced by TQM practitioners in higher education institutions. A list of these potential barriers to U.S. institutions was prepared to determine the effects of these barriers on the institutions, the level of difficulty they create, and from where they originate. It is postulated that some barriers are more difficult to overcome than others and may originate from internal sources, such as staff and management. An awareness of the existence of these barriers, their sources, and the potential effect on the institution could provide the means by which they could be overcome.

Reasons for Implementing TQM

Every organization has a reason for implementing TQM as a result of situational, environmental, or organizational factors. The authors believe that it is a basic notion that every TQM organization aspires to achieve continuous improvement in terms of products or services at the lowest cost and with everybody's participation. During literature review, the authors found that there are some common reasons that influence TQM process. The authors seek to establish whether this observation occurs among U.S. higher education institutions as well. The strength of the reasons, if any, is also examined in the research.

Critical Success Factors

Critical success factors are the key areas of activity in which favorable results are necessary for the success of an organization. Hofer and Schendel[22] believe that critical success factors vary from industry to industry. However, Rockart[23] found from his survey of several companies that there is a generic set of critical success factors among the companies, although there are some variations. In the present research, the researchers determine the TQM critical success factors for higher education institutions. In many research works, researchers start with a large number of variables that are derived by extracting important aspects of TQM implementations reported in the literature. These variables are grouped into corresponding factors by using factor analysis and narrowed down to several mutually exclusive groups (for example, measurement of critical factors of quality management[38] and measurement of customer's perceptions of service quality[39]). In this research, the authors refer to the pyramid model and use its principles and core concepts as the critical success factors. U.S. higher education institutions are examined in terms of the relative importance of these factors in their TQM process. The researchers also investigate whether there is a presence of other factors not covered by the pyramid model.

Thiagarajan[40] has used a three-point scale in a measuring instrument he developed to categorize critical factors of services and manufacturing organizations into three groups: first-level factors, second-level factors, and third-level factors. Another classification of critical success factors is by using four levels of criticality and three dichotomous attributes. The four levels of criticality in descending order of strengths are: factors linked to success by a known causal mechanism, factors necessary and sufficient for success, factors necessary for success, and factors associated with success. The three sets of dichotomous attributes are: standing/instigating, direct/indirect, and enhancing/inhibiting. In the present research, the researchers developed a ranking scale to indicate the relative importance of the critical success factors. The sense of importance given on the factors may not be reflected by the amount of effort placed on them during TQM implementation. In this research, the contributory effect of differences between critical success factor rankings and institutional involvement on the factors are examined.

Relationship between TQM and Organizational Performance

TQM proponents and practitioners claim that the TQM process influences organizational performance. However, organizational performance is measured in many different ways, such as business excellence in EQA, quality and operational results as well as customer satisfaction in MBA criteria, and other measures developed at higher education institutions such as the performance measure of critical processes at Oregon State University.[2] Other measuring instruments, such as those provided by Saraph et al.[38] and Parasuraman, Berry, and Zeithmal,[39] do not measure the TQM process but are related to quality of service. At present, there does not exist a measuring instrument to measure critical success factors of TQM process. The authors foresee the need to develop a measuring instrument on the TQM critical success factors of higher education institutions derived from empirical study.

Data Collection and Analysis

The study population is represented by 294 quality directors of U.S. institutions listed in the *Quality Progress,* a monthly magazine of the American Society for Quality, September 1997. Institutions in the listing are described as being involved in quality in administration or the curriculum development areas of the institutions. The authors have designed a questionnaire to explore the extent of the institutions' quality involvement, reasons for implementation of a quality management process, implementation barriers, the critical success factors, and the indication of quality performance and organizational performance. The questionnaire contains 49 quality-related questions in 12 pages. Although the questionnaire is quite lengthy, the types of responses sought were mostly single or multiple response. Quality directors of institutions were also required to provide reasons for implementing TQM processes and give their rankings. They were also required to rank the critical success factors.

The questionnaire was pretested by senior staff at Sheffield Hallam University who are involved in quality in administration, research, or teaching. After several reviews, the questionnaire was finalized for distribution. A cover letter was included to explain the purpose of the research, how the respondents were selected, and how they could benefit from the survey. The researchers ascertain that research results are reported in aggregate only and that the anonymity of the respondents is guaranteed. For convenience, a mail questionnaire survey on U.S. higher education institutions was chosen for the research. The survey was sent out on February 2, 1998, giving a total of 72 replies, or 24.5 percent returns. The institutions are divided into public and private institutions to compare their data. The breakdown of public and private institutions was 51 (70.8 percent) and 21 (29.2 percent) respectively.

Before analysis, the data underwent several preanalysis treatments, including error check and data editing. The most common errors were nonresponse, inconsistent responses, and wrong entries. Most nonresponses were ignored for computation. Inconsistent response was corrected based on researchers' best judgment when comparing it with other related responses. Wrong entries, which often occurred in ranking-type questions, were corrected based on question requirement (for example, when a respondent used a larger set of ranking scales than provided by the question).

Nominal-type data were first given numeric codes before they were used for analysis. In the SPSS package, which was chosen to analyze the data, nonresponse was dealt with automatically by keeping it out of computation. Before data collection and during questionnaire design, the researchers postulated what variables and their relationships they wished to examine. Therefore, during the preanalysis stage, variable development was a straightforward step, whereby the variable names were chosen and a variable list was prepared based on the questions in the questionnaire. The types of analysis performed on the data were descriptive analysis and cross tabulation, although correlation for ordinal and interval data was also computed. Preliminary tables and values of variables were generated by computer for subsequent interpretation.

General Findings

The conclusions of the research are divided into five parts:

1. General information of institutions and extent of TQM implementation

2. Reasons for TQM implementation

3. Approaches to critical success factors

4. TQM and institutional performance

5. Implementation of quality control circles

Some General Information on Extent of TQM Implementation

The results of TQM implementation are described as follows.

- About half of U.S. institutions are small in size (less than 5000 full-time enrolled students, or 49.1 percent).

- Higher education institutions in the study population have a mean age of 75.8 years.

- A large proportion (70.9 percent) of U.S. institutions are implementing TQM.

- Most old and new institutions have adopted TQM in the last 10 years (96.5 percent). Thus, the practice of TQM does not depend on the age of the institutions.

- Most institutions (68.4 percent) give great importance to meeting a customer's expectations, similar to business organizations.

- Lack of customer awareness among employees is a general drawback for institutions in order to measure customers' expectations. 11.1 percent of the institutions indicate that they have full customer awareness by all their employees.

- Although there are non-TQM institutions practicing so-called quality management (54.2 percent), our research indicates that they have adopted some TQM processes.

- Many small to medium-sized institutions (73.1 percent) are able to implement TQM for the whole institution due to the fact that it is convenient for them to cover the entire organization.

- The research indicates that the role of leadership is the most important factor to promote TQM in institutions. TQM is introduced by the leadership in about 77.4 percent of the institutions.

- Although a large proportion of institutions has adopted TQM in the academic area of the institution (74.1 percent), there is scope for improvement in order to manage the complexity and the changing nature of the organizations.

- In general, there is a large number of quality councils and teams in U.S. institutions (41.5 percent and 84.9 percent, respectively). However, it is clear that higher education institutions in the United States require quality management consultants and other experts to implement TQM properly (use of consultants—17.0 percent).

- The survey indicates that some of the barriers to TQM implementation (for example, lack of commitment, insufficient knowledge, and fear of failure) originate from organizational members. Sometimes these barriers are more difficult to overcome than other barriers in the institutions.

- Lack of quality culture exists among organizational members in various institutions, which can be developed by engaging quality experts for training and education. The proportion of institutions that have a high level of expertise in TQM is 25.9 percent. However, 63.5 percent of institutions use consultants only occasionally.

- It has been found that quality culture has not yet been widely adopted in most U.S. higher educational institutions (47.2 percent). It is therefore necessary to develop quality culture where leadership can play a more important role.

- For quality motivation, U.S. higher educational institutions tend to provide sociological and psychological rewards to employees (recognition—77.4 percent, organizational support—52.8 percent, and quality award—32.1 percent). Very few institutions provide economic rewards (job promotion—5.7 percent, and bonus—3.8 percent).

Reasons for TQM Implementation

There are 36 causal factors for quality management that can help respondents to improve quality, as shown in Table 2.1. Many of the factors in the list are related and could be combined to give a number of unique causal factors:

1. To be competitive
2. To increase the number of meaningful academic programs
3. To satisfy customer and accreditation requirements
4. To upgrade student performance

1. To be competitive.

2. To develop customer/student satisfaction.

3. To adhere to government influence.

4. To improve staff morale.

5. To build image.

6. To increase efficiency and productivity (includes processes and academic programs).

7. To obtain continuous improvement.

8. To encourage teamwork.

9. To minimize costs.

10. To increase number of meaningful academic programs.

11. To satisfy industry requirements.

12. To upgrade student performance.

13. To increase revenue and ensure self-reliance.

14. To improve financial position.

15. To create value driven employees.

16. To provide high level of service to internal and external customers.

17. To meet future plans.

18. To Improve effectiveness (includes processes).

19. To resolve current problems and overcome weaknesses.

20. To inculcate positive culture (e.g., corporatization and positive work ethics).

21. To manage change.

22. To survive.

23. To improve management.

24. To obtain feedback on actions to guide future decisions.

25. To improve communication.

26. To capitalize on employee talents and innovativeness.

Table 2.1. Reasons for implementing TQM in U.S. higher education institutions.

> 27. To develop and provide opportunities to entire institution's community.
>
> 28. To benchmark against best practice.
>
> 29. To improve work environment.
>
> 30. To improve decision making.
>
> 31. To improve planning.
>
> 32. To satisfy accreditation requirements.
>
> 33. To promote interest of lead faculty and individuals.
>
> 34. To initiate team and individual empowerment.
>
> 35. To improve the organization and its processes.
>
> 36. To improve student recruitment and retention process.

Table 2.1—*Continued.*

5. To increase revenue and self-reliance

6. To improve management

7. To improve communication

8. To capitalize on employee talents and innovativeness

9. To develop and provide opportunities for an entire institution's community

10. To benchmark against best practice

11. To improve decision making

12. To improve planning

13. To initiate team and individual empowerment

14. To improve the organization and its processes

The following conclusions are made about the causal factors for institutions in the United States.

1. The institutions are mature by way of their assessment of unique causal factors which relate to strategic development processes.

2. The presence of many factors that relate to quality improvement in U.S. institutions indicates their commitment toward developing the organization's quality culture.

3. The institutions are concerned about both process and results.

4. The institutions are customer-oriented in their TQM process.

5. The institutions operate at a broad level (long-term strategies).

Approach to Critical Success Factors

• From our survey, we have found that there are nine TQM critical success factors which can be attributed toward U.S. higher education system. Their ranking is given in Table 2.2.

• It has been found in our survey that leadership is the highest ranked TQM critical success factor, which provides strategic management. The weight for leadership based on a scale of 1.0 for least critical to 10.0 for most critical is 9.5. The weight is calculated from rank values given by respondents.

• The survey also indicates that the role of leadership is less demanding during TQM implementation activities. The weight is based on above scale taken during the implementation activities. Its weight of 8.3 during implementation indicates some lack of understanding about importance of leadership in the TQM implementation process.

• A moderate to strong correlation between the importance of critical success factors and the emphasis given to them during TQM implementation has been found (Spearman correlation = 0.8061).

• Most respondents (76.9 percent) believe that the ranking of critical success factors changes over time.

Critical success factor	Ranks
Leadership	1
Continuous improvement	3
Prevention	9
Measurement of resources	8
Process improvement	5
Internal customer satisfaction	4
External customer satisfaction	2
People management	7
Teamwork	6

Table 2.2.   Ranking of critical success factors.

TQM and Institutional Performance

- Most private institutions (81.0 percent) use measures based on financial condition, which depends on customer satisfaction. This is because the survival of private institutions depends on their financial performance. We also believe that business excellence can be achieved through customer satisfaction.

- Performance indicators are widely used in U.S. institutions (69.6 percent). However, the use of performance indicators has been criticized by many researchers as they merely "indicate" level of quality and not the measuring of the actual quality level.

- Most institutions have reported that, overall, they enjoy good to excellent organizational performance (86.1 percent) and quality management (92.9 percent).

- In general, the survey indicates that the TQM institutions outperform non-TQM institutions in organizational performance. The proportion of TQM and non-TQM institutions that have good to excellent organizational performance is 92.3 percent and 78.8 percent, respectively.

- Good performance is associated with good organizational performance for both TQM and non-TQM institutions (Spearman rank correlation = 0.7263).

- There are moderate interests within the institutions to expand TQM to cover wider quality activities (45.6 percent).

Implementation of Quality Control Circles

There are only nine cases of quality control circle (QCC) implementations among the institutions surveyed. However, some interesting findings among the QCC practitioners are discussed as follows:

- There is no evidence to suggest that institutions that implement a QCC program would also practice TQM.

- Examples of reasons for success of individual QCCs are knowledge of quality, persistent support by the department head, commitment, and teamwork. These factors are also part of the TQM philosophy and principles.

- Many QCC programs are still operating after several years of implementation. The proportion of QCC programs that still exist after five years of implementation is 37.5 percent. However, QCCs provide three of the TQM critical success factors: leadership, teamwork, and management by fact.

- Only one U.S. institution has suspended its QCC program citing "lack of commitment" and "change of management" as the reasons for suspension. These factors are not only barriers to QCCs but also to TQM.

- Seventy-eight percent of those who have QCCs (nine institutions) believe that the QCC program has improved performance or has the potential of improving performance.

- Teamwork is the most important factor for success of QCC programs, suggested by seven of the nine institutions. This is also an important concept for TQM.

Conclusion

From our study it is clear that for higher education institutions to achieve business excellence, it is necessary for them to adopt a TQM process. The critical success factors which provide the TQM business excellence can be achieved by developing quality culture using the Kanji[17] TQM pyramid model. According to Kanji,[41] the higher education system has to be guided through the TQM principles and core concepts by top management leadership in order to achieve business excellence (see Figure 2.4).

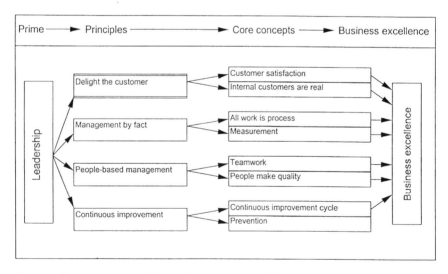

Figure 2.4.   Prime, principles, and core concepts of TQM.

TQM is suitable for all higher education institutions regardless of age, size, and type of control (whether public or private institutions). Higher educational institutions are organizations that strive to meet customers' expectations in all areas of quality or service. To do this, the institutions must identify the presence of various groups of internal and external customers. However, it is found from the survey that most U.S. institutions lack customer awareness. In addition, the institutions also lack knowledge in TQM and provide insufficient quality training to employees. Thus, quality consultants and other experts could be engaged for training, educating, and development of quality culture. TQM consists of principles and concepts that can influence quality culture. The quality culture can be developed by adopting the universal total quality culture model of Kanji and Yui[36] (as shown in Figure 2.2). This model can be used in conjunction with the concept of quality culture to be customized in individual institutions (as shown in Figure 2.3).

There are numerous causal factors for introducing quality management given by institutions which require them to improve quality. Some of these factors are unique to individual institutions. By examining the causal factors, it is found that U.S. institutions are concerned about the strategic development of their institutions and strive to perpetuate a culture that influences customer satisfaction and, thus, business excellence. From these observations, it is also concluded that TQM can be applied to institutions to solve problems as well as improve quality in general.

There are nine critical success factors for higher education institutions compiled in the research. These factors are critical because if they are implemented properly, the institutions will achieve business excellence. These factors are useful because they can be used by managers for missions, policies, and decision making. The highest ranked critical success factor indicated is leadership, which is the prime in Kanji's TQM model. It serves as the driving force to move the institutions toward their goals. In the process of reaching those goals, the institutions are confronted with many barriers that are difficult to overcome. However, many barriers originate from organizational members themselves by way of resistance to change, lack of commitment, and fear of failure. If quality can be nurtured into the senses of all people in the institutions, then organizational members will engage in the cooperation and commitment required of them.

The present research has shown that TQM institutions outperform non-TQM institutions in organizational performance (see Table 2.3). There is a higher proportion of TQM institutions that have good to excellent organizational

	Institutions' quality performance		Institutions' organizational performance	
Level of performance	TQM %	Non-TQM %	TQM %	Non-TQM %
Excellence	15.4	12.1	10.3	6.1
Very good	35.9	30.3	33.3	27.3
Good	41.0	51.5	48.7	39.4
Fair/poor	7.7	6.1	7.7	21.1

Table 2.3.   Quality and organizational performance of TQM and non-TQM institutions.

performance and a lower proportion of fair to poor organizational performance. This result is consistent with previous research works carried out in various sectors of the economy.[36,42] Performance indicators are widely used for evaluating the performance of organizations in the United States and Europe. The Malcolm Baldrige Quality Award and the European Quality Award systems use performance indicators to assess quality. However, many authors believe that performance indicators do not portray the actual quality level of institutions' processes but merely provide "indicators" of quality.

However, customer satisfaction as one measure of performance is a key feature of TQM because it contributes to business excellence. This agrees with Austin[43] and Schmitz[44] that the continuing institutional self-examination should focus on the institution's contribution to students' intellectual and personal development. With the help of this survey, our findings indicate that the student is one of the key customers in higher education institutions along with other stakeholders such as the public, industry, parents, and the government. To produce a TQM model in higher educational institutions, it will be necessary to incorporate all of these customers.

References

1. Spanbauer, S. J. 1989. *Measuring and Costing Quality in Education.* Appleton, WI: Fox Valley Technical College Foundation Report. Spanbauer, S. J. 1995. Reactivating Higher Education with Total Quality Management: Using Quality and Productivity Concepts, Techniques and Tools to Improve Higher Education. *Total Quality Management* 5-6:519-537.

2. Coate, L. E. 1990. *Implementing Total Quality Management in a University Setting*. Oregon State University Report.

3. Doherty, G. D. 1993. Towards Total Quality Management in Higher Education: A Case Study of the University of Wolverhampton. *Higher Education* 25(3):321–339.

4. Clayton, M. 1995. Encouraging the *Kaizen* Approach to Quality in a University. *Total Quality Management* 6(5 & 6):593–601.

5. Idrus, N. 1995. Empowerment as a Manifestation of Total Quality: A Study in Three Countries. *Total Quality Management* 6(5 & 6):603–612.

6. *The Star*. 1998. UK Varsities Loose Their Goose. Kuala Lumpur, Malaysia. 5 April.

7. *The Star*. 1998. Asia's Woes Likely to Hit Aussie Education. Kuala Lumpur, Malaysia. 24 January.

8. Lozier, G. G., and D. J. Teeter. 1996. Quality Improvement Pursuits in American Higher Education. *Total Quality Management* 7(2):189–201.

9. Burkhalter, B. B. 1996. How Institutions of Higher Education Achieve Quality within the New Economy. *Total Quality Management* 7(2):153–160.

10. Sherr, L. A., and G. G. Lozier. 1991. Total Quality Management in Higher Education. *New Directions for Institutional Research* XVIII(3):3–11.

11. Kells, H. R. 1995. Creating a Culture of Evaluation and Self-Regulation in Higher Education Organizations. *Total Quality Management* 6(5 & 6):457–467.

12. Barnett, R. 1992. *Improving Higher Education: Total Quality Care*. Buckingham: Open University Press.

13. Seymour, D. T. 1992. *On Q: Causing Quality in Higher Education*. New York: MacMillan.

14. Holloway, J. 1994. Is There a Place for Total Quality Management in Higher Education? In *Developing Quality Systems in Higher Education*, edited by G. D. Doherty. London: Routledge.

15. Doherty, G. D. 1994. The Concern for Quality. In *Developing Quality Systems in Education*, edited by G. D. Doherty. London: Routledge.

16. Tribus, M. 1994. Total Quality Management in Higher Education. In *Developing Quality Systems in Higher Education*, edited by G. D. Doherty. London: Routledge.

17. Kanji, G. K. 1996. Implementation and Pitfalls of Total Quality Management. *Total Quality Management* 7:331-343.

18. Narasimhan, K. 1997. Organizational Climate at the University of Braunton in 1996. *Total Quality Management* 8(2 & 3): 233-237.

19. Ho, S. K., and K. Wearn. 1996. A TQM Model for Enabling Student Learning. *Innovations in Training and Education International* 33(3):178-184.

20. Hackman, J. R. and R. Wageman. 1995. Total Quality Management: Empirical, Conceptual, and Practical Issues. *Administrative Science Quarterly* 40(2):309-342.

21. Daniel, D. R. 1961. Management Information Crisis. *Harvard Business Review* 39(5):111-121.

22. Hofer, W. C., and D. E. Schendel. 1978. *Strategy Formulation Analytical Concepts*. St. Paul, MN: West Publishing Company.

23. Rockart, J. F. 1982. The Changing Role of the Information Systems Executive: A Critical Success Factors Perspective. *Sloan Management Review* (fall):3-13.

24. Yang, H. L. 1996. Key Information Management Issues in Taiwan and US. *Information and Management* 30(5):251-267.

25. Boynton, A. C., and R. W. Zmud. 1984. An Assessment of Critical Success Factors. *Sloan Management Review* (summer):17-27. Burello, L. C., and D. J. Zadnik. 1986. Critical Success Factors of Special Education Administrators. *Journal of Special Education* 29(3):367-377.

26. Jenster, P. V. 1987. Using Critical Success Factors in Planning. *Long Range Planning* 20(4):102-109.

27. Cooper, R. G., and E. J. Kleinschmidt. 1996. Winning Business in Product Development: The Critical Success Factors in New Product Development. *Journal of Product Innovation Management* 12:374-391.

28. Atuahene-Gima, K. 1966. Differential Potency of Factors Affecting Innovation Performance in Manufacturing and Services Firm in Australia. *Journal of Product Innovation Management* 13:35-52.

29. Gowan, Jr., J. A., and G. R. Mathieu. 1996. Critical Factors in Information System Development for a Flexible Manufacturing System. *Computers in Industry* 28:173-183.

30. Udo, G. J., and C. I. Ethie. 1996. Critical Success Factors for Advanced Manufacturing Systems. *Computers and Industrial Engineering* 31(1/2):91–94.

31. Burello, L. C. and D. J. Zadnik. 1986. Critical Success Factors of Special Education Administrators. *Journal of Special Education* 29(3):367–377.

32. Nelson, R. R. 1991. Survey of Knowledge and Skill Requirements. *MIS Quarterly* 15(4):503–521.

33. Pellow, A., and T. D. Wilson. 1993. The Management Information Requirements of Heads of University. *Journal of Information Science* 19(6):425–437.

34. Dervitsiotis, K. N. 1995. The Objective Matrix as a Facilitating Framework for Quality Assessment and Improvement in Education. *Total Quality Management* 6(5 & 6):563–570.

35. Kanji, G. K. and M. Asher. 1993. *Total Quality Management Process: A Systematic Approach*. Carfax: Abingdon.

36. Kanji, G. K., and H. Yui. 1997. Total Quality Culture. *Total Quality Management* 8(6):417–428.

37. James, P. T. J. 1996. *Total Quality Management: An Introductory Text*. New York: Prentice Hall.

38. Saraph, J. V., R. G. Schroeder, and P. G. Benson. 1989. An Instrument for Measuring Critical Success Factors of Quality Management. *Decision Sciences* 20:810–829.

39. Parasuraman, A., V. A. Zeithmal, and L. L. Berry. 1985. A Conceptual Model for Service Quality and its Implications for Future Research. *Journal of Marketing* 49:41–50.

40. Thiagarajan, T. 1995. An Empirical Study of Total Quality Management (TQM) in Malaysia: A Proposed Framework of Generic Application. Ph.D. diss., University of Bradford, Post Graduate School of Studies in Management and Administration.

41. Kanji, G. K. 1998. An Innovative Approach to Make ISO 9000 Standards More Effective. *Total Quality Management* 9(1):67–78.

42. Terziovski, M., A. Sohal, and D. Samson. 1996. Best Practice Implementation of Total Quality Management: Multiple Cross-Case Analysis of Manufacturing and Service Organizations. *Total Quality Management* 7(5):459–481.

43. Austin, A. W. 1986. Measuring the Quality of Undergraduate Students: Are Traditional Approaches Adequate? Unpublished presentation notes to the Texas Education System, p. 56.

44. Schmitz, C. C. 1993. Assessing the Validity of Higher Education Indicators. *Journal of Higher Education* 64(5):530–541.

Chapter 3

A TQM Model for Value-Based Customer-Supplier Relationships

JOHN D. HROMI

Introduction

This chapter deals with supplier-processor-customer relationships and the role of each in increasing the effectiveness of such partnerships. It offers answers to problems that may arise in implementing total management concepts. Tools for evaluating suppliers, operation guidelines for the processor or producer, and means for understanding the customer are provided. These are brought together through an understanding of the supply chain system. The presentation goes beyond traditional aspects of supply chain management. It introduces a more encompassing approach for each element in order to better understand the system.

Brought to the fore is a relatively new use of the *wheel*, an assessment device, by the supplier, producer, and customer for measuring the degree of progress in achieving leading-edge goal characteristics in their relationship.

Recently, researchers and consultants at the Center for Integrated Manufacturing Studies at the Rochester Institute of Technology developed some fresh ideas about supply chain management and customer-supplier relations.[1-4] Their work gives an added dimension to the basic elements that are shown in Figure 3.1.

Two customer-supplier conditions are prevalent. The manufacturer or processor must meet customer expectations, whereas, the supplier must satisfy the processor's requirements. In either case, the customer derives a capability from having capable suppliers. Therefore, a customer-supplier relationship (CSR) is the degree of bonding that exists between two companies based on the values exchanged between them. Delighting the ultimate customer is the main focus of their combined efforts.

When the value exchange is balanced (win/win situation) as shown in Figure 3.2, then the relationship is strong and will be evidenced by a high level of trust. If the value exchange is one-sided, then the relationship will be short-term.

Delighting the Customer

J. T. Schirmer, a senior consultant working with the Center for Integrated Manufacturing Studies, uses a cause and effect diagram to illustrate some factors that determine what it takes for a company to delight the customer. As shown in Figure 3.3, the supply chain is a major part of the strategy that is consistent with a successful company's vision. It is important to recognize that in today's business world, companies cannot achieve competitive advantage without a responsive supply chain, which is essentially comprised of contractors and subcontractors

Figure 3.1. Basic elements of the customer-supplier relationship.

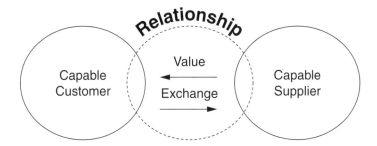

Figure 3.2. Customer-supplier relationship.

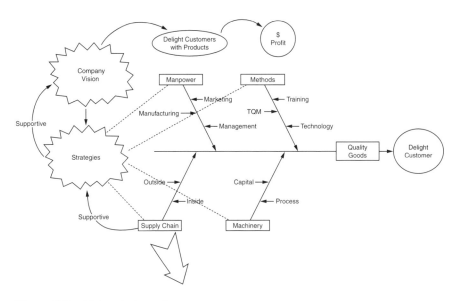

Figure 3.3. Vision-strategy-plan.

© J.T. Schirmer. Used with permission.

bound together to produce superior quality products for the ultimate customer. Companies and organizations that work together effectively constantly attempt to improve relationships with each other through cross-functional teams and direct lines of communication between the interfacing companies.

It has been said by many researchers that 70 percent of sales costs are directly related to materials and material-related costs, which are derived to a large extent from the supply chain. By adding design quality and responsiveness as supply-chain issues the ability to achieve customer delight is enhanced. Unfortunately, without a vision, a corresponding strategy, and a workable plan this won't be accomplished.

Supply Chain Management

Figure 3.4 focuses on the process of optimizing flows in the supply chain for the benefit of the entire chain. Crucial to the process are information flow, material flow, product flow, and cash flow. An interruption in the system flow weakens the entire process. Hence, system efficiency is a function of each of its elements. For example, manufacturing should cooperatively involve design, production scheduling, materials management, purchasing, and so on. It is interesting to note that marketing in a successful company is also an integral part of the process of optimizing flows in the supply chain for the benefit of the entire chain. In addition, coordinated shipping, handling, and storage are key issues in a smoothly functioning chain. Feedback is also a vital element in open communications between those who comprise the supply chain.

For example, think of the supplier and the customer who interface solely at the sales and purchasing levels, respectively. As shown in Figure 3.5, this limited interchange has been expanded to include a free flow of information between the customer's manufacturing and quality activities and those of the supplier(s). Further, the customer-supplier relationship need not be limited to the manufacturing and quality functions. Even though the flow chart offers a conceptual framework for supply chain management, there are other considerations.

There are at least two conditions that must be present within companies in order to drive customer-supplier relationships successfully. In Figure 3.6, Schirmer refers to these as the *will* and the *way*. The will should create the "conditions for excellence" or "climate," so that all parties within an organization would be motivated to use the most current tools to improve customer-supplier relationships. Of course, the way is the "methods and application" part of the equation. In other words, everyone throughout the supply chain must have the

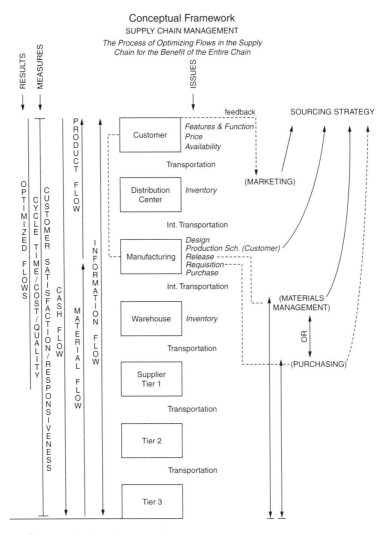

Figure 3.4. Supply chain framework.
© 1995 by J.T. Schirmer. Used with permission.

will and desire to develop seamless relationships within the multifaceted system. Then, there must be a strong belief and confidence that each element in the chain has the ability to interact in such a way that moving from one element in the chain to another can be done smoothly. The extent to which this can be done needs to be monitored in the Plan-Do-Check-Act sense.

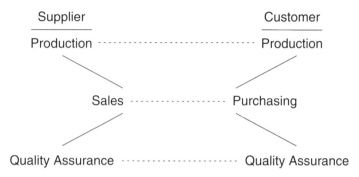

Figure 3.5. Total quality relationship.

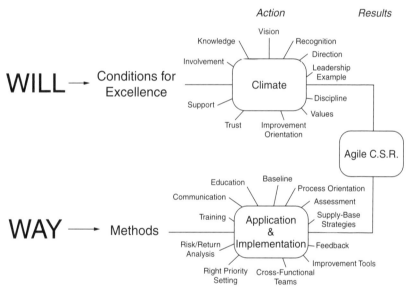

Figure 3.6. Customer-supplier relationship requirements.
© 1996 by J.T. Schirmer. Used with permission.

The Wheel Model: A Vehicle for Dialogue

The three wheels in a sense can be regarded as a tool set. One assesses the capability of the customer, another the capability of the supplier, and the third assesses the results of the relationship. Traditionally, assessments were aimed primarily at suppliers. Now, the wheels provide a means for not only assessing the elements of the customer-supplier relationship, but also to provide a basis

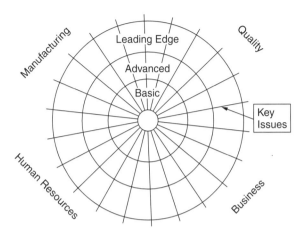

Figure 3.7. The wheel.

for a healthy dialogue and direct communications between cross-functional teams.

Figure 3.7 illustrates the structure of a wheel, which is comprised of three concentric circles through which pass 25 equally spaced spokes representing key issues. Each circle measures a level of progress toward a worthy goal, like customer delight. Moving out from the hub, the circles advance from basic, to advanced, to leading edge. Key issues can be categorized as manufacturing, quality, business, and human resources. In the "Results of Relationship" wheel, key issues may include total supply time, technology and/or knowledge transfer, safety and environment, time to market, total defects, and so on. For example, "total defects" may be plotted in the basic region as > 200 ppm, in the advanced region as 50–200 ppm, and in the leading edge region as < 50 ppm. Hence, on one graphic, the relative position of up to 25 key issues of customer-supplier relationship can be observed in their various stages of accomplishment.

Key issues may appear as clusters on the wheel. For example, a grouping of key issues may include quality system, quality assurance, and safety and environment. Figure 3.8 illustrates how results and targets for this cluster of key issues provide insight into quality management where the basic question may be, "Are we producing the right things well?" In this example, a wedge from the wheel offers a comprehensive snapshot of the organization's capabilities and results relative to its long-term objectives.

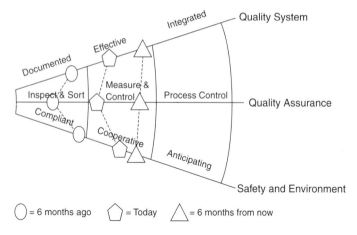

Figure 3.8.   A cluster of key issues.

Six months ago, an organization produced the right things barely well enough to maintain a place in the market. Today, it produces them well enough to be competitive and is improving. In another six months, the organization intends to be producing products and services well enough and to be improving fast enough to be potential industry leaders in three years. Other wheels may have greater specificity.

Reaching the Wheel's Leading Edge

To achieve the leading edge of the wheel through continuous improvement, a company should

1. Select a key product or service

2. Engage customer and supplier in a joint assessment

3. Assess its capabilities as a customer and as a supplier

4. Exchange information and develop a consensus

5. Develop an improvement plan

6. Assess relationship results

7. Recognize and reward achievers

Conclusion

In today's world, suppliers are more selective of the customers with whom they can partner, just as customers are more demanding and thus more selective of suppliers. Regardless of whether the company is a customer or supplier, the relationship issue must be addressed to be competitive in the future. Tools such as the wheel provide a comprehensive perspective and dialogue for continuous improvement throughout the customer-supplier chain.

Acknowledgment

I am indebted to Mr. J. T. Schirmer for sharing with me in meaningful discussions the development of the wheel concept described in this chapter. Much of what has been presented here is a result of our close relationship.

References

1. *The Wheels: A Vehicle for Dialogue—Capable Customer*. 1996. Rochester, NY: The Center for Integrated Manufacturing Studies Report, Rochester Institute of Technology.

2. *The Wheels: A Vehicle for Dialogue—Capable Supplier*. 1996. Rochester, NY: The Center for Integrated Manufacturing Studies Report, Rochester Institute of Technology.

3. *The Wheels: A Vehicle for Dialogue—Results of the Relationship*. 1996. Rochester, NY: The Center for Integrated Manufacturing Studies Report, Rochester Institute of Technology.

4. *Manufacturing Excellence*. 1997. Rochester, NY: WXXI, a public broadcasting company for the Rochester Chamber of Commerce. Videocassette.

Chapter 4

Integration: The Key Word for Quality-Based Organizational Transformations

Tito Conti

Introduction

The fad season in relation to quality seems to be declining. It takes time to completely be rid of the distortions that success inevitably brings. Quality-related consultancy is still, all too often, taking advantage of the inability of managers to sort out the good from the bad. The institutions that flourished, meanwhile, are thanking the quality explosion for making them more focused and perpetuating their own success rather than understanding and reasoning what is really good for the enterprises and the economy. ISO 9000 standards and total quality management (TQM) have often lost their good name because of wrong presentation, overselling, or acquiescence to short-term customer demand. As a result, talking of quality strategies today has become counterproductive.

Beyond tactical reasons, however, more substantial reasons suggest using the word *quality* with some moderation. Progress in quality in the last decade has gone far beyond the traditional concept of product quality and even customer satisfaction to embrace the whole organization. Quality is no longer a product or service-expected attribute, but an attribute of the organization itself as a *system;* that is, of its functions and its processes. However, quality is still widely perceived as a separate entity instead of as an attribute of each and every organizational entity as well as of their "products" and "services." In some cases, the perception of its intrinsic pervasiveness has generated bitter reactions. Perhaps those perceptions or reactions can be corrected by deemphasizing the attribute—through a more frugal use of the word *quality*—and emphasizing the substantives (for example, business planning, resource management, new product development, etc.). But the effort should go in the direction of convincing management that each of those substantives should be critically reviewed with the aim of enhancing competitive advantage. In doing so, implicitly or explicitly, TQM approaches and tools should be widely used. Paradoxically, success in quality requires that quality "disappears" as a separate entity in the organization, absorbed and metabolized by the already accepted management and organizational concepts. The dichotomy between quality objectives and business objectives should disappear. That means that quality has to be *integrated into business.*

The aim of this chapter is to discuss how *integration* is the key word for quality transformations and why *the ability to integrate* is the name of the game today. *Integration* can have different meanings. Since at least two of those meanings are important for quality-based organizational transformations, we shall try to make the appropriate distinctions. The first meaning is *to integrate quality concepts into organizational and management concepts and practice.* As already observed, quality is not separate from business. It is the yardstick for managerial excellence for any aspect and at every level of business. The top executive who understands how quality tools can be integrated into the various areas of management and promotes such integration in his/her company creates a more competitive "machine." The second meaning refers to *a second form of integration*, which is not usually critical for the small business but becomes increasingly important as company dimensions increase. This dictates the ability to reach an integrated vision of all the company's strategic goals and the integration would help achieve various company subsystems (generally known as functions) into a unified, harmonious whole geared toward those strategic goals. This does not mean eliminating functional responsibilities; rather, it means stressing the need for cross-functional cooperation. Above all, in the interests of unified management of key processes, which cut horizontally across the various functions, it also means extending the quality approaches to the entire company to be winners in product-related processes. This avoids the need to start from scratch every time the company wishes to maximize the effectiveness and minimize the cost and time of a new result. The quality concepts and tools used to generate good products and services for the customer can be easily adapted to impact the environment, human resource management, financial management, sales and relationships with business partners.

Integration of this level of concept, however, is based on one condition: the top executive of the company takes on the role of "architect" for organizational change. This in turn requires a combination of competence and vision that would allow him/her to see what others fail to see, to do what others fail to do, and to be different. The key to competitive success today is integration of diversity, not compliance with standards.

How Integration Can Help

An astonishing number of company capabilities that play a strategic role in enhancing competitiveness can be improved—often to a dramatic extent—by the use of quality concepts and tools at the appropriate levels. Yet, most of the companies that have embarked in TQM do not use those concepts and tools at the strategic levels. The reason is simple: quality is considered a technical issue related to products and services, not so much to strategic internal processes like business planning, human resource development, decision processes, and company organization. Quality is not allowed to interfere with strategic capabilities, which are the prerogative of top management. It is pointless to expect significant contributions from quality until top management allows quality tools to enter the hallowed halls in which strategy is decided. In other words, until management demands that *quality be integrated into business*, very little will happen. Very often, TQM presentations omit this strategic dimension. But, it confirms the fact that top management must become autonomous in deciding the company's organizational architecture and in setting guidelines for the people responsible for organizational engineering. The following is a list of strategic capabilities that would strongly benefit from integration of quality concepts.

1. Reading and interpreting market expectations and anticipating market trends; setting competitive goals accordingly

2. Planning the *means* of achieving goals through improvement, transformation, reengineering, and creation of new capabilities for gearing the company system and processes to achieve the planned goals

3. Developing and motivating the workforce, releasing potential, and focusing effort on goals

4. Managing processes to ensure maximum precision and minimum cost in achieving goals

5. Reducing process cycles in order to improve competitive effectiveness (time-to-market) and efficiency (containing working capital)

6. Managing business partners (suppliers, distributors, etc.) in order to optimize the effectiveness/efficiency of the "value chains" (maximum value for the end customer at minimum global cost)

7. Enhancing company flexibility and the ability to adapt rapidly to change (change management)

Some of the above items, with their focus on value perceived by the customer and on reducing nonconformity, stem from conventional quality concepts, while the others go beyond the listed descriptions. They give us an idea of the progress in quality over the last 20 years: from product/service quality, quality perceived by the customer, and customer satisfaction to the organizational roots of each quality entity. They reflect a rational, deeper investigation of the causes of problems, whose sources can in many cases be traced right back to the company's "systemic factors" that are directly controlled by top management. For example, the greatest desire of business executives is to be able to develop new products quickly (compete in terms of time-to-market) and to launch defect-free products. Very few succeed. Most continue to suffer despite all urging, rewards, and penalties. What the second group fails to understand is that errors, redesigns, and changes are technical problems with organizational roots and that only top management can introduce the architectural changes (concurrent engineering) together with the necessary expertise and rigorous process control to weed out sickly growth. The only serious approach to eliminating defectiveness before products are marketed is through close integration of all the company functions responsible for product development, production, marketing, and support to coexist. This is an example of *functional integration*. The second type of integration we are discussing is normally a result of the first: the integration of quality concepts into business concepts and practice.

To understand the above list of strategic capabilities, especially for those items that link with quality, it is necessary to adopt the modern approach. This vision takes quality perceived by the customers and stakeholders (*quality of results*) as its starting point, but focuses above all on the *quality of the means*; that is, the processes and company factors on which the ability to generate quality depends. This conceptual advancement is vital. It keeps us from being quality focused on the specific techniques needed to generate products/services that satisfy customer expectations, and allows us to focus on a concept that embraces the entire company structure base. It is based on the managerial and organizational factors that allow quality (value for the customer, the company, and stakeholders in general) to be generated at minimum cost.

Now let's see how this concept can influence the strategic capabilities listed previously.

Ability to Compete in Terms of Value Perceived by the Customer

The Japanese in particular have developed systems to identify latent and potential market needs which are considerably more efficacious than conventional market research techniques. These systems include the Quality Function Deployment (QFD) technique and the concepts of Kano model. Companies that do not incorporate these methodologies into new product/service planning (because they are unaware of them or because their specialists do not use "quality tools") automatically undermine their competitiveness in terms of value perceived by customers. Moreover, methodologies like QFD remain a powerful technical tool since they require a multifunctional approach to development of the company to work properly. It also assists in organizational integration.

Planning Improvements/Adjustments/Reengineerings Enable Company Capabilities

This is a key strategic issue and will therefore be examined when we look at self-assessment and improvement-planning aspects.

Employee Motivation and Empowerment

This is a tricky issue. In many companies, fear of external interference has provoked a negative reaction from the human resources function. The fact is that quality can make a significant contribution to job enhancement. Involving people in identifying, diagnosing, and resolving organizational problems (in addition to technical problems) and encouraging active participation in self-assessment is an extremely powerful way to strengthen motivation. People's potential is enormously underutilized. Constant improvements in standards of education and standards of living and wider access to information and greater social interaction have always been found to fuel a growing need for self-realization. Taking steps to unleash this potential in the workplace, not just in weekends, is a major challenge for the management and an important opportunity for both the employers and employees. Greater spontaneous contributions to the company from its workers are a stimulus for greater competitiveness.

Efficiency in Operating Processes

Top managers who wish to avoid high-flown disquisitions on quality and adopt a practical approach should take process management as their starting point. Process management concerns the ability to achieve goals (by minimizing variability and therefore defectiveness) with minimum outlay in costs and time. If more than a few industries have reduced their defect rates by a factor of 100 or even 1000 over the last 20 years (for example, electronic chips), this is due to improvements in process management. Large businesses have found that the greatest advantages come when an organizational approach, together with a technical approach, is taken in process management. In other words, when *cross integration* is encouraged, and when functional organizational barriers that often prevent large companies from competing with more agile players in terms of costs, speed, and quality are lowered.

Relations with Business Partners

TQM models in general, and the improvement-oriented business models derived from them in particular, have paved the way to a more rational and integrated approach to management of relations with all stakeholders and business partners. Using process management criteria to manage the value chain is another way to maximize value for the end customer and minimize global costs and time.

Organizational Flexibility

Once again, cross-functional integration is the way to overcome the rigidities typical of bureaucratic-functional organizational models. Flexibility is the attribute of lean, flat companies that stress the importance of horizontal integration. Process management and teamwork enhance flexibility and readiness to change.

Self-Assessment: The Key to Integration

If self-assessment is correctly implemented, it can put companies on the right track to integration. The author stresses *correctly implemented* because the self-assessment approach adopted by many companies today is defective and has lead them to nowhere. The reason, as always, is the power of management positions. Thanks to the incentive provided by the quality awards, the idea of self-assessment is now widely accepted, but many companies suffer from drawbacks of implementation being focused on "scores" rather than on improvement. For top management, the idea of achieving a magical number that shows (or is presumed to show) where the company or a company division stands in relation to leading players is more appealing than the idea of self-assessment as a diagnostic tool for improvement. Once again, managers should be asking: Will I give my company a competitive advantage by doing exactly the same as everyone else?

The models and self-assessment approaches used by the awards criteria are becoming *de facto* standards. This is perfectly acceptable for measuring purpose: establishing a starting point (the company's opening position) and periodically measuring subsequent progress. Standard weights and models are needed for this and the award models fit the bill when applying for the awards. But, for the company that wants to improve performance in relation to competitors, standards are no longer enough. It must adapt the model to its specific competitive situation. In other words, its implementation of self-assessment must be aimed at identifying weaknesses in relation to strategic goals rather than at obtaining a number.

Management must be clear about the various purposes that can be served by assessment. The choice of model and approach will depend on what the company aims to achieve. If *a priori* assessment of the products and services of quality management and the assurance system is the goal from the customer's interest and the potential supplier's viewpoint, ISO 9000 assessment is amply suitable. If the company also wants to check the effectiveness of its quality management and assurance system, then customer satisfaction results must be taken into account. Additionally, if the company wants to verify the ability of the entire company to satisfy customers, shareholders, employees, business partners, and society, then it will need a TQM model of the sort used by the quality awards (EQA, MBA, Deming Prize, etc.). However, the purposes of TQM assessments themselves can differ. Comparative assessment against other companies (or among different divisions in the company) and improvement-oriented assessment should be differentiated. In the first case, the assessment focuses on obtaining reliable scores (the difficulty of which is often underestimated). In the second, it aims to identify performance weaknesses and diagnose the underlying causes. This is a demanding exercise: identifying the root causes of problems within processes and the company system is often extremely difficult.

When self-assessment focuses on the company's critical results (for example, gaps in performance compared with goals and/or with reference competitors) and on its new strategic goals, it enters a new strategic dimension. It attempts to identify the reasons for critical results and the weaknesses that prevent it from achieving its strategic goals, so that appropriate action can be taken. Thus, self-assessment and the consequent strategic improvement plan become an integral part of total business planning.

The best place to begin integrating quality into management is at the planning stage. Planning is the basis for achieving competitive results. However, it often suffers from a weakness that can be remedied by a diagnostic approach. The weakness is as follows. The company cycle is subdivided into two main phases: planning and implementation. If, as often happens, results are not in line with goals, it is not customary to conduct in-depth analyses of processes and systemic factors in order to pinpoint the root causes of the gaps. In fact, many companies lack an appropriate reference model: processes are vague concepts, systemic factors are hardly ever mentioned. As a result, no critical analyses of previous failures are conducted in the interests of the subsequent or future planning cycle and it tends to repeat the same overestimates or underestimates of the company's ability in relation to its goals. Introduction of an analysis, diagnosis, and adjustment phase at the end of every implementation phase, before proceeding to the next planning stage, is a major step toward corporate maturity. This phase is self-assessment.

To repeat using quality terminology, the *Plan-Do* approach is replaced with a *Plan-Do-Check-Act* approach, where the introduction of the *Check* phase (and of the subsequent *Act* phase, which consolidates the positive findings of the check and makes the necessary adjustments) signals a desire for extensive changes in organizational behavior. Diagnosis of failure is the basis for continuous improvement and for turning the company into a learning organization. The Deming Cycle, or the *Plan-Do-Check-Act* cycle thus graduates from being purely a technical tool into a cycle which, year after year, is repeated by management to lead the company toward the goals that are so difficult to achieve and maintain.

Integration of self-assessment into the company planning cycle also implies integration of improvement planning. Improvement planning (in the broad sense of the sum of incremental and large-scale improvements) is the inevitable conclusion of self-assessment. Figure 4.1 illustrates the integration of business planning (strategic and operational), self-assessment, and improvement planning. Strategic planning and the year-end critical results provide the input for self-assessment. Self-assessment focuses not on quality but on business goals (or, at a more general level, on the company's strategic goals) in order to identify any process and systemic weaknesses that might prevent these goals from being achieved. The output from self-assessment is channeled back to strategic planning with suggested improvements/reengineerings, which will either be accepted or lead to adjustments in goals. The subsequent operational planning phase will proceed at two fully complementary levels; that is, at business operation level and improvement operation level, the latter comprising all of the measures to be implemented on processes and the company system to enable the company to achieve its business goals. Figure 4.2 illustrates inputs for self-assessment. It shows that an in-depth analysis of the company's capabilities must take into account three factors: the *voice of the market* (customer satisfaction results, vendor ratings, etc.), the *voice of the company's processes* (the readings provided by internal process indicators), and *the voice of the company* (everyone who works in the company whose contribution is essential to help the diagnosis identify the root causes of problems).

The Second Type of Integration

For many years, conventional wisdom held that making profits should be the absolute priority for the business organization, almost to the exclusion of all

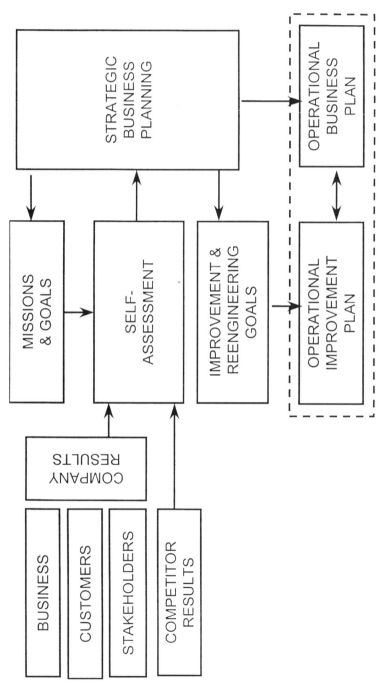

Figure 4.1. Integration of self-assessment and improvement/reengineering planning into business planning.

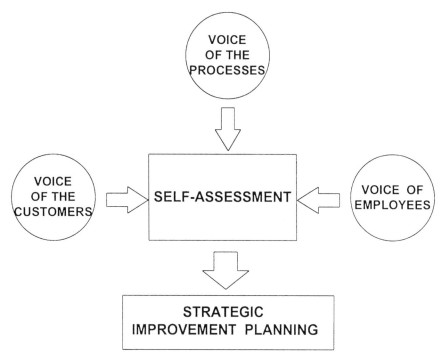

Figure 4.2. Inputs for self-assessment.

other goals. Fiercer competition, however, has put the customer back into a key position. Winning the customer's preference has always been essential for lasting business success, but never more so than today with the structural surplus in supply. Similarly, increasingly aggressive competition suggests that the company will not be able to compete at the level of customer satisfaction unless focus on the customer becomes a key corporate value. Customer satisfaction (or, customer preference) must therefore be a primary goal of the company, *on a par* with its business goals. Subsequently, focus on the customer has been extended to all groups with legitimate expectations of the company; in other words, to the company's "stakeholders," or all the parties who are bound to the company by a contract or by some formal mutual relationship, which provides for them to offer specific contributions in exchange for specific benefits. In short, achievement of business goals (satisfaction of the company and its management), achievement of customer preference, and mutual satisfaction in relation to stakeholders remain the three basic aims or missions of the company.

Examination of competitive success factors suggests that long-term business prosperity requires a balanced approach to the satisfaction of the three groups (company, customers, and stakeholders). This means the company must have an integrated vision combining all three missions into a balanced whole. Separate visions inevitably spell dissatisfaction for one group or another and will ultimately undermine performance. Figure 4.3 represents the company's individual missions in relation to its holistic mission. The use of a circle is deliberate, to suggest the intrinsic symmetry of the company's relationship with customers, stakeholders, and business results. The stakeholders group is subdivided into four categories: shareholders (who contribute financial capital), employees (who contribute human capital, intelligence, and labor), business partners (who

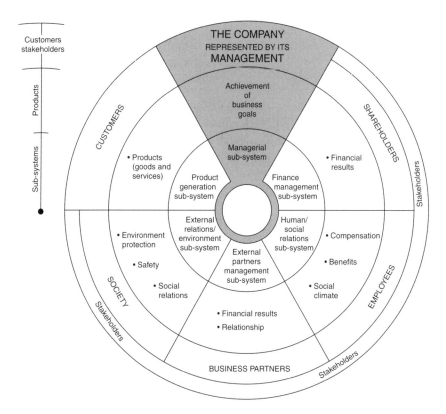

Figure 4.3.   The company as a system that generates products to satisfy the needs of a variety of customers/stakeholders.

(From Conti, T. 1997. *Organisational Self-Assessment.* London: Chapman & Hall. Reprinted with permission from Kluwer Academic Publishers, The Netherlands.)

offer various types of value), and society (which provides the benefits of the physical, social, and cultural environments, etc.).

Management must therefore learn to set explicit strategic goals for each of the three missions. This is something of a departure from normal practice, which at best sets specific strategic business goals, rarely sets the customer satisfaction/loyalty goals, and almost never sets the stakeholder satisfaction goals (what the company expects from stakeholders).

Once an integrated system of goals has been set, the means adopted to achieve those goals will vary and should be integrated. Small businesses will naturally tend to make an integrated response to the various problems they face because the links among them are somewhat clearer. The large organization, with its functional divisions, tends to lose sight of the integrated approach and adopts a heterogeneous set of policies in relation to and within the business, customers, and stakeholders groups.

Although the functional approach to the division of labor was a necessary step in corporate development to permit management of complexity, it tends to become a constraint as competitive pressures increase. The competitive crises experienced by today's Goliaths facing the Davids who arrive on the market as the barriers to entry prove the point. To survive, the large organization has policies in place to slim down. But downsizing has not proven to be an effective cure, just as crash diets are not the answer for the overweight. Subdivision into agile operating units and streamlined staff functions is a possible solution, but the more the organization subdivides the greater the need for coordination. Flexibility does not cancel out the benefits of greater operating autonomy. Integration is the answer, no matter how difficult to achieve, because it conflicts with the vertical, bureaucratic-functional organizational approach, which seems to be ingrained into some managers' thinking.

A correct understanding of TQM will foster an integrated vision of the managerial system and a process-based vision geared to continuous improvement. As the underlying layer of various subsystems, the inner circle in Figure 4.3 represents the unitary nature of the company system. Figure 4.4 is another illustration of how the company subsystems converge toward an integrated, mission-driven vision, based on processes and the principle of continuous improvement. The TQM models used by the awards and the business models highlight the fact that this unitariness is the result of strong leadership and integrated strategic planning. In Figure 4.5, which represents one of these models,[1] the company's goals or missions are shown on the right (the same missions as

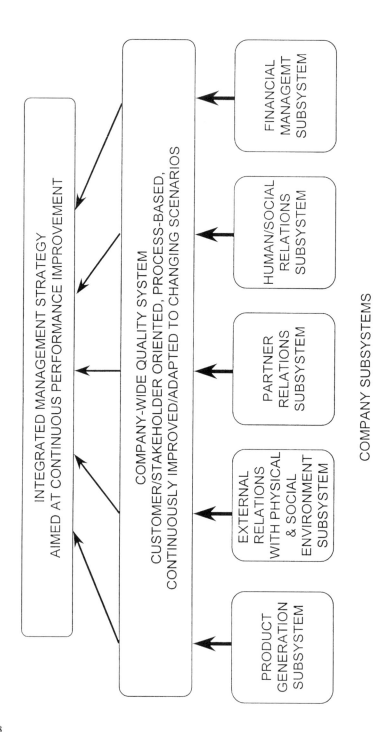

Figure 4.4. A continuous-improvement strategy aimed at business excellence, based on a company-wide quality system.

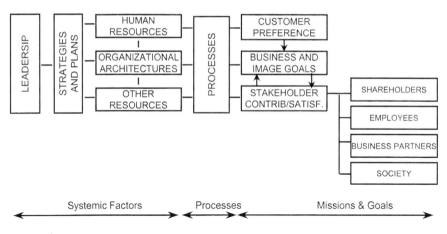

Figure 4.5 The model.

in Figure 4.3); the left side and center represent the factors—the levers—used by management to achieve its missions. Leadership is both the driver and the integrator of the organization. Its task is to first promote a consistent, balanced planning approach embracing all the various goals, and then create organizational solutions that make the best use of human, financial, and technological resources yielding processes capable of achieving goals with minimum cost and time.

As discussed earlier, this integrated vision of management tends to eliminate the vertical barriers among company subsystems and recreate unitary processes cutting horizontally across the company. At a general level, it tends to optimize management of the company's main value chains to maximize end quality and minimize global costs. Since these chains do not stop at the company gates, but extend to suppliers on one side and distributors or large customers on the other, the effectiveness of integration is directly proportional to the degree of involvement of all business partners.

Conclusion

In today's competitive situation, the idea that some simple, lasting solutions can be found to complex variable problems is an illusion. Standards do not offer competitive advantages and the succession of managerial formulas has been considered at best as tesserae in a mosaic, useful to the extent to which management is able to put them together to build an approach geared to suit the individual company's needs. Quality is a differentiating factor. Saying that quality should be integrated into management is the same as saying that quality tesserae can be used together with the other managerial tesserae, to build a practical, personalized mosaic capable of generating competitive differentials. Quality tesserae are key elements of the mosaic. They link and connect. They provide cohesion and synergy. Best of all, they integrate the business-oriented tesserae. The first, fundamental form of integration is the integration of quality concepts and tools with management concepts and practice. Management must accept the introduction of quality tesserae into the business mosaic. Once this mosaic has been created, the company will discover how potential quality offers a tool for integration; first, by integration of and focus on the company's missions and goals, and then by integration of the management system that sets out to achieve these missions and goals.

Integration as described in this chapter is a major challenge for management today. It is also a cultural challenge because it requires management to accept the idea that previous experience and competence is no longer sufficient. New skills are needed for more efficient and effective management in today's complex technical and social system.

Reference

1. Conti, T. 1997. *Organisational Self-Assessment*. London: Chapman & Hall.

Chapter 5

Quality Certification Scheme for Integrated Safety Management Systems in Shipping Industries

ALAIN-MICHEL CHAUVEL

Introduction

Under increasing pressure from authorities and clients, maritime transport companies are being forced to provide proof of the quality of their management and organization. Possession of a uniform set of statutory certificates, usually referring to technical regulations and codes, is no longer sufficient to demonstrate a company's good management techniques. Companies have to comply with new mandatory international requirements, culminating in certification of provisions for safety on ships and prevention of pollution risks. They also have to meet the requirements of their clients, and prove that personnel on each ship possess the skills needed to ensure that all the tasks involved in proper functioning of the ship are performed. The administrative arrangements needed to handle all these new requirements may seem complicated, expensive, and difficult to implement, or even appear to conflict with profit-earning considerations.

This chapter presents the key items in each of the new reference standards in order to identify the points they have in common. It also offers a new view of certification, helping to simplify the system.

Present Systems

The two main references to be taken into account are the International Safety Management (ISM) Code, and ISO 9002 standard concerning quality. In addition to these two documents, however, there are the mandatory requirements of the new Convention on Standards of Training, Certification and Watchkeeping for Seafarers (STCW).

Because of their individual areas of application, management of each of these three reference documents involves different aspects. They may overlap, but never duplicate one another. Each constitutes a system, the first common point being the work needed to implement them, keep them operational, and prove that they offer an adequate response to all the relevant requirements.

ISM Code

Adopted in 1993 by the International Maritime Organization (IMO), the purpose of the ISM Code is to manage safety on ships and prevent pollution of the marine environment. In 1994, the Code was incorporated into the Convention on the Safety of Human Life at Sea (SOLAS) as the new chapter 9.

The ISM Code contains the following requirements.

- Objectives concerning safety and environmental protection

- Policy to be implemented by the company

- Company responsibility and authority

- Person or persons appointed to provide ship/company liaison

- Ship's captain responsibilities and authority for implementing company policy on board

- Resources and personnel needed to achieve company goals

- Establishment of onboard operational plans

- Preparation of personnel for emergency situations

- Notification and analysis of nonconformities, accidents, and potentially dangerous incidents

- Maintenance of the ship and its equipment

- Control of documents concerning ISM Code requirements

- Verifications, examinations, and assessments to be carried out by the company

- Certification, verification, and inspection of conformity to the ISM Code

All the provisions to be introduced by the company form the safety management and pollution prevention system. The regulatory nature of the Code makes it a mandatory obligation for companies in the maritime transport sector.

The ISM Code comes into effect according to a timetable.

- July 1, 1996, for passenger ships and ro-ros sailing between ports within the European Union

- July 1, 1998, for all passenger ships, oil tankers, chemical tankers, gas tankers, and bulk carriers and high-speed cargo ships of at least 500 grt

- July 1, 2002, for all other cargo ships and mobile offshore platforms of at least 500 grt

STCW Convention

The STCW Convention, adopted by IMO in 1978, defines standards for training, certification, and watchkeeping for seafarers. This Convention, which was revised in 1995, reinforces all the criteria for eligibility of seamen, and requires proof of the effectiveness of measures introduced to satisfy the intentions of the Convention.

Chapter A of the Convention covers minimum compulsory standards for the qualification and certification of the skills of seafarers, apart from general provisions for implementation of the Convention.

- Requirements for master and deck department

- Requirements for engine room department

- Requirements for radio personnel

- Specific requirements concerning certain types of ships

- Requirements concerning safety, emergencies, medical care, and conditions of survival at sea

- Conditions for maintaining certification of seamen during the transitional period provided for in the Convention

- Requirements to be respected for watchkeeping at sea in order to ensure the safety of those on board during a voyage

Chapter B of the Convention is a guide containing a set of practical recommendations for implementing the provisions and requirements put forth in chapter A. The regulatory nature of the STCW Convention means that there is no way that maritime transport companies can avoid it. All these provisions concern maritime administrations, training bodies, and companies.

Every company must be able to prove that seamen on board its ships possess the skills needed to perform the functions assigned to them. They also have to set up a further training program to maintain and even develop such skills.

The STCW Convention is to be implemented internationally according to a timetable.

- February 1, 1997, the Convention comes into force internationally

- August 1, 1998, each maritime administration is to submit to IMO its intended program for meeting the minimum qualification requirements for seamen sailing under its flag.

- February 1, 2002, each maritime administration has to certify its seamen in accordance with the new STCW requirements, and issue fresh certificates of the new stipulated models.

However, until February 1, 2002, maritime administrations may continue to recognize and approve seamen's qualification certificates in two cases.

- If the training program started prior to August 1, 1998

- For seamen who entered active seafaring life prior to August 1, 1998

ISO 9002 Standard

ISO 9002, adopted by the International Organization for Standardization in 1987, concerns quality management within the framework of contractual relations between a company and its clients. The basic intention of this standard is to provide a client with adequate reassurance that the expected service will meet his or her requirements. The standard, which was revised in 1994, is intended for all industrial-sector and service companies.

ISO 9002 requirements concern:

- Company responsibility

- Implementation of a quality management system

- Review of the contract signed between the company and its client

- Control of documents concerning the requirements of the standard

- Purchasing

- Control of purchaser-supplied products

- Identification and traceability of the product or service covered by the contract

- Control of product or service manufacturing processes

- Inspection and testing to ensure conformity of the product or service

- Control of measuring and test equipment

- Inspections and test status

- Control of nonconforming product

- Corrective and preventive action undertaken by the company

- Handling, storage, packaging, and delivery

- Quality records

- Internal audits of the quality system

• Personnel training

• Statistical techniques used to validate product or service conformity

All these provisions, implemented by the company, form the quality management system.

The status of such standards means that ISO 9002 is neither a legal obligation, nor a set of rigid rules. It offers a way of achieving voluntary improvement in the quality of a company's services and of demonstrating it. However, with the passage of time, and as experience increases, clients are increasingly demanding its implementation.

A more detailed analysis of this standard, alongside the ISM Code, shows the clear benefits that companies can draw from an effort to reconcile the requirements of both internationally recognized reference documents.

Comparison and Links among the ISM Code, STCW Convention, and ISO 9002 Standard

An individual reading of these three reference documents could suggest that shipping companies are faced with an inextricable puzzle, in which not all the pieces fit together. It is difficult to perceive any coherent whole.

The ISM Code covers safety and prevention of pollution risks, while the STCW Convention covers the competence of shipboard personnel, and ISO 9002 the quality of service. Taken separately, each reference document might seem to require the development of specific systems to meet specific requirements (see Figure 5.1). This involves the correspondence of means to requirements.

Seen from this standpoint, there is an obvious temptation to see the whole matter as a proliferation of constraints. Such a picture hides any suggestion of benefits for a company bold enough to venture into the area. The only likelihood seems to be extra costs at an operational level, and a growing number of outside interventions to check, survey, audit, assure, and issue certificates that will require subsequent monitoring. In the absence of proper understanding of each document, one can look forward only to unnecessary duplication of activities that offer no real added value, or even act as brakes on company growth. Without some preliminary reflection on how to integrate these new requirements into the company, failure is certain.

	ISM Code	STCW Convention	ISO 9002 Standard
Field of application :	Safety at sea and pollution prevention	Training, Certification and Watchkeeping	Quality assurance of services
Applicable to :	Ship management Shipboard operation	Administration Training Colleges Ship Management Shipboard Operation	Contractual relationship between customer and supplier
Purpose : **Demonstrate** **compliance with**	The safety and pollution prevention requirements	The training, certification and watchkeeping requirements	The customer quality requirements
Means : **Implementation of**	A Company Safety Management System	A Company Crew Management System	A Company Quality Management System
Scheme of **certification :**	Shore-based audit : "Document Of Compliance" Ship audit : "Safety Management Certificate"	Company audit : "Certificate of Compliance"	Company audit : "Quality System Approval"
Validity :	5 years Subject to audit	5 years Subject to audit	5 years Subject audit
Compliance :	Mandatory	Mandatory	Voluntary

Figure 5.1.   Comparison among ISM Code, STCW Convention, and ISO 9002 Standard.

In order to succeed in the changes required by these new documents, and remain in business, the following steps are needed.

- First, it must be recognized that whether one is for or against these new reference documents they have become unavoidable. If you do not agree, go to a gymnasium, write the names of the documents you most detest on a punching bag, and hit it as hard as possible until you are utterly exhausted. The names will still be on the bag, as visible as when you started. Clearly, you have to learn to use them in order to continue progress.

- Second, all three documents need to be analyzed objectively in order to find out what they have in common (see Figure 5.2). This will help you avoid the unnecessary duplications that are wrongly seen as inevitable in these evolutionary approaches. The specific features of each reference document need to be identified. These are the points that deserve a specific, or even complementary, approach. There are few of them, compared with what is in common. They are often the points that lead to the issue of a new reference document in order to make up for shortcomings in an existing text. Unfortunately, hidden in an often confusing text, they hardly seem to justify a new document. Once identified, they are extremely useful, for they show the value, sometimes in a more explicit way, of the more abstract requirements of earlier documents.

- Third, a single system should be constructed from these reference documents. This is where the term "Keep it simple, seaman" (KISS) takes on its full meaning, helping avoid the traps and errors of transposition, coordination, monitoring, and updating of a company system.

- Fourth, responsibility for the system should not be entrusted to a single person. Remember Parkinson's Law, that any work expands to fill the time available for it. Unless you observe this law, the person will soon need deputies to do a job that, in fact, requires only person. Entrust coordination to a single person, and assign responsibility for the necessary action to each department manager.

- Fifth, do not delegate your own responsibility at the level of the system you have adopted. Delegate action by giving individuals the authority needed for them to assume their own responsibilities within their own functions. Otherwise, sooner or later you will be faced with the consequences of Murphy's Law, the basic principle of which is that whatever can go wrong will go wrong.

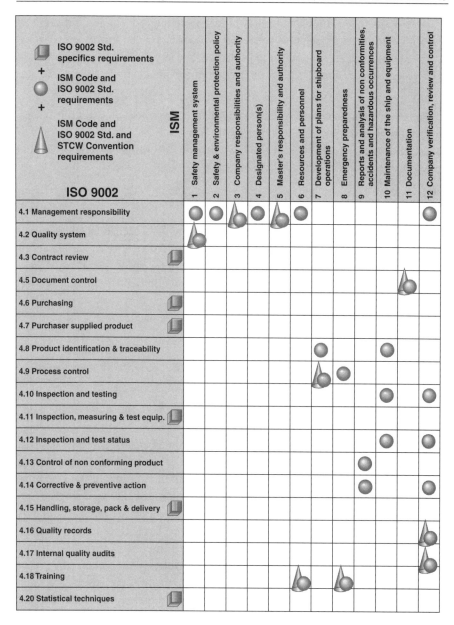

Figure 5.2.   Links among ISM Code, STCW Convention, and ISO 9002 Standard.

Note:

Cubes represent specific ISO requirements.
Circles and cones represent links among the ISM Code, ISO 9002 Standard and STCW Convention.
Cones locate specific STCW Convention requirements, in relation to the ISM Code and ISO 9002.

Following this somewhat philosophical examination, on the progress of implementation of these new reference documents, it is worth returning in practical terms to the second point of the list. In 1994, Bureau Veritas published a correspondence chart for the different requirements of the ISM Code and ISO 9002.

Figure 5.2 illustrates these correspondences, now accepted by the profession, but it also shows the links that exist with the requirements of the STCW Convention. This should help in the construction of a single system, before the certification project is actually launched.

Certification of Integrated Systems

The introduction of these new reference documents, which contribute to the improvement of safety at sea, has given rise to the idea of specific certifications for each system. Because of the timetables laid down for implementation of these documents, companies will be faced with a growing number of audits, ashore and on board their ships, in order to validate the measures they have introduced to meet the requirements of each such document. These audits cover:

- Safety management at sea and prevention of pollution risks

- Quality system management, against the background of client/supplier relations

If each system is kept in isolation from the others, the number of audits needed to prove conformity is bound to increase as the reference documents progress. This large number of audits can even militate against the very aim that is being sought, namely safety at sea, in its most effective sense. Repetition of audits is bound to create such confusion that audited companies will be incapable of grasping the full implications of each audit, specific to a single reference document. They may even find contradictions among the reports issued by the various assessors, and this will be all the more likely because the requirements of different reference documents do in fact sometimes overlap. For example, the ISM Code deals with many requirements relating to the competence of personnel on board. ISO 9002 also refers to this issue. However, the STCW Convention is clearly much more precise about such requirements than the ISM Code and ISO 9002 combined.

This is only one example. Figure 5.2 shows the zones common to all three reference documents. It is therefore advisable to rethink the certification of such systems, giving up a sequential approach for one based on balancing out requirements. This will make it possible to reconcile the idea of certification with a company's expectations of progress. In order to achieve this goal, Bureau Veritas has developed a new approach, the aim of which is to integrate all of these systems into a single certification operation.

A New Certification Scheme

The new certification scheme for integrated systems is quite straightforward. It comprises:

- Initial certification for a period of five years
- Maintenance of certification by means of combined annual audits

Initial Certification

Initial certification comprises four steps (see Figure 5.3):

1. Company needs are analyzed to ascertain the scope of the systems to be taken into account for certification purposes.

2. All of these documents, describing provisions introduced by the company, are covered by a single document review, for the purpose of checking conformity to the requirements of the selected reference documents.

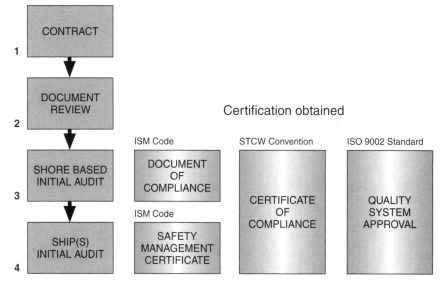

Figure 5.3.   Initial certification.

3. Shore-based operations undergo an initial audit of company procedures. At this stage in the certification process, it is already possible to issue the document of conformity to the ISM Code.

4. Shipboard operations then undergo an initial audit, based on specific procedures for each type of ship. When the audit confirms that the systems employed meet reference document requirements, all certificates are issued together for a five-year period.

- Safety management certificate for each ship, under the terms of the ISM Code
- Certificate of conformity of management for the company, under the terms of the STCW Convention
- Certificate of approval of the company quality management system, under the terms of ISO 9002

Maintenance of Certification

Maintenance of certification (see Figure 5.4) is based on a similar principle, involving annual audits that cover all the reference documents adopted. This avoids any unnecessary duplication of such audits.

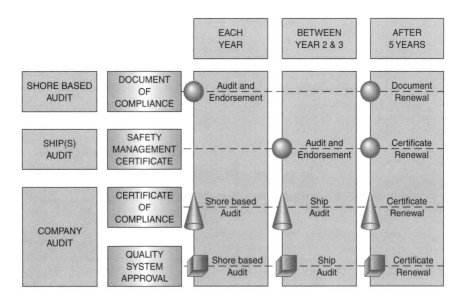

Figure 5.4. Maintenance of certification.

- Onshore operations are audited annually

- Onboard operations are audited once, between the second and third year of validity of the certificates

When the five-year period has elapsed, all certificates are renewed, following an audit performed on the anniversary date of the original certification.

Benefits of the New Scheme Certification

The new scheme certification displays many advantages in favor of the certification of integrated systems. There are major benefits for the company:

- Greater flexibility in the choice and definition of the management system

- Integration of reference documents into a single system simplifies the documents involved

- All selected reference documents are covered by a single contract

- Duplication of audits for certification and its extension is eliminated

- All certificates are issued together, for a period of five years, by the Marine Division of Bureau Veritas

Conclusion

This chapter has shown that a mere possession of a uniform set of statutory certificates for shipping industries is no longer sufficient. Companies must now comply with all mandatory international requirements. A scheme has been developed to compare and link various international standards and conventions with ISO quality program standards in order to help simplify the shipping industry's integrated quality management systems.

Chapter 6

Insights on Quality Process from the Perspective of Sociology

TIMOTHY E. WEDDLE

WILLIAM A. GOLOMSKI

Introduction

One of the models used by those who advocate a scientific or systems approach is what Robert Bellah calls total technical control.[1] One tries to develop the best model, the best systems, and the best procedures. Then, one chooses a perspective or reference point from which to select and design an organizational structure and some measures of optimization. In global companies the assumption usually is that one approach fits all cultures. But why not only use the Malcolm Baldrige National Quality Award criteria, or the ISO 9000 series, or QS 9000? Because they do not address the social questions that have to be addressed in today's world. Everyone is aware of these problems, but sociology brings them into sharper focus.[2] Sociology is concerned with the study of society and its various parts during the industrialization of society today and in the past two or three centuries.

Paid work takes place within an organizational context. People within an organization have their own world view, complete with a set of values and a shared interpretation of meaning. There may be multiple groups within an organization, and individuals can affiliate with more than one group. Each group interprets what is going on around them according to their world view. In this social context, there is no one definition of the "correct" quality approach. Rather, quality is interpreted, created, and continuously renewed within each social group. The driving question from this microsocial perspective is: How does the diversity of group interests and quality approaches become melded to become the products and services of the organization?

What is work? How are the benefits to be shared? Who determines how it should be organized? What are the hours to be worked? How can one have pride in work? Who should determine what the safety and health conditions of employment are? Under what conditions should the weekly hours of work be reduced to enable work sharing? How does society rank the prestige of jobs? What is the relationship of salaries of CEOs to first-level workers? How does one balance the expectation of a smiley face by flight attendants as a customer preference versus the stress caused by unruly or boorish customers? Why are women paid less? Why do we expect workers of different cultures, genders, and ages to be happy working together? What are the implications of using contingent workers to employee training, socializing, quality, productivity, safety, and teamwork? What does work in a good corporation mean? What are professions? These are all questions that have relevance to quality and that benefit from sociology analysis.

What Is Work?

Product and services are actualized through work. We are interested in activities that people engage in when they have the expectation of consumption based on their performing the activity. Work is an activity, but not all activities that people engage in meet the definition of work. For example, this definition of *work* excludes many necessary activities such as uncompensated child care or, in a democracy, voting. Although child care is a necessary and valued activity, it does not carry with it the expectation of consumption. Similarly, voting is necessary to perpetuate the political system in a democracy, but the activity of voting does not carry with it the promise of future consumption. This means that it is not the activity of work that promises consumption, but the social relationship of the activity. In a market economy, we think of work as activities performed for the promise of a wage. The expectation of consumption related to work carries with it the implication of a social relationship. In other words, we use the term *work* to refer to a social relationship where on one side of the relationship a person performs an activity, and on the other side of the relationship a person promises to provide the worker with access to consumption. This conception of work is sometimes given the special name of *labor*.

A person participating in work may see different perspectives of his/her end product. For example, an auto mechanic working on a car engine sees the totality of the car engine. The mechanic knows when the engine is fixed, and that it was his/her work that allows the driver to start the car and drive away. Take in contrast to the auto mechanic a person on an assembly line. The person on the car assembly line may see a particular part of the assembly, but he/she may not be aware of what the final product looks like. For example, a person building a component of a brake subassembly in a parts plant may not be aware of the type of finished car that uses their brake subassembly in the completely assembled car. The conclusion here is that some workers, like the auto mechanic, see the totality of their product or service, but some workers only see their particular fragment of the work effort. As a result, quality consciousness requires special effort so that employees can relate their work to something socially useful, even if the car driver is unaware of their component.

The social framework for labor can take several forms. One form of social framework is exemplified by the sole proprietor auto mechanic working on a car. The auto mechanic has sole responsibility for the engine repair, and the customer has sole responsibility for accepting the work of the auto mechanic and paying the mechanic (fulfilling the expectation of access to consumption). The social framework becomes more complicated when the work becomes more fragmented. For example, the person who makes a component in a brake assembly plant is part of a division of labor. The presence of a division of labor typically carries with it a hierarchical organization. The hierarchical organization embodies all of the tasks performed by the sole proprietor auto mechanic. These tasks include the acquisition and set-up of land and capital, as well as identifying the customers of the work and defining the necessary labor tasks. In the case of division of labor, the hierarchical organization intermediates between the customer and the worker. The customer pays the organization in return for the finished good. It is left to the worker and the hierarchical organization to apportion the payment from the customer to the various product contributors.

The social framework of work also carries with it the implication of community.[3] People who work together have a common shared object in the form of their work product or service. They are part of a division of labor that requires their participation. They are mutually dependent on the hierarchical organization, and ultimately the customer, to find value in their labor. People working together share jokes. They participate in shared rituals, such as coffee or tea breaks. And, very importantly, people working together have a world view that is unique to them. The world view is used by the members of the community to interpret their experiences at work, and perhaps beyond the job. For example, workers could view that their work is valued by the organizational hierarchy and by customers, so that they willingly participate in quality circles and constantly strive for improvement. In contrast, workers could develop the view that their work is not appreciated by the organizational hierarchy, that they are viewed as commodities to be replaced by automation or organizational downsizing as soon as the opportunity presents itself, in which case they might delay improvement efforts to preserve their access to consumption as long as possible.

In summary, what is *work*? Work is a special alignment of social factors, where an individual performs an activity with the expectation of consumption. Work can take place within the context of a range of social relationships. In the simplest form, a sole proprietor provides a work product directly to the customer. In the more complex form, a hierarchical organization mediates the factors of production, including the labor of individuals, in providing a product or service to a customer. Work also mediates the formation of communities with world views that are formed based on the specific experiences of the people within that community. Their world view mediates between them and all that they do in the work setting, including quality activities.

Who Is Accountable for the Organization?

In sociology there is the puzzle of the free-rider.[4] A free rider is someone, or a group, that benefits from the effort of others, but either contributes less or does not contribute at all because they can achieve the benefits without contributing their effort. For example, in a call center the group of service workers responsible for responding to customer inquiries may have one person who only takes easy calls, or fewer calls, and lets the others carry the load. Who is responsible for the success of the call center? Is it the other workers in the call center group who are responsible? Is it the other workers' job to take up the slack created by the free rider? Is it management, in the form of the call center supervisor?

For example, on a quality team one member might not volunteer for assignments outside of the team meetings, and let the others on the team carry the load. Who is responsible for the success of the quality team? Is it the job of the other team members to continue to do extra work because of the free rider? Is it management, in the form of a team sponsor, who needs to intervene?

At the corporate level, a company can be bought out by corporate raiders who then fire the former managers, liquidate the pension plan for the pension assets, eliminate jobs, move jobs to cheaper labor markets, or sell off a factory or division to another company with a lower pay scale. What is the responsibility of the corporate raider for the organization, or are the corporate raiders only responsible to themselves?

It is rational for each group in an organization to better their position relative to the other stakeholders. Each of the groups are in competition with one another for scarce resources. The better price break that a customer gets means that there are fewer profits available to pay workers, management, and to invest in capital assets. The more that management is paid means that there is less for the workers. The more that the workforce is paid means that the company needs to charge more for their product or service. Each group wants the best that they can get. The workers want higher wages and benefits, management wants bigger bonuses, and the customer wants the best deal. In this grab-bag for resources, what holds the organization together? Who is accountable for watching out for the future of the company, or is each group like the free rider who wants more for themselves, while the others carry more of the burden?

Sociology provides some insight as to how organizations stay together instead of disintegrating from everyone acting in their own rational best interest. The sociological response is that there is a moral force that holds the groups and the organization together. In communist China, we might say that foreign currency is needed and that the organizations need to be successful to further modernization. Everyone needs to contribute for the good of China. In Europe, the moral force of worker rights has resulted in laws that effectively provide for two-tier boards of directors with union participation on them. In the United States, labor strife at United Airlines with pilots and mechanics was resolved by employees getting ownership in the majority of stock and having representatives on the Board of Directors. In the United States, the moral force is that free markets and efficiency provide for the fairest distribution of resources among the population. Quality provides a contribution to overcoming the free rider problem by making it everyone's job to take responsibility for their part of the organization by focusing on their customers and constantly striving to improve everything that they do.

The final answer as to who is accountable for the future of the organization is a paradox. No one is accountable for the organization's future, including top managers who would liquidate the business if it provided them access to enough resources. What holds an organization together is a moral force that provides incentives for each group to forgo free rider status for the good of the organization. Ultimately everyone is responsible for the future of the organization because of a shared moral dimension. A belief in a quality philosophy which includes focus on the customer is part of that shared moral belief.

Sharing the Benefits of Work

Before one can determine how the benefits of work might be shared one has to explore who owns our work. In the cases of agriculture and underdeveloped economies, parents own the earnings or results of work of minors. In many developed economies minors usually own the money they earn. In very poor families, minors are expected to share part, or all, of that which they earn. In communist economies, the state owns the means and results of work, and decides how much money, housing, health care, and other benefits to give to all citizens. The state, the collective farm, and the factory are viewed as collectivities with a common interest. There might not be any incentives for improving quality and productivity. One is persuaded to put aside individual interests for those of society.

In the case of self-employed people, the individual benefits from his/her own work and improvements. Where external stockholders control the company, there is pressure for the benefits of increased productivity to go primarily to them, and to upper-level executives and managers. Profit-sharing and gain-sharing systems are not growing to the extent that the percent of workers involved is increasing. Distribution companies, such as Wal-Mart, capture the benefits for themselves and not for those in manufacturing. The pressure is to reduce the purchase price from vendors and, moreover, in many cases, to deduct 1 to 4 percent of the purchase price as an allowance for defective product. There is no cost incentive for the manufacturer to improve quality except through increased customer satisfaction.

Family-owned companies, and companies closely held by the officers of the company, except for highly leveraged companies, have incentives for improvement primarily at the managerial and executive levels. These are based on attaining company goals and attaining individual goals. Most bonuses given to all employees are based on achieving company goals and longevity with the firm.

In capitalistic societies we find two other major sources of contention on wages and salaries. The first has to do with difference in profits by industry. For decades the auto and steel industries had a wage and salary structure far above that of other industries. Their employees worked no harder nor smarter than those in other industries. Their oligopoly power enabled them to extract money from the economy to support their desire for higher profits and benefits to employees. In the long run this was self-correcting as new competitors emerged throughout the world, and new cost-reducing and quality-improvement technologies emerged. A second source of contention has to do with regional differences. Generally wages are less in the South in the United States than in the North. There are exceptions. The differences in California are reversed—wages are higher in southern California than in northern California. This is mainly a rural versus urban comparison. But the cost of government can also be a factor when we compare states and cities. As competitive factors affect costs, managements try to contain or reduce lower-level employee wages as a means of trying to be competitive.

Sharing benefits is viewed by employees as an issue of fairness. If the company is increasing in profitability, they expect wages and benefits to increase. Stockholders might want the same money to be used for business expansion, or an increase in dividends. Issues of fairness are converted to issues of power.

Quality-improvement projects that result in modest gains do not result in a demand for gain sharing. When large gains occur, and the financial benefits go to the upper levels of the organization, employee motivation goes down, and it is harder to get employees to work on new projects. In publicly held companies with unions, any increase in profits is viewed as a subject for negotiation. Management might have a variety of capital improvement, acquisition, and market development projects in mind. In some European nations, regardless of profits, multicompany negotiation occurs between unions, manufacturers' associations, and the government.

Total quality management (TQM) cannot be sustained with intrinsic motivation if the wage and benefit sharing system is viewed as unfair by the employees. In some companies when executives or managers implore employees to improve profits or the plant will close, the message has no positive impact. The employees think that they heard the same message before and the plant did not close down. Furthermore, if profits improved, the executive and managerial levels received a disproportionate share of the gains. The first-level employees think that if the plant closes, they will find another similar job with no loss in their standard of living; they think that the executives and managers will not easily, or maybe never, find another job as good as the one they have. Therefore, speeches imploring employees to improve profits are perceived as self-serving for the interests of those at the top.

Pacific rim companies are a special case. There is such a surplus of labor that executives can easily replace dissident employees. Very high benefits to owners and executives continue without a lot of social unrest. In European countries, with powerful unions, there are not sufficient incentives for entrepreneurs to start or expand ventures. Powerful unions have reduced profits to the extent that the companies cannot secure capital for local expansion. Employees have shared in too much; and the ability of governments to provide social benefits will decline because of the inability for growth in taxes. Expansions occur elsewhere.

In China, and similar developing nations, growth in profits is claimed in taxes for large scale infrastructure and regional development projects. The worker observes no individual gain for hard work, and is less receptive to TQM and campaigns for quality.

Most of the analyses of sharing are based on economic considerations. There should, and will, be an increase in sociological analyses of sharing gains. Employees will not tolerate others getting a large unearned share of the profit increases of a company.

How Is the Organization of Work Determined?

The stated rational goal for work organization is to provide the highest levels of efficiency and quality. However, sociology says that there is more to work organization than rational decisions. There is also the issue of group interest. Specifically, there is the organization problem of acquiring and maintaining information.

A brief historical background is of interest here. Before industrialization, craft workers passed on the knowledge of how to do a job through long apprenticeships. The knowledge about how work was performed was held by the craft system. For example, making buggy wheels required knowledge about what were the best type of wheels to use on the local roads. The local crafts-people from long years of trial and error knew the best wheels for the local roads. With industrialization, craft knowledge became less important. The advent of mass assembly meant that people were required who could learn a simple job. The knowledge about how to put together the assembly line and defining mass assembly jobs fell to management and engineers. Organizations grew that had ever increasing middle management ranks to handle the information and trust needs of the organization.

In modern industry, work organization has been continuously rationalized through the use of scientific management approaches and application of technology. The knowledge about the business is held in the middle management ranks of the organization. The owners of the organization do not in general have the detailed knowledge about production processes and product technology. This information is held by the middle management ranks of managers, engineers, and, increasingly, the technicians.

How is the organization of work determined? It is in the best interest of middle management to hold onto the knowledge of the organization.[5] This article is being written at a time of persistent announcements of organizational downsizing and reengineering. In these reorganizations, middle managers are losing their jobs. This is because the power to make decisions about the organization is reflecting the change in location of information. For example, in a bank a Vice President may have had responsibility for a client. The VP would have had responsibility for knowing the credit worthiness of the client and the history of the client with the bank. With computer systems, information about the customer that was known only to the VP previously might now be readily available in a computer data bank. The reason for the VP job was to hold the client information. With automation, the VP is no longer required. Their job can be performed by someone at a lesser salary by just looking information up on the computer. Similarly, in continuous manufacturing the process information is instantaneously available to everyone in the organization. For example, prior to automation a supervisor walked through the plant and monitored what was going on. The supervisor then reported to a higher-level manager, who in turn reported to the plant general manager, who in turn reported to someone at corporate. Information was passed with a significant delay due to the chain of command. With automation, a disruption in a process can be reported through a computer network in real time to a corporate office. Layers of middle management become redundant, and hence become reorganized.

The quality movement must also take some responsibility for corporate reorganization. Quality has involved workers in the work process. Self-directed teams are a glaring example where education of the workforce and worker participation in the design of work has reduced the need for middle-management supervisors. Again, the redistribution of knowledge within the organization accounts for the power to define the organization of work.

Why Have Work Teams Become So Prominent?

Work teams have been a prominent theme of the 1990s. Much of this interest in work teams was generated by the quality movement. Quality demonstrated the advantages of having people work in groups. Amazing leaps forward were made in product quality and productivity. The advantages of using teams are so obvious that with hindsight, we ask: Why weren't teams the focal point of workplace organization all along?

The reasons for the slow adoption to teams are historical. The development of mass production resulted in large industrial sectors in steel, followed by consumer automotive. Workers were needed who could fit into the production process, performing unskilled assembly jobs. The work was designed to allow a poorly educated worker who had perhaps only recently moved to an urban area from an agricultural area to perform the job. The strategy for job design was to assign specific tasks that could be repeated. The story of Ford Motor is well known. Ford applied the logic of job design developed for the steel industry and applied it to mass manufacturing. Workers were assigned individual tasks and held individually accountable. The focus on the individual allowed for better control by management over the individual's work effort, the consolidation of knowledge about the production process with middle management, and the breaking up of groups that might otherwise be a risk for labor unrest. All of these reasons are in addition to the need to take a poorly educated, unskilled labor force and put them into productive activity. But to retain good workers, higher wages were paid than generally available elsewhere so that employees could buy cars and make other purchases to stimulate the economy. The success and dominance of the auto industry led to a domino effect in new industries, such as aerospace, defense, and chemicals.

Clearly times have changed. Instead of an unskilled labor force performing defined tasks, we have service workers and knowledge workers who need to adjust the manufacturing process for continuous improvement. Instead of middle management protecting their monopoly on organizational knowledge, we see workers being trained in the tools of work management. The capital of a modern company is its knowledge resources. The use of teams leverages the knowledge within a company. For example, if there is an opportunity to improve the production process, a team composed of the people who know the process best can be assembled and work through the concepts as well as the practical issues of improvement. Why is this better than having a central production expert handle all improvement issues? The central expert does not have all of the knowledge that the team has. This highlights the phenomena that knowledge about the work process is distributed among the team. When the knowledge of the team is put together, the knowledge is greater than any one individual has. Some executives misunderstand what participation means. They bring in everyone for a meeting, listen, and then decide what to do. Teamwork involves using the best resources in the organization to come up with a solution and in many cases empowering the team to implement the solution. In brief, teams are more effective because educated workers hold a knowledge base that provides a powerful lever for improved processes and improved profits.

Occupations and Professions

During the last 50 years there has been an erosion of the status of the word *profession*. At one time it was restricted to medicine, law, theology, and the military. It referred to an occupation that required many years of study, an agreed-upon code of ethics, a means for practitioners to discipline those who violated the code of ethics, and independent judgment by the practitioner as to what was best for those receiving the services of the professional. An *internship* eventually qualified one to be a professional. In some countries there is a university degree beyond the master's degree called the licentiate degree. In other countries there is licensing of professionals. The case of the military professional has several exceptions that will not be covered here. Professionals had higher status in society because of their dedication to the welfare of their clients.

Those in other occupations wanted the prestige of professionals and adopted one or more of the criteria. One was licensing, which dentists, engineers, cosmetologists, and teachers used. In some cases, practice was restricted to those licensed. This is the case with dentists. Engineers who sign blueprints that affect public safety, as civil engineers do, have to be licensed. Mechanical and other engineers who worked within companies are exempted from licensing in the United States by what is called the *industrial exclusion*, even though they might design products that affect safety. One could then ask whether or not both licensed and unlicensed engineers are equal professionals.

At one time, in some countries, one could be qualified to be a professional with only an internship with no college education. This is changing in most countries. The term *physician* or *surgeon* requires a university education, taking an internship, passing a licensing exam, and joining a medical society that has the authority to discipline. The title is restricted in medicine. In engineering there is no restriction. A locomotive driver may be called an engineer; a power plant operator who goes through an apprenticeship may be called a stationary engineer; in some countries, a mechanic who works a certain period of time in repair and design might be called engineer; and finally, those who work in software might be called systems engineers or software engineers. An occupation may take on the trappings of a profession.

Another meaning of profession is *anyone who works for pay*. So, we have professional singers, professional athletes, and professional salespeople. We find, in surveys, the response "a professional does his/her job well whether as a laborer, a politician, or a housewife." Thus, there is a desire not to have a distinction between occupations in general, and the subset called *professions*.

Professions at one time also indicated status or class in society. But, with the desire to call almost any job a profession, if one is dedicated to it, the term in the old sense is used primarily by regulators and academics. The independent physician, although few in number, is still respected.

One in a profession was unquestionably dedicated to quality. There was some criticism of medical doctors not attending conventions to learn, and not reading professional journals. There was criticism that far too few physicians and surgeons lost their licenses because of poor quality work. There was criticism that those who worked for large clinics, or large hospitals, or health care corporations, or in government health plans, could not provide care in the best interests of the patient. Cost came first, quality second.

In the future the concept of profession will continue to be broadened and will represent competency and concern. Those older aspects that were associated with class status will diminish. Intensive education will still be associated with professions. The other occupations might not be called paraprofessionals, a title that neither nurses nor elementary school teachers like, but researchers who study occupations still use it.

Using sociological concepts of professionalism are of great help in understanding the quality movement.

What Are the Hours to Be Worked?

Experts in the field of sociology look to the future and see a world without work as we know it.[6] The sociological perspective is that we are engaged in the deployment of computer technology. Computers are increasingly capable of replacing much of the work that is done today. These sociologists see the analogy to the maturation of industrialization, which moved labor from the farm to the factory. Industrialization grew on the ability to transfer power into mechanical motion. The use of mechanization was a triumph of technology. The introduction of mechanization is welcome where it takes the place of brutal manual labor, dangerous environments, or extends quality capabilities. For example, in auto manufacturing the job of body shop painter is performed in an environment loaded with airborne particles, and has high defects because it is difficult to repetitively hold the paint stream steady. When the job of body shop painter was replaced by robots, workers were happy because they no longer needed to work in the messy environment, and they were no longer criticized for defects. However, the machine is unwelcome where it either makes work harder or eliminates worker jobs.

The computer allows the continuation of the displacement of human work that was begun with mechanization. For example, in a chemical plant automatic process control can continuously monitor the in-line sensors and instruments. If the temperature requires adjustment, the computer can make the indicated adjustments. The chemical process the computer controls allows the plant to operate without the worker. Work to manually watch dials to monitor temperature and other variables is not required to be performed by people. The computer allows the process to function "smarter."

The computer can also displace workers who are not performing or monitoring machines (for example, reading an X ray). The machine can be developed to look for patterns in the X ray that indicate a problem. There is the potential to rely totally on the X ray and to eliminate the radiologist. This is an example where intellectual work performed by a person can be potentially eliminated by a computer using artificial intelligence. As another example, the screening of credit risk by a bank could be automated. The bank computer could be set up to access all relevant credit references for a person in multiple databases. Using credit risk algorithms, the credit check work that was previously performed by a person could be handled through rapid access to the credit applicant's financial files by a computer. Again, the need for the person is eliminated. Note that this is not the replacement of a person by an increasingly smart mechanical machine; it is the replacement of a person because of the ability to create knowledge without human intervention.

These points, that increasingly smarter machines are replacing jobs, and that increasingly intelligent computers produce knowledge, bring us to the prospect that jobs as we know them will dwindle, just as agricultural jobs dwindled. Within the prospect of dwindling job prospects, what are the appropriate hours of work?

When work is eliminated, there are choices. One choice is to eliminate workers along with the jobs. We can use the rationale that when farming jobs were being eliminated, new jobs were being created in the factory. We can say that although we do not know what the new jobs will be, the market system will take advantage of available workers and put them to work at a profit. Another choice we have is to say that it is the responsibility of society to provide jobs for people who want to work. If society takes responsibility, then there are alternative solutions to eliminating workers such as reduced work hours or job sharing. Sociologists say that the situation is not unlike the Great Depression when jobs disappeared overnight. There was social pressure to standardize a reduced work week, and to try experiments in reduced work hours. This is found in many European countries where the work week is less than 40 hours, and vacations are longer than the rest of the world.

In addition to the weekly hours that an individual works being a function of the overall amount of work available, there is the consideration of the rationalization of work and of social preferences. Service businesses face peak and off-peak periods of demand for service. The hours to be worked can be matched with the peak demand. For example, a call center taking reservations for airline travel knows the typical periods of high-load call volume. The hours to be worked are rationalized when the available workers taking calls are matched against the expected call volume. There are some workers who might prefer reduced work hours. For example, a worker with young children may value having time with his/her children. In this case, the worker may prefer a job with reduced hours.

In summary, there are many pressures for jobs to be structured beyond the traditional work week. The issue for quality is to anticipate work hour flexibility, and to include all workers in the continuous quality effort.

How Can One Have Pride in Work?

Pride in work is an individual feeling. Workers feel something from inside themselves that gives them the feeling of pride. However, the sociological explanation for the feeling of pride looks not inside the worker, but rather outside to the worker's community.

The feelings that we have about ourselves are based on our reflections about what we have done and what we have accomplished. The criteria we use for judging our behavior comes from outside of ourselves. When we join a group, we observe what others around us are doing. We use our observation of their actions to give us cues about what is expected and acceptable. These cues are reinforced when we take an action. We can see the reaction of others to our behavior. The reactions of others reinforces the cues that we have of what is expected and acceptable. We see ourselves reflected in the expectations and responses of others. The internalization of cues from others around us are sometimes called *norms*. Norms tend to exist as a system, with the system of norms making up the norms of a culture. In brief, sociology says that a group has a culture that includes a system of norms and shared beliefs. Workers feels pride when they are operating within the system of norms, and receive a positive reflection of themselves back from their community. The key to the sociological explanation of pride is not the individual, but rather the culture that surrounds the individual and the ability of the individual to learn the culture. This sometimes causes problems for immigrants.

The sociological explanation of pride says that an individual's feeling of pride is culturally specific; that is, the norms and values of a culture are internalized by the worker and used internally to feel pride. This explanation of pride implies that what constitutes a feeling of pride will vary across cultures. For example, in the United States a worker may be inclined to feel pride by performing a heroic individual act. A customer may have a complaint about service, and the worker feels pride because they responded quickly to the complaint. In Japan, workers may feel pride because their group has performed well, as measured by there being no complaints to respond to. They take pride not in an individual achievement, but rather in the success of the group.

Even within the culture of China, Europe, Japan, or the United States, a worker belongs to multiple groups. Each group carries with it its own set of norms and values that provide an internal point for reflection by the worker. Specifically, the worker is a member of a family relationship. The family can have a shared set of values, including perhaps religious beliefs. These family-center norms are used by the worker in feeling pride about his/her work. For example, if the religious value system says that individuals should take pride in being of service to others, then someone doing personal service such as a doctor or nurse can feel pride by helping others, even if he/she has just done the "routine" during the day. Another worker may belong to a family belief system that says that money is the beginning and end of the reason of working. There might be no pride in the contribution of the work to benefit others, but only in the amount of money earned.

In addition to being a member of the country (for example, China, Japan, Europe, United States, South Africa, Australia, South America, Canada, Mexico) and the family, the worker is also a member of a work group. The work group has its own set of values. For example, a group of doctors may value more highly another doctor who has a large practice. The measure of pride may be the amount of money earned. This same doctor may have a religious belief system that values helping the sick and injured. The doctor may take pride in talking the language of success and income when talking to physician colleagues, and discussing patients whom they have helped when they are at home. As another example, software salespeople may discuss the number of sales they have made when they talk to other salespersons, and talk about how their software provides a benefit to society when they discuss it with members of their church. In brief, pride has multiple dimensions and is relative to the cultural system of norms that are relevant in a given situation.

The flip side of pride is the feeling of shame. Shame occurs when a person feels that they have not met the norms of their group. For example, workers participating on a quality team may take on assignments outside of the group meeting time because they would feel shame if they let all of the work fall to other members of the group. They are not seeking pride for their contribution, but rather are avoiding shame. The reality of overlapping group membership can cause contradictory feelings for a worker. For example, doctors who have religious beliefs that stress helping others and charity, may have a conflict if they refuse charity cases because of the potential negative impact on their income. On the one hand, the doctor is valued by their colleagues because of their success as measured by income, and on the other hand they feel shame because they have strayed from family-oriented values. As another example, an employee in the Federal Counselor service felt shame when one of the cmployees elsewhere was discovered to be a spy for a foreign government.

The feelings of pride and shame are the energy that drives quality. Where the greater society holds quality products and services as a norm, the company and its members are motivated by internalized pride and shame to focus on quality. Within the organization, the culture of quality can either cause workers to create quality or disregard quality.

How Are the Safety and Health Conditions of Employment Determined?

It is easy to blame the market system for a disregard for worker safety, health, and the environment. The easy criticism is that capitalists want to maximize their profits, so they maximize profit at the expense of the workers and environment. However, how does failure of the market system explain the state of the environment and the working conditions that prevailed in the formerly communist states of Eastern Europe? The answer is that work conditions of safety, health, and environment are not solely shaped at the workplace. They are conditions that are influenced by the norms of society as well.

The "correct" condition of safety, health, and environment is a negotiation between the participants at the workplace. An individual at the work site is in a poor position to negotiate for improved working conditions that ensure their health and safety. If a worker is in fear for their job, then the employer is in a position to dictate working conditions. If the worker does not like the working conditions, then they can leave. For example, a chemical factory may have airborne particulates that are known to cause birth defects when a pregnant woman is exposed to them. The company has the option of investing significant capital to reduce the environmental hazard, or in denying jobs to pregnant women. It is situations like this that workers ban together to improve their working conditions.

One response of workers is to negotiate working conditions as part of the labor contract. It is not unknown for work stoppages to occur because of disputes over working conditions. Where a single worker cannot effect change, the worker collective can. But even the ability of the worker collective to remove workplace safety and health issues is limited by the extent of their bargaining strength. If jobs are scarce and there are other workers who can be brought in who will accept the working conditions, then the position of the workers is relatively weak.

In situations where labor is ineffective in negotiating improved health and safety, a larger collective is needed to confront the business owners. The larger collective is the broader society, where business and labor appeal to the government's legislative and administrative functions for relief. In the United States, deplorable working conditions were exposed by journalists and authors. The whole of society became involved to mandate health and safety for workers. But there are limits on the ability of governments to mandate health and safety conditions. Companies have the option of moving their operations from the purview of governments with stringent health and safety requirements to jurisdictions where labor has less say, and the government tilts in favor of the company.

The issues of workplace health and safety are within the scope of the quality movement. Quality projects include a dimension of projects related to health and safety. Quality projects focused on health and safety improvements are included within the priority system that allows time to work on projects and makes investments to implement improvement solutions.

Job Prestige

The prestige of occupations and jobs is socially determined. There are a variety of ways to design studies of job prestige. One of the best is to develop a list of jobs that can be labeled with one of a few additional words such as *lawyer, supreme court justice, politician, policeman, quality control manager, hotel housekeeper,* and others. Each of these is written on a card. The person interviewed is requested to arrange the cards from highest prestige to lowest, with no ties. A rank of 1 would be given to the highest, 2 to the next highest, and so on. The respondents are chosen based on the question you want to answer. Some might be:

1. Among those in the last year of high school, how will the ranking help us to forecast the fields on which students are unlikely to concentrate?

2. What is the relative prestige of quality control, quality engineering, engineering, science, and management as determined by adults who work for a salary?

The rankings of the respondents are averaged and the results ordered from highest to lowest. We might ask some qualifying demographic questions to enable us to have analyses by various groups (for example, gender, age, education level, occupation, and country).

Figure 6.1 shows the truncated results of a 1998 study of 1000 adults in the United States, chosen at random.

Occupation	Ranking
U.S. Supreme Court Justice	98
Professor	73
Medical Doctor	61
Senator	56
Teacher	55
Local Religious Leader	47
Engineer	41
Policeman	40
Quality Control Director	39
Military Officer	34
Congressman	25
Quality Assurance Director	24
Lawyer	22
Professional Athlete	20
Businessman	18
Entertainer	18
Banker	18
Union Leader	16
Garbage Trucker	10
Hotel Housekeeper	6

Figure 6.1. Relative prestige.

Determination of Ratios of Highest to Entry-Level Compensation

There are several measures of organizational effectiveness. One is the number of steps or levels in an organization between the lowest-level person in an organization and the person at the top. It is this that we will concentrate on.

In the Roman Catholic Church you have the member, the priest, the bishop, the cardinal, and the pope in an organization with over one billion members. At one time within engineering management in General Motors there were 13 levels between an engineering technician and the Executive Vice President of North American Auto Operations. In commercial organizations we would expect global, multiproduct firms to be more complex and to have more levels in the organization chart. One would expect that the greater the number of levels, the larger the ratio between the highest paid employee and the entry-level person. There are exceptions such as partners and managing directors in investment banking firms on Wall Street. There are few levels and very large salaries at the top.

A rule of thumb used in large manufacturing organizations is that a person should earn approximately 80 percent of the salary of the person at the next level. A person at the top who earns $100,000 per year would have a person eight levels below earning a little less than one-fifth of the top salary. Executives who earn over $1,000,000 per year might have those at the entry-level who earn $5.15 per hour, the minimum wage, or $10,700 per year, or one-hundredth of their salary. In organizations such as this motivation for quality and productivity improvement is common, but not as effective as it might be.

We know that money is not the top motivator of employees, except for those in need of the basics of life and the respect that comes from the ability to share the basic social goods of the majority of citizens.

We know that in U.S. investment banking and law firms salaries with bonuses for partners are over $500,000 a year, and that there might be less than five levels in the organization chart. Those at the bottom are in clerical support; those at the top have graduate degrees or professional degrees. A ratio of $1,000,000 to $20,000, or 50 to 1 is not unusual in a firm with 200 employees. The professional skill of the partners is recognized by all and not contested. The difficulty is in establishing incentives for first-level people. Tradition, and paying no more than the local competitive conditions, determines what those in administrative jobs are paid.

Manufacturing, retailing, government, and transportation salary ratios are based on competitive conditions. Wages for those at lower levels are based on local competition. Those for the top levels are based on a national or multinational market for executive talent.

The question rises as to whether the ratios are the same across developed nations. They are approximately the same in Japan, the United States, Germany, and the Netherlands, if you include nonsalary benefits, deferred income, and the present value of retirement benefits. Nonetheless, there are advocacy movements in Europe and the United States to reduce the ratio. In Norway, according to Academician Asbjorn Aune, the culture would not tolerate the high ratios that we have in the United States at Disney, even if the CEO was able to dramatically reverse the losses and increase stockholder wealth tremendously. Equity for employees is also an issue, and if not addressed, high ratio will be demotivating.

Losing Your Identity at Work

In the October 9, 1998, issue of the weekly newspaper *Isthmus*, of Madison, Wisconsin, there is an advertisement for Winston cigarettes. In the left page we see a waitress, facing us as she pauses from her work. In the right page of the ad we see the following:

I'm a damn good waitress. If you want an actress, go see a movie.

This ad reflects the concern than many employees have, especially those in the service industry. Arlie Hochschild, in a study of flight attendants, found a high level of discontent because of management expectations that they always be upbeat and frequently smiling.[7] They also complained about the problems of some passengers drinking too much, or being rude, or having unreasonable expectations. They were expected to follow the dictum "The customer is always right," regardless if they were or not.

In that customer satisfaction model of the firm, employee satisfaction and employee motivation are reduced. Those who provide customer services in these situations are not considered social equals. They are expected to lose their identity for the benefit of the organization. Henson, in his book *Just a Temp*[8], also discusses demeaning comments made by full-time employees of a company. They make no attempt to learn a person's name, but call out, "Hey temp," when getting the attention of a temporary employee.

Work design should not only focus on productivity, but on the needs of employees to be treated with respect and dignity.

Gender and Income

In early cultures the whole family worked together to provide for their needs. As society evolved, specialization occurred and families bartered with others for goods and services. Eventually money was used as a medium of exchange and was earned primarily by men. The work of women in households and farms was not considered paid work. As the industrial revolution took hold, men were considered heads of families and paid more because it was believed that they needed more. Income was based on status and perceived need, but not on value added.

The recent concept of income parity is based on concepts of value added. But even here it is socially constructed. Certain jobs are considered "men's jobs" and pay more even though they do not add greater value. Even "value added" is a socially constructed concept. Profit is a matter of definition in a multiproduct firm. When direct costs are determined they are gender biased. The work of men is considered more important. The work that men did at one time might be easier today because of robots and ergonomic considerations, but the relative wage level has not changed. Some work that was considered women's work, such as typing, is now done by men on their word processors. The salary of men has not gone down as a result of doing lower salary work.

Trying to achieve parity is a political issue in which a widespread desire for fairness becomes embedded in the law. As recently as 20 years ago women received 65 percent of the pay of men for the same job in the United States. Now it is at about 85 percent. Again, such inequities lead to a lack of full participation in the quality improvement activities of the firm.

Figure 6.2 shows an excerpt of a 1990 study involving 150 women in both the United States and Japan who work in businesses and who were asked the question: Is your participation in quality improvement projects less because of the unfairness in pay to women?

Cultural Diversity

There is a great deal of difference from country to country on the acceptance of cultural diversity in society, in neighborhoods, and at work. The main issue is, what culturally determines the identity of a group, and how does that help to hold the group together? The cultural determinant in the Middle East is theology, which results in theocracies. Ethnic purity in the former Yugoslavia, Japan,

Country	Percent
Japan	14%
USA	41%

Figure 6.2.   Response to a survey.

China, and Korea is another example. Some nations are trying to welcome those from other cultures, but with difficulty. Among them are Germany, Sweden, and the United Kingdom. The United States and Canada have welcomed many, but need the leadership of politicians to reinforce the desire to welcome the oppressed, academics, and entrepreneurs. This has worked to the advantage of the latter two nations.

Cultural diversity has led to changes in outlook in science, engineering, and business. When one looks at the birthplace of members of the U.S. National Academy of Sciences and the National Academy of Engineering, a disproportionate number were born outside of the United States. When one looks at lists of the officers of the largest 500 companies in the United States as listed by Fortune magazine, again a disproportionate number were born outside the United States. One could argue that they were talented people who could succeed anywhere if given the opportunity. More opportunities were available in the United States.

Another way of looking at it is that people of various cultures have different insight on problems, which can be built on to the advantage of the organization. Solectron is the only company that has won the Malcolm Baldrige National Quality Award twice in the large manufacturing company category. At the time of the first award, the chairman was Chinese, the president Japanese, the VP of Operations was Arabic, and 30 other national and ethnic groups were represented by recruiting choice. Dr. Chen, the Chairman, observed that in an organization where respect for the ideas of others is fostered, discussion will enable one idea to be built on another. The diverse insights in a multicultural group of employees is richer, and more creative, than those of a monocultural organization.

This is not to say that one should have diversity without any concern for employee qualifications. Given a choice, one should not avoid those of other cultures. Care must be taken within organizations to sensitize employees to realize that other cultures are no more exotic to us than we are exotic when viewed by others. The concentration should be on the help we give to others so that everyone can reach his or her potential. No national or ethnic group has a monopoly on talent.

Contingency Workers

This is a fancy name for part-time workers. Seasonal workers in agriculture, restaurants, and in vacation areas have been used for over a century. What is new is the use of contingent employees as a means of giving some full-time employees job security.

There is no commitment to have employees when you do not need them. A fast food restaurant has peak business primarily during the times of the three meals of the day. A direct mail merchandiser who sells through catalogues might have 50 percent of its yearly business from October through December. A manufacturer supplying the mail-order firm would affect the staffing of their suppliers and affect staffing of transportation companies. For some manufacturers it might be less costly for them to supplement the workforce with contingent workers. Some companies use contingent workers because they are not certain as to how many they will need in the future. Government regulations might make it very costly to lay off a full time employee in terms of severance pay, unemployment compensation, and a continuation of social benefits.

There is some work that a minimally trained worker can do as a substitute worker. If a receptionist, secretary, or clerk is ill, or on vacation, or on a pregnancy leave, companies will use the services of a business that can furnish such employees with no long-term penalty to themselves. In many large Japanese manufacturing companies, worker cooperatives are hired for some categories of work.

From the contingent employee point of view we have another perspective. Some temporary employees might have been laid off, or are reentering the market after having raised a family. They want a stable job with health benefits. They hope that a part-time job with a company will lead to a full-time job. They get a rude awakening. Some employers do not want to hire them. They want a certain percentage of their employees to be part-time workers. Some temporary worker agencies require the employer to sign a contract prohibiting the user of their employees to hire them until six months have elapsed since the last assignment. If they do, they must pay one to three months salary in lieu of an employee search fee.

What happens to productivity? What happens to quality? What happens to teamwork? All go down. In part this is due to lack of experience on the job, in part it is due to not having an informal network to help get things done, and in part it is due to being considered an "outsider" even though organizationally part of a team. A survey report of over 300 CEOs in the United States by the Malcolm Baldrige National Quality Award Foundation was reported on June 30, 1998. A major trend identified by 71 percent of the CEOs was "a need for improved management of the use of more part-time, temporary, and contract workers." Either the effect of using contingency workers is not measured carefully, or only the economic aspects are measured.[9]

From a societal point of view we have a group of people who are marginalized, and can not participate in the benefits of society. From a power point of view, they have no power to affect changes.

How Is Identity of Self Related to Work?

People identify themselves with their jobs. For example, "I am a lathe operator," "I am a doctor," "I work at Toyota." However, in each of these examples people identify themselves in different ways. "I am a lathe operator" identifies someone to a specific job skill. "I am a doctor" identifies someone to a profession. "I work at Toyota" identifies someone to a company.

Historically, people have identified themselves with what they do. Prior to the industrial revolution, and even at the start of the twentieth century, most people were engaged in agricultural production. People were farmers. In the United States today, there are groups of workers who migrate to follow the harvesting of crops. Their job affiliation is as a farm laborer. Their pride is in the ability to harvest crops. The measure of quality is the affiliation with crop picking. In computer software, there are workers who travel from project to project at different companies. Their loyalty is much like the migrating farm laborer, they work on a project, and when their part is complete they move on to the next project. Whether or not the project is at the same company is not a material consideration. These migrating technical workers travel to projects anywhere in the world. As another example, sailors would go to a shipping hall to wait for the next available ship. The ownership of the ship did not matter. They just wanted to sign on as a ship hand. The common thread for these workers is that their identity is with the work they are doing. They do not have a permanent job, but rather have a permanent job skill or occupation. They are dependent on larger owners of land and capital for their work, but their identity is with their work.

In contrast to the worker who is totally identified with his/her work is the worker who owns the capital that employs his/her work skills. For example, doctors in the United States are stereotyped as having both the skills of medicine and ownership of their own private practices. Another example is a chef who owns his/her own restaurant. The chef employs his/her own skill and resources in the work. The chef is affiliated with the restaurant as well as with his/her skill as a chef, just as doctors are affiliated with their own private practices as well as their medical skills. Their efforts on quality focus on the success of the professional operation.

Workers who are employees of a company have traditionally carried over the idea of affiliation with a skill, occupation, or profession. A worker who says "I am lathe operator who works at Toyota," is saying that they identify with a specific job skill. The job skill just happens to be being put to use at Toyota. A worker who says, "I work at Toyota as a lathe operator," is primarily affiliated with Toyota but also is affiliated with the skill of a lathe operator. A worker who says "I work at Toyota," is identified with the Toyota organization and is flexible with regard to job skill.

Quality has been a prominent focus from moving employees of organizations from "I am a lathe operator" to "I work at Toyota." The mechanism for this movement has been the reorientation of work from a skill-centered orientation to a flexible skill-set orientation.[3] With the flexible skill-set orientation, workers participate in teams. The team is responsible for work production. The worker contributes within the team, and is cross-trained to handle all of the jobs assigned to the team. Quality and the reorganization of work has changed the way that workers identify with their work. The historical predominance of skill-center work identity is breaking down in the face of the quality movement.

Conclusion

Quality is not achieved exclusively through a defined set of procedures and rules. If it were, then one set of rules and methods would have universal applicability. Quality is done by people with different norms, values, and shared interpretations of the world. The practice of quality must include consideration of where it is located socially, and what quality means to the people in the setting. Anything less has the potential for missed opportunity or failure. We think that the field of sociology offers insight on how the stakeholders of an organization absorb the concepts and methods of quality, and helps explain the variation of successful practice in different settings. There are three major areas where sociology can have an important tangible impact on organizations.

1. Sociological impact analysis (cost/benefit analysis) is used to a great extent in public policy analysis, but rarely in quality-related issues at organizational and individual levels. This can provide a companion to the usual cost of poor quality analysis.

2. Helping to determine accountability in organizations.

3. Improving the understanding of what effect one's personal identity, profit sharing, pride, cultural diversity, and organizational structure have on organizational and societal health.

References

1. Bellah, R. N. 1992. *The Broken Covenant: American Civil Religion in Time of Trial.* 2d ed. Chicago: University of Chicago Press.

2. Giddens, A. 1987. *Sociology, A Brief But Critical Introduction.* 2d ed. New York: Harcourt Brace Jovanovich.

3. Casey, C. 1995. *Work, Self, and Identity.* London: Routledge.

4. Collins, R. 1992. *Sociological Insight.* New York: Oxford University Press.

5. Suboff, S. 1988. *In the Age of the Smart Machine.* New York: Basic Books, Inc.

6. Aronowitz, S., and W. DiFazio. 1994. *The Jobless Future.* Minneapolis: University of Minnesota Press.

7. Hochschild, A. R. 1983. *The Managed Heart: Commercialization of Human Feeling.* Berkeley: University of California Press.

8. Henson, K. D. 1996. *Just a Temp.* Philadelphia: Temple University Press.

9. *The Nation's CEOs Look to the Future.* http://www.quality.nist.gov

Chapter 7

TQM as Winning Strategy in Public Sectors

MADHAV N. SINHA

GEOFFREY H. BAWDEN

Introduction

Total quality management (TQM) has received a great deal of attention in many organizations in the last couple of decades. It is now being accepted more than a passing management fad. Even the skeptics see that the methods and philosophies of TQM can help all sorts of organizations and be utilized in all processes, improve all working environments, and eventually better serve the community and general public.

One of the greatest challenges of TQM in recent years has been its applicability away from its heartland territory in manufacturing and private sector service enterprises to the biggest service business of its kind, namely the public sector (government) organizations. For the fact that implementing TQM is a major organizational change that requires a transformation in the organization culture; processes; strategic priorities; and individual attitudes, beliefs, and behaviors equivalent to no less than a total paradigm shift, two classic impediments have been recognized for government organizations entering into the TQM way of doing business. First, it has remained an issue of debate whether to try to implement TQM in governments because of its existing age-old badges of uniqueness, massive size of operation, built-in bureaucratic culture, variations in individual organizational characteristics, and so on. Secondly, the question of belief that TQM is concerned only with manufacturing organizations has distorted many of the public sectors' administrative mindsets for its implementation.

As a result, many public sector organizations wasted years on conducting feasibility studies, reading reports, generating their own short-term alternatives, proposing program-of the-month, listening to the experts from the quality fields, attending seminars of very little value, trying to choose between "more with less" and "less with less," strategizing for restructuring, reorganizing, and so on. One can only conclude that the focus on quality and citizen satisfaction focus of doing business has remained long overdue in government organizations.

The Winds of Change

By other names, other than TQM, government organizations and their public sector agencies have always searched for models of management and experimented with many of their internal ideas, marked by many terminological differences in traditional government administration theories. As far as the financial crises were concerned, these were handled in one of three ways: raising taxes, cutting services, or closing the programs. Looking for alternative ways of delivering public service was not seen, until recently, through "better with less" ideas grounded in the practices of TQM methodologies. In the meantime, the unstoppable winds of change were coming.

It started happening precisely through the public outcry against spiraling tax increases, high inflation (in the late 1970s), dissatisfaction with quality of service delivery, and the fiscal and performance dilemmas when public sector organizations began to look for reaping the benefits of TQM and its accumulated knowledge, just as the private sectors had done following the Industrial Revolution.

There were other flurries from winds of change at play simultaneously. Customers (citizens) had changed. Business boundaries began changing. Environmental consciousness had taken a dramatic turn. The world-wide network of interdependent national and international economics changed into an increasingly global economic system. Since Adam Smith wrote the theory of moral sentiments and *The Wealth of Nations*, a change from *shareholder* to *stakeholder* mentality had emerged. Recently, the growth of media power (Internet included) has made it possible for everyone to be aware of events, where access was previously difficult. Private sectors have started gearing up for being socially responsible. Social accountability standards (SA 8000) have come into the limelight with a set of social criteria to be followed similar to the quality management standards (ISO 9000 and ISO 14000 standards). Indeed, changes began taking place everywhere more rapidly than anticipated. Public sector organizations did clearly feel tremendous pressure along the way to change; that is, to move from *treating the symptoms* to creating situations where *proactive judgments* and *breakthrough* initiatives are to be made part and parcel of government business portfolios, both for short-term and long-terms goals. Good news is just starting to appear.

A Progress Report

TQM as a cohesive frame of reference for significant improvement of economic and human development for examples in the public sector management, on the massive scale, emerged in the United States for the first time in federal government in 1993. "From Red Tape to Results: Creating a Government That Works Better and Costs Less," was the title of a report of the National Performance Review, released in Washington, D.C., that was called by quality professionals as one of the most dynamic documents of the day.[1,2] Drs. Joseph Juran and Armand

Feigenbaum, who were both asked by the U.S. Vice President to contribute to the report by participating in "Reinventing Government" sessions, were pleased to see the U.S. government's solid commitment and actions.[3] The shear volume of the work, using TQM principles, that has since emerged from that time clearly seems to dispel many misconceptions of the skeptics about quality in government.[4,5,6]

There are similar management reform initiatives being hailed as examples of great successes in Canada, the United Kingdom, and other European countries at all three levels of governments, namely at the national, provincial, or state and municipal levels.[7-12]

Specific applications of quality improvement and quality assurance, respectively, in monopoly government agencies—as far different from commercial organizations and hanging on to the noncompetitive market—are beginning to take root. Signs of progress are beginning to appear in many government reports and can be found in the following itemized list.

- Recognizing customers and their needs

- Streamlining operations and workforce

- Management innovation and flexibility

- Fiscal management reform

- Systems and process reengineering

- Defining vision, mission, and purpose

- Creating partnerships with community and businesses

- Using computer technology, Internet

- Teams and empowerment

- Training and education of employees

- Delegating authority

- Cutting red tape

- Doing more with less

- Regulatory reform and paperwork reduction

- Setting world-class customer service standards

- Managing by results

Emerging Strategies

From the results seen so far, it is apparent that the institutionalization of TQM in public sectors is helping the government to accomplish "better with less" systematically in the following four major areas.

1. Elimination of wastes

2. Increase in productivity

3. Leveraging of more uses of nongovernmental resources

4. Improvement in the bottom line, budgetary situations

In addition, the application of TQM is beginning to redefine the administrative infrastructure and mindsets on several other fronts:

1. The application of TQM tools and techniques has begun to reshape the existing *command and control* methodology by reorienting managers' actions from arbitrary command to an emphasis on leadership, teamwork, and continuous learning in the articulation and development of shared values. The validity of TQM is beginning to appear to have an appeal to authorities. When authority is delegated broadly and in task-oriented terms, the hierarchical dynamics of control are making impacts through undisturbed *executive functions* and *administrative powers*. This is an encouraging development.

2. The old management models in public sectors that hardly differentiated between management and leadership are beginning to change through identification and focus on meeting and exceeding the needs of one's customers. Many organizations have started requiring that managers participate simultaneously into the evolving new relationships between purposes and instrumentalities. Through this dynamic relationship, a premium is being placed on using organizational weaknesses as opportunities and employees' strengths as resources for meeting and exceeding citizens' needs and aspirations. This is being done through teams (both internal and external to the organization) for simplifying decision making.

3. There are many public sector examples of how *shared visions, stretched goals, clear* and *measurable objectives* are proving to be more holistic and sensitive to citizens' and stakeholders' needs. The actions taken are gradually being found to be conducive to effective implementation when commitment from and agreements amongst all major players are considered and practiced.

4. Developments in information and communication technologies are arguably benefiting many public sectors. Many departments are using technology to overcome barriers of distance, time, job functions, and cultural differences in search of best solutions.

5. In many of the public sector organizations previously preoccupied with rule-driven mentalities, the advent of TQM methodologies is helping to build more reliable mission-driven management models. Performance indicators and critical success factors are being developed and examined in areas and quantities never before examined and many of these are similar to the private sector businesses.

6. Accountabilities, performance measurements, and incentive factors are being revisited in light of encouraging results with respect to empowerment and continuous learning cultures that are slowly emerging.

7. Many public sector authorities have also begun addressing the question of *management by facts*. This, of course, has meant greater collection of operational data than ever before. Even if not all data are hard and tangible (compared to the manufacturing environments), they often embrace customer satisfaction issues through surveys of external customers (for citizens' input) and customer opinion questionnaires applied to internal customers to get an outline of meaningful work agenda.

Growing Pains

TQM in the public sectors is presently undergoing "growing pains." The language of "customers" and "profitability" still seems to baffle many managers who find it hard to accept the "total" philosophy in the wake of a long history of having to work under authority, control, command, and bureaucratic procedures. The cultural legacy in many instances is suffering from "lack of employee involvement" and "individual group of silos," while other institutions are continuing to struggle with finding the right mix of various TQM models based on many national quality awards criteria. Still many others are going ahead with cultural transformation seminars, team building exercises, employee surveys, training in TQM tools and techniques, and addressing the broader issues of technological change, privatization, business process reengineering, benchmarking, and job redesign.

Recognizing Critical Success Factors

There is a clearly identified need for change and the development of change management strategies in public sector organizations. Change for what, one may ask? The answer is: change for total improvement. Effective change, however, would not take place overnight and in many instances catalysts are needed to kick-start the service quality initiatives. Careful planning and execution of processes are necessary. Top management involvement from the outset is a must. Deliberate targeting of areas or departments where quick tangible results are possible is required in the beginning (fast tracking). Constant employee communication strategy is important, but not the information overload. Recognition and reward scheme must be put in place. Commitment, involvement, and participation have to be considered as a continuum in order to create an environment of change. Demand of workers (internal customers) for genuine participation in decision-making and opportunities for personal development must be considered alongside customer orientation to let the self-management capacity increase. Finally, as more and more public sector agencies and departments buy into the TQM philosophy, or go into the mode of project-by-project improvement work habits and form task forces to find solutions, the concept of finding leaders from within (described in the next section) should be allowed to emerge for reputation and making things happen.

New Requirements of Leaders and Leadership

In public sector organizations, the complexity in defining and finding a leader is compounded by severe difficulties that need deep soul searching starting from political forces of tradition at one end and the genuineness of regular managers and internal champions at the other.

How can leaders be developed or, more appropriately, where can they be found? The practice of TQM cannot develop in a vacuum and must have a relationship with the contemporary field of practice of process of governance. This relationship must include the recognition of the ways in which the public sectors are approaching new demands and current issues. While the role of elected representatives will always have a stronger influence, the contributions from permanent positions of internal management must provide the much-needed foundation material for new forms of practice.

In a recent article, "Leading Learning Organizations,"[13] Peter Senge asks the question, "Why do we cling to the view that only the top can initiate significant change?" He asks further: "Is it just our willingness to give up a familiar mental model? Is it the fear of stepping out of line without the imprimatur of the hierarchy? Perhaps, also, there is an element of self-protection—the comfort of being able to hold someone else, namely top management, responsible for the lack of effective leadership."

Peter Senge's observations, commentaries, and proposals are indeed an eye-opener for all organizations, public or private.

In a fast-changing society and for organizations of tomorrow, it is unlikely that methods which worked in the more static conditions of rigid hierarchical years (under the guidance of one or two leaders at the top level) will be appropriate and to support the development of people at different levels. Now there is a need for several leaders at all levels in the organization: leaders in the front-line and bottom level, leaders in the middle management level, and leaders at the top, such as executive leaders. Leaving aside the discussion of development of such leaders at all levels, which is a subject by itself, the following issues are of significance.

1. *A need to think of finding the leaders from within.* If the drive for change in the public sector has risen from a business pressured and customer-focused concern, then TQM and process improvement initiatives may offer many quantitative measures of success, but the continuance of this success will depend as much on top executive leadership as the leadership of middle and bottom-rank management.

2. *A need to think of aligning different levels of leaders.* The need to gather information and the need to manage customers' expectations throughout the "contact sphere" of organizations will necessitate a view to achieving as close an alignment as possible not only between managers of all levels but between leaders of all levels.

3. *A need to support change through leadership in change management.* As the concept of service delivery is going through a rapid perceptual change from being part of a complex whole entity to becoming a smaller and more independent part, there must be a recognition for learning about the tactics of change management. The issues of interconnectedness of leadership, interdisciplinary development of multi-skilled workforces, creation of a suitable teamwork environment, and so on add further requirements for managers' and leaders' roles in the organizations.

Conclusion

There is nothing inherent in government service organizations that ought to lead to the rejection of TQM. Indeed, the evidences are on the contrary. There are vital signs of a new culture of professionalism and recognition of the importance of satisfying citizens' requirements wherever the TQM principles are being tried under different names and program initiatives. Yet, there are evidences that TQM is being pursued systematically by only a minority of government organizations and public sector agencies. The new "citizen-centered" orientation would mean that everything that contributes to societal advantage, from business and community prosperity to good schooling of children to better health and safety, ought to be recognized and taken care of in the same way as world-class private sector components do to strive and stand behind their products and services. No matter under what name or slogan a TQM journey is under taken, the evolutionary changes will continue to sweep across public sectors. Taking the long view will make public sectors more effective today and will carry the citizens through uncertain times in the future.

References

1. National Performance Review Report. 1993. Creating a Government That Works Better and Costs Less. Washington, D.C.: U.S. Government Printing Office. NPR's extensive library on government reform through quality principles can be accessed through the World Wide Web (http://www.npr.gov).

2. Gore, A. 1996. *The Best Kept Secrets in Government*. Washington, D.C.: National Performance Review Report, U.S. Government Printing Office.

3. Stratton, B. 1993. How the Federal Government Is Reinventing Itself. *Quality Progress*. December: 21.

4. Osborne, D., and T. Gaebler. 1992. *Reinventing Government*. Reading, MA: Addison Wesley.

5. Kanji, G., ed. 1998. Total Quality Management. *Managing Innovation in Public Services* 9(2 & 3): May.

6. Sinha, M. N., E. Stephenson, and J. Cumberford. 1999. Sustaining Political Leadership in Quality: A Case Study of Quantum Improvement. Paper presented at the 53rd Annual Quality Congress, American Society for Quality, Anaheim, CA, May. Sinha, M. N. 1998. Ch. 21 in *The Best on Quality*, Vol. 9. ed. Sinha, M. N. Milwaukee, WI: ASQ Quality Press.

7. Naschold, F. 1996. *New Frontiers in Public Sectors Management: Trends and Issues in State and Local Governments in Europe*. Berlin: deGruyter.

8. Brooks, I. and P. Bate. 1994. The Problems of Effecting Change Within the British Civil Service: A Cultural Perspective. *British Journal of Management* 5: 177–290.

9. Audit Commission. 1986. *Performance Review in Local Government*. London: HMSO.

10. Bendell, T., L. Boutner, and J. Kelly. 1994. *Implementing Quality in the Public Sector*. London: Pitman Publishing.

11. Boston, J., J. Martin, J. Pallot, and P Walsh, eds. 1991. *Reshaping the States; New Zealand's Bureaucratic Revolution*. Auckland: Oxford University Press.

12. NORMIDTEC. 1995. *An Evolution of Investors in People and National Qualifications, Executive Summary*. Birmingham: Bostock Marketing.

13. Senge, P. M. 1996. Leading Learning Organisations. In The Drucker Foundation Future Book series, *The Leader of the Future*. F. Hesselbein, M. Goldsmith, and R. Beckhard, eds. San Francisco: Jossey-Bass Publishers. Senge, P. M. 1990. *The Fifth Discipline: The Art and Practice of the Learning Organisation*. New York: Doubleday.

Other References

1. Flynn, N. 1993. *Public Service Management*. New York: Simon and Schuster.

2. Hunt, V. D. 1993. *Quality Management for Government: A Guide to Federal, State and Local Implementation*. Milwaukee, WI: ASQC Quality Press.

3. Kirkpatrick, I., and M. Martinez Lucio, eds. 1995. *The Politics of Quality in the Public Sectors*. London: Routledge.

4. Leach, S., J. Stewart, and K. Walsh. 1995. *The Changing Organisation and Management of Local Government*. London: MacMillan.

5. Walsh, K. 1995. *Public Services and Market Mechanisms*. London: MacMillan.

Tools, Techniques, Technology, and TQM

Chapter 8

Transferring Quality Using Technology

GREGORY H. WATSON

Introduction

One of my most rewarding experiences as a volunteer member of the American Society for Quality (ASQ) board of directors was serving on the Futures Study Team. This team was challenged to think futuristically about what the world will be like in the year 2010 and how different possible scenarios could affect the practice of quality. We created four scenarios to understand the potential outcomes of future events based on current, observable trends.

The first step in this journey was the building of scenarios for analysis of what will happen in the future by the Futures Study Team. Scenario planning provides us with alternative views of potential future events; however, it is not the truth of the scenario or the relevance of its outcome that is most important— it is the ability to transition from today's condition to the future. When a large discontinuity in that pathway exists, then changes must be made. A different approach to the future extrapolates from today's situation to the future state. The extrapolation approach is particularly good when an end state has been clearly envisioned and the current state is known. Then, one can extrapolate forward from today to determine what actions will take us to the desired state— in our case to the time where basic quality is sown throughout society, advanced quality methods have been integrated into all professions, and quality specialists have developed new competencies.

When the extrapolation takes place, and the transference of basic quality skills to the masses has been achieved, we see that a significant transition has occurred within the quality community. It is especially significant that this trend existed across all scenarios studied by the Futures Study Team. The trend was the change that occurs in the quality profession as a result of technology and its profound potential impact on organizations to solve problems and manage their bodies of competitive knowledge. This trend requires quality professionals to accept greater personal accountability for the outcomes of their efforts and to build an increased competence in the application of technology to our body of knowledge. In other words, we become knowledge managers through the enabling application of technology.

This chapter examines the projected influence of technology on the quality profession, based on the background investigations of the ASQ Futures Study Team.

Living in the Knowledge Age

What is knowledge and how can an organization manage its body of knowledge? Knowledge management is an approach for sharing knowledge using technology as a creative enabler to evaluate contextual information that incorporates new experiences, resulting in actions that provide unlimited growth potential.[1] In other words, knowledge management is a way to apply technology that links the organization's body of knowledge with the minds of individuals facing current business decisions to help them make better judgments about potential actions. Quality tools and methods provide an analytical basis for such problem solving. John A. Young, former CEO of Hewlett-Packard, once commented on the reason for making a significant investment in information technology by saying that a personal computer on each worker's desk has created a virtual network for problem solving and sharing ideas across the whole company. Knowledge management provides a means for linking contextual information about problems with the people who are solving the problem using information technology.

Managing the Knowledge Transition

Is the future best foretold by such famous cartoon characters as Pogo and Dilbert? As Pogo succinctly states: "I have met the enemy and he is us." Sometimes people are their own worst enemies—we resist the extension of our experience into new areas through fear of performance or a Ludite-like "technophobia." Advanced tools cannot be reserved for the sole use of professionals. Knowledge tools are like religious faith: they become more meaningful when they are shared. As the Greek poet Aeschylus said, "it is the knowledge of useful things that makes one wise." What are the useful things in the body of quality knowledge, and how can technology be used to communicate them in the decision-making process?

Kaoru Ishikawa claimed that 80 percent of the problems encountered in business could be solved by applying the basic quality tools. This thought can be extended by using the Pareto principle to postulate that 80 percent of the remaining 20 percent can be solved using advanced quality tools. This means a company could be successful (solving 96 percent of its problems) when quality tools are used throughout the organization. But if, as the Futures Study Team concludes, there are fewer quality professionals in this future organization, who will do the training and how will the organization assure that its front-line workers are knowledgeable in using these tools, in both reactive and proactive modes, to solve current problems and inhibit future ones?

As Scott Adams, the creator of Dilbert, observed, "All the technology that surrounds us, all the management theories, the economic models that predict and guide our behavior, the science that helps us live to 80—it's all created by a tiny percentage of deviant, smart people. The rest of us are treading water as fast as we can. The world is too complex for us. Evolution didn't keep up."[2] This truism, spoken by a dissatisfied customer of the quality movement, implies that quality practitioners will be challenged in transitioning their knowledge to the masses, especially in finding a way to transfer their knowledge so that the masses will find it useful in their application.

This means that such a transfer of knowledge must apply the learning principles that work for adults, which focus on providing new, profound knowledge that is applicable to the task at hand, not knowledge for the sake of knowledge. As Adams also observed, "Everything I've ever learned in my entire life can be boiled down to a dozen bullet points, several of which I've already forgotten."[3]

It can be expected that people will forget what they are told, so what can be done to remind them to apply these tools and methods to their work? This is where technology comes in. Before discussing the technological enablers, however, remember the pseudosolutions that should be avoided.

We should avoid being placed into either the *Lone Ranger* or the *Socratic* role. The Lone Ranger quality professional is created whenever one individual is called on to solve all of the organization's quality problems. In a similar manner, the Socratic quality professional is created whenever one individual becomes a full-time teacher of basic skills or a team facilitator of problem-solving groups (who typically do not want external participation in resolving their problems). To be successful in the long run, line managers need to acknowledge and solve their own problems; that way they will take long-term responsibility for preventing the recurrence of such problems. So, how can a future be envisioned that achieves good for society by applying the quality professional's skills to reach this desired outcome?

The Driving Force of Change

One of the forces driving the conclusions of the ASQ Futures Study Team was globalization stimulated by shrinking boundaries among business due to electronic commerce. Today, we are routinely confronted by change, but most of us are unable to tell the difference between changes that merely present a mild inconvenience in our daily lives and changes that will revolutionize the way we work. As Arthur C. Clarke once said, "Any sufficiently advanced technology is indistinguishable from magic."[4] The role of the technologists is to innovate new products and applications developments that keep the magic going. For non-magicians, however, this is a most disturbing world with disappearing buildings and floating tigers, not to mention quarters that appear out of thin air.

How can we become settled and live successfully in such a magical world? We must learn to embrace change—to seek it and not be afraid of a new and different world. As John A. Young, former CEO of Hewlett-Packard, decreed in 1985, "If you're going to be successful in the electronics industry, then you've got to learn to love change. If you don't like change, then you should go into the beer industry where the most successful beer makers work hard to preserve the traditions of the master brewers."[5] However, with today's microbreweries and other innovations, it appears that technology and change may have penetrated even these most hallowed halls. The truth is that there is no business immune from change that is stimulated by new technology.

Business Factors in the Knowledge Age

Peter Drucker christened this new age the *knowledge age*—a time when information is a dominant factor and the economic value of knowledge is becoming greater than the economic value of durable goods. In this age, the act of creating new knowledge will be synonymous with designing a new product, and people will be valued for what they know, not just what they do. Information will become a freely traded commodity, just as food and consumer electronics have been.

In this future age, wars may be fought over copyright, trademark, or patent violations instead of border disputes. As Nicolas Negroponte, Director of the MIT Media Lab, pointed out, "being digital is to reflect on the difference between bits and atoms."[6]

The future of the business world will not be in physical trade, reflected by our current trade policies, but in electronic bits that store the knowledge that is central to an information economy—the physical world (atoms) will be less important than the world of ideas (the electronic world of bits). It seems that Plato was right when he suggested in *The Republic* that the world of ideas (neurological bits) is as important as the physical world!

What will be the character of the emerging world? One planning premise is that successful future companies will take advantage of their knowledge bases of intellectual property and will seek to find ways to use this property to better serve their customers.

The most successful companies in this knowledge age will integrate quality thinking into their business model, creating a holistic or integrated enterprise. Many of these critical success factors come from successful quality management and can be summarized as:

- *Vision-directed:* Closing the gap between the current state of the business and the vision of its future is the strategy of the organization. Mutual understanding and support for the organization's vision of its "desired state" are required to harness the energy of its members to pursue the greater goal of organizational success.

- *Values-driven:* The organization's common culture and shared set of beliefs build collaborative, committed relationships among its stakeholders—both internal and external—and networks of collaborators among unrelated businesses that share common interests.

- *Customer-focused:* The organization exists to serve its customers and considers customer expectations in all phases of its business life cycle—from new product development to field service. The voice of the customer is heard clearly and used as a compelling source of information about what products to design and what changes need to be made in the organization's customer service model. The organization is an active solicitor of feedback and maintains excellent relations with its targeted customers.

- *Process-controlled:* All work is managed as processes and these work processes are not only documented and measured, but use the in-process measures to guide the operation so that outcomes meet targeted results. Adaptive feedback and control mechanisms are one element of the information age that has been around for some time, but will grow in sophistication and application as technology becomes more advanced.

- *Team-based:* Putting two heads together has been demonstrated to be better than having a single head dedicated to a problem. Teamwork will continue to be required—even in the way that future factories will be designed. According to the tongue-in-cheek prediction of management consultant Warren G. Bennis, "The factory of the future will have only two employees: a man and a dog. The man will be there to feed the dog. The dog will be there to keep the man from touching the computer."[7] Now that's the ultimate in teamwork.

- *Quality-engineered:* Work processes must be quality-engineered to prevent defects in output, reduce operating cycle time and waste, and eliminate lost productivity. The companies that take these steps forward move closer to a goal of *six sigma* operation—working at a level where problems are a rarity because failure opportunities have been both anticipated and eliminated at the process design stage through the application of advanced quality methods.

- *Technology-aided:* Organizations have come to realize that technology is not a panacea, but can provide a competitive differential when applied to an organization that has its processes controlled and quality engineered. Technology for the sake of technology did not prove itself, as General Motors demonstrated by its 1980s-era investments in automated factory equipment projects that did not make any impact on its bottom-line financial or market performance. In the final analysis, appropriate technology used at the appropriate time will win.

- *Results-oriented:* Organizations must be focused on achieving the results described in their vision. These desired results will be defined in their strategic plans and all of their action plans will focus on delivering the long-term result—the vision—while meeting the short-term commitment to financial excellence expected by stockholders.

New Sources of Knowledge—New Sources of Competition

Although most quality professionals have dedicated their careers to microeconomic considerations—the business of a firm—the quality professionals of the future must concentrate on a more macroeconomic world—a world that is affected by global politics and emerging sources of business competition. We will not only be concerned with what our historical competitors are doing, but also what potential or latent competitors—those with the resources and capability to compete against our firm, if they should so choose—are going to do.

Years ago, the U.S. Postal Service and the United Parcel Service (UPS) had a friendly monopoly on the transportation of packages within the United States. Competitors (including FedEx) emerged, along with the rise in popularity of the fax machine. FedEx has been a direct competitor focused on the movement of "atoms" for business. The fax represents the movement of "bits" and is a competitor of a different sort. FedEx also directly competes against airlines, representing the old way of doing things—(moving physical packages). But, the fax machine is a competitor of a different type—a virtual competitor that has been spawned from the womb of technology to move virtual packages such as documents and mail via the Internet and World Wide Web. The Internet takes this competition one step further toward electronic commerce, thereby changing forever the dynamics of the "information dissemination" industry.

In the knowledge age, competition can come from a variety of unanticipated sources because it will be easier to compete when the traded commodity is "bits of knowledge" rather than the physical presence of a product. These companies must consider the possibility of virtual competitors—as Joel Barker has preached for over a decade, "What would happen if an excellent company shifted the paradigm of business and discovered a completely different way of doing things?"[8] The digital world provides just the sort of mechanism that companies can use to leverage the paradigms of their business models.

Meaning for Quality Professionals

Consider by analogy how this affects our colleagues in finance. In the old world of atoms, being a bean counter was a much simpler and more friendly occupation. One merely had to differentiate between pinto, lima, and brown beans, and in more complex situations, between baked, boiled, or refried beans. However, in this digital world, the beans have become bits and the practice of auditing has shifted from collecting the beans in jars and counting the beans (auditing and reporting) to a new model that is based on performance management and analysis of real-time operations to maximize financial considerations. This means that many of the old paradigms that have been part of business will shift over time as the digital representation of our world becomes more important in our lives. What does this mean for a quality professional?

For one thing, it means that we cannot act like ostriches and put our heads in the sand, pleading technological naivete or fear of technology. We must face this emerging technological challenge head-on because, as Mikel J. Harry, founder of the Six Sigma Academy, often preaches to people that he trains as black belts, "We don't know what we don't know."[9] It will become more important for us to gain knowledge of what we don't know to explore the limits of our knowledge than it will be to plow the fertile field of our past history.

In the future, we will be able to collect data so easily that we will be tempted to analyze data that are easy to obtain, which is not necessarily the data that we need to characterize the performance of our work systems. This means that we must become more proficient in sorting, searching, and converting data to our requirements, rather than taking the easy way out and producing reports because these data are readily available. Care will be required to identify meaningful measurements that provide actionable findings and to assure that we construct information systems to report on meaningful metrics. As Bill Gates, founder of Microsoft and widely acknowledged technical guru, has aptly observed, "The computer is just a tool to help in solving identified problems. It isn't, as people sometimes seem to expect, a magical panacea. The first rule of any technology used in a business is that automation applied to an efficient operation will magnify the efficiency. The second [rule] is that automation applied to an inefficient operation will magnify the inefficiency."[10] Gates' statements, or rules, seem to reinforce the need for process management and problem solving in the world of the future—two of the fundamental roles of quality professionals.

What Technological Changes Will Affect Our World?

What global trends and techno-shifts will change today's world and what effects will reach far into our future? Some of the major trends that are changing today's world:

- Technological breakthroughs will continue to be introduced to society. In a recent product announcement, Intel claimed that Moore's law (each new generation of microchip electronic memory will have twice the capability of the prior generation at half the cost) is dead. It is producing a new technology that will provide multipliers of capability, rather than merely a doubling of capability—thereby significantly enhancing the ability of its customers to perform new operations using the emerging technology.

  This trend has enormous implications for quality and process control applications. As computer processing power and speed of access to data increase, so do the complexity of the problems analyzed and the number of sources of data then expands exponentially.

  This is due to the interconnection capability that extends beyond a single machine to the factory floor and beyond. This increase in problem complexity and interconnection density for data sources may preclude the use of traditional quality control techniques and push the envelope to develop new areas for information processing and data transformation applications.

- Despite a need for a unique cultural identity within businesses, there is a strong movement toward standardization of business practices—uniqueness seems to have its practical limits. Standardization is necessary when the hardware and software that different companies produce must work together in a single operating system (as is obtained in the open system architecture for computer systems) or when the operations of business processes must work across the boundaries of a number of collaborative firms.

• Electronic commerce and global communications will change the way we work and live. They will provide business capabilities between individuals and companies that could not have existed previously. They will also be the means to establish new economic entities that had not been considered previously (an outgrowth of networks, special interest groups, and forum and chat groups).

What will be the outcomes of these shifts on our global society? No prediction can be completely correct; however, the roots of the future can be observed in the past. By observing the choices made and developments of the past, we can chart a future view that is "roughly right" from our historical perspective. Some possible projections include the following:

• Economic entities will be more important to the world than will be the individual nation-states. Although the types of economic entities will most probably change, they will rise to dominate the nation-state in influence.

• Regional trade affiliations will be more important than national political parties.

• Global businesses will influence international relations more strongly than the political agendas of local or national governments.

• Technology access will be critical for national economic growth.

Fortunately, technology is an enabler that accelerates the deployment of quality methods to the appropriate point of application by multiplying the availability of tools and techniques to the points of need that are distributed throughout an organization. Which technologies will play a role in this future knowledge management process and allow quality professionals to leverage the lessons learned from their experiences? Consider the following set of technologies that could enable the achievement of this possible future state.[11]

• *Expert systems*: These are computer programs that capture the knowledge of experts as a set of rules and relationships used for such applications as problem diagnosis or system performance assessment. This technology permits the thought patterns and lessons learned by the "gray beards" to be consolidated and used by "green workers" to evaluate their problems directly using the expert system as a mentor in their problem-solving process. It provides the foundation for many of the "smart learning systems" that are part of the crystal ball system.

- *Relational databases*: These are databases with logical pointers that create linkages among different data elements to describe the relationships that exist between them. This technology permits logical relationships between data elements to be preserved within the operating system for consistent application across the entire organization.

- *Groupware*: This is computer software that allows a number of users to access the same document, data set, or program simultaneously. It permits a group of people to create and modify a common document (whether it be a proposal, set of data, or research report) in real time.

- *Agent technology*: This technology permits a surrogate computer program to learn and think like the individual it represents (either a computer user or a master expert). It serves to monitor a preprogrammed set of conditions or adaptively learns what is important to the host by monitoring frequent activities and emulating those that pass a certain test (for example, the host does this about three times a day, and therefore the agent will do it continuously while operating in the background of the host's other activities).

- *Electronic books*: This technology allows an individual to create a personal electronic notebook that specifies information used on a regular basis. It may be used to compile a personal collection of data or software that is helpful in certain task-related activities. In its simplest form, the book is merely a text document that is downloaded to a product similar to a personal data assistant, which has smart applications included, such as agent technology that monitors relational databases or an expert system algorithm.

- *Adult learning theory*: This theory holds that the experience of discovery is the best teacher, and grounding new learning in past experiences is the best approach for getting people to change their behavior. Learning is a process of active inquiry, not passive consumption. Thus, to learn effectively, individuals must learn as part of a larger team that shares their desire to know. Adult learning theory can be applied to individuals in an organization and supplemented by agent technology, expert systems, or individuals who become virtual team members through participation in internal or external networks that are formed based on communities of competence.

- *Contextual information:* This is information that fits a particular context or situation. For instance, when a shipment is made from a factory, certain information becomes relevant. Every time a shipment is made these types of information are automatically linked for a basic report that is recorded as the activity, along with any exception data that are provided by monitoring systems, to describe events that occur outside the regular process.

- *Adaptive systems:* This technology permits a system to learn from data patterns or repetitive situations by monitoring data flows to detect, characterize, and record patterns in events that describe the actions taken under similar sets of circumstances.

Since information technology will become critical for business, it is most important for us to understand what direction this technology will be taking in the future. Although information technology has become the single most important factor that differentiates between success and failure in the competitive global economy, it is not on a linear path for technological development. Today information technology consists of two different technology categories which will ultimately converge and drive many future developments for business:

- *Telecommunications technology and the Internet:* This technology consists of wide area networks (including the Internet), telecommunications protocols, data transmission technology, and network management systems that assure both personal privacy and economic security. The convergence potential of telecommunications technology comes from the choice as to where intelligence should be located—on the network, or at the control of the user? This choice is not as straightforward as it seems on the surface. We already have given up personal choices to computer systems that select news articles for us to read, determine when a security check needs to be made based on our buying habits, and sort our incoming messages for significance.

- *Personal computing, networks, and thought machines:* This technology includes such elements as personal computers, high-speed modems, optical storage devices, artificial intelligence, agent technology, relational databases, local area networks, and groupware computing environments. The potential convergence for personal commuting with telecommunications comes from the merging of computer technology with modems, cellular phones, and personal data assistants in order to integrate our personal "information environment."

The fact is that these two technologies are on a potential collision course and many businesses that support these technologies may become the candidates for mergers and acquisitions as multinational companies seek to position themselves to dominate the global market share of these highly valuable technological areas. No matter what these potential ramifications will be, consider what the outcomes of these technological shifts will mean for businesses:

- Automated, real-time access to business data and information sources will be available to monitor business developments as they occur, taking much of the guesswork out of decision making and eliminating time lags that occur due to end-of-the-reporting-period book closure delays.

- This extensive access to information will pressure management teams to "urgently" develop new products (either goods or services) that will both meet the observed requirements and anticipate the desires of the ultimate customers. However much the time-to-market for new products is shortened, it will not be sufficient to deliver this requirement for urgent breakthroughs that serve the specific needs of customers.

- As the knowledge of competitor moves becomes more certain, and the understanding of the factors that motivate a competitor's choices emerge, the faultless execution of strategy and enhanced productivity of operations will be the battle trenches for business. No delays will be given in order to correct design or operating problems or to correct a misperception of the market.

- As product offerings merge and lose their distinctive quality, the level of service that an organization offers will become a critical product differentiator.

Implementation of these technologies will not be without problems. They tend to raise issues of the ownership of intellectual property, the right of the individual to privacy, and the ethical and legal issues that arise from the spread of false information about people or companies. Putting these issues aside, what will this "brave new world" mean to the community of workers in our quality profession?

Defining a Learning System

How can these technologies be integrated into a comprehensive learning system? First, consider an analogy that describes this type of learning system: playing a video game where the participant gets caught up in a virtual conversation with the gaming environment. The challenge in designing a system that permits this type of interactive dialog is that the prospective audience's reaction can have thousands of permutations in its learning experience. Designing such a computer-based learning machine requires the art of interactive storytelling. In this art, the storyteller recounts a tale, and when the audience responds with a question (or a hiss, boo, cheer, or some other linguistic expression), the story-teller adapts and responds to this new stimuli. This type of interaction is less rigid than the print media that most people have become accustomed to using for training and expressing thoughts. A significant difference is that the written media are linear, and the learner must follow the instructional pathway that has been proscribed by the teacher. Knowledge is gained by imitating the pattern of the teacher. In an interactive session, it is the learner who controls the pattern of learning and determines the sequence, topics, and depth of learning that is achieved. This approach supports an empowered view of organizational learning where each person learns what they need to know and when to apply it to their problem. In the words of Mathew Arnold, a British poet (1822–1888), "I am wandering between two worlds, one dead, and the other powerless to be born."

How Do Techno-Shifts Change the Work of Quality Professionals?

We should begin thinking about the future of the world by observing that the various disciplines of management (planning, finance, marketing, engineering, operations, personnel, information systems, and quality) have taken different paths in their evolution. It should not be surprising that the practitioners of these disciplines have developed unique cultures, values, and vocabularies in their efforts to coexist as an "identifiable vocation" within the milieu of the organization. However, this creates just the problem that drives top management crazy—the disciplines of management become wrapped up in the care and feeding of their functional disciplines while ignoring the greater value of their business processes that deliver value to their external customers. The organization that reinforces functional thinking in the vocational subcultures therefore perpetuates this strong disconnect and builds high walls that serve as boundaries to the free flow of the business. The organization of the future will be more of a virtual organization that eliminates these boundaries and disconnects through the appropriate application of technologies.

Virtual presence through teleconferences and videoconferences eliminates much business travel with its time lost from working and the often aggravating and frustrating experiences that come with it. However, it is not clear that a company will just make a few purchases and then walk into the new era. As Soshana Zuboff has said, "Unless informing is taken up as a conscious strategy . . . it is unlikely to yield up its full value. The centerpiece of such a strategy must be a redefinition of the system of authority that is expressed in and maintained by the traditional . . . division of labor. The informing process sets knowledge and authority on a collision course. In the absence of [a] strategy to synthesize their force, neither can emerge as a clear victor, but [and] neither can emerge unscathed."[12]

Knowledge and authority confront one another. This transition requires leadership and planned change. Teamwork and group-ware drive knowledge to the lowest level of authority and are the driving forces that encourage an organization to consider restructuring its decision-making processes to push the decisions down to the level where the information is best understood—in most organizations this is the true meaning of empowerment. So, what will be the impact on quality professionals?

- Greater access to information will mean that any failure of a company with one customer will be visible to all customers. Global communications will be so readily facilitated that a company's one-time problem could appear as a major failure. Therefore, greater emphasis will be placed on faultless delivery of products and services to customers (following the philosophy of Six Sigma!).

- Getting products right during their design will be a priority that gives added emphasis to reliability engineering for both hardware and software products.

- Maintaining predictable manufacturing processes will lead to greater emphasis on process characterization, monitoring, control, and adaptive correction systems.

- The need to understand the voice of individual customers will lead to an expanded use of statistical sampling and analysis techniques in the survey of customers and will drive companies to use direct customer communications as the primary vehicle for collecting and analyzing customer data.

- In order to assure that every *moment of truth*—the direct interface between an organization and its external customers—becomes a competitive discriminator, an organization will need to measure, monitor, manage, and improve the quality of its service to customers.

So, how will these trends change the way that quality professionals work in the future? Some of the trends that we should consider as potential developments include:

- The technical content of our work will increase. Does this mean that quality will merge with information technology?

- The breadth of a professional's expertise will be highly valued. Does this mean that quality will merge with industrial engineering?

- Human interaction will become more important to the success of individuals who work in this field. Does this mean that quality will merge with human resources?

- The value-added contribution of quality professionals will focus on two applications, one that is focused on the application of high-technology quality (reliability and test engineering, advanced statistics, etc.) and the other emphasizing strategic application of quality methods to the business and its customers.

While it is unclear what potential professional consolidations will take place in the future, it is significant that each of these proposed mergers represents a choice that has already been made by at least one Fortune 100 firm over the past few years. To prepare ourselves for a transition, we should observe the words of H. G. Wells, who in 1920 said, "Human history becomes more a race between education and catastrophe."[13] Our new mantra: Educate to avoid catastrophe! As Bill Gates said in his book *The Road Ahead,* "Education is society's great leveler. . . . Part of the beauty of the electronic world is that the extra cost of letting additional people use educational material is basically zero."[14] This means that while technology continues to change, we must create a robust means to educate people about how that change will affect them and give them the tools that prepare them for the new future.

Since the rate of technological change will probably continue to accelerate, we must create an ability to anticipate change, integrate new concepts into our business models, and build on proven work processes. These will be the critical success factors for achieving and maintaining operational excellence in the knowledge world. As is true today, the reliance on competent people and using business alliances and partnerships to extend the capability of the firm will be fundamental keys to success. In order to achieve this level of performance, both executives and quality professionals will need to become technologically astute in order to lead their firms into the twenty-first century.

We must learn to wield digital hammers and use electronic nails—the tools of the next generation!

As the great British statesman Winston Churchill once forecast in *Onwards to Victory*, "The empires of the future are the empires of the mind."[15] We must prepare ourselves for the new competencies of quality in order to have a leadership role in the future. Perhaps we should follow the admonition of Bob Galvin, former CEO of Motorola, who rated his top managers on their ability to anticipate change and to commit to its preparation. What will it take for quality professionals to prepare for this changing world? "In a time of drastic change, it is the learners who inherit the future. The learned find themselves equipped to live in a world that no longer exists," said Eric Hoffer.

Tomorrow Has Become Today

The change of name of the American Society for Quality is merely an outward signal of an inward change that has already occurred in the world around us. It is a sign that ASQ now recognizes and welcomes this shift and is seeking to align itself with this emerging broad application of quality—even to the point of making a change in the ASQ mission statement from a focus on "quality" to "performance excellence" in recognition of this transformation in quality thinking. This trend gives a much more extensive prominence to the meaning of quality—quality is not just a subject for technical professionals, it now belongs to the masses.

Quality is no longer just what we do at work. It is now an activity that has a prominent place in other aspects of our personal lives, such as our civic community or religious congregation—it applies equally to our volunteer work with the girl scouts and primary education, or our church where we conduct meetings, define problems, interpret data, and make decisions.[16,17]

The same challenge to personal capability occurs during the greening of business management: a maturing process for individual managers, the outcome of which is the profound knowledge of how each of the components of a business system produces a value that contributes to the systemic effectiveness of the organization as a whole. When management becomes mature, the functional fights between reigning organizational fiefdoms pass away and a collaborative spirit exists where people, processes, and information are equal contributors to business success, replacing the stereotypical management paraphernalia of laudatory titles, executive perquisites, span-of-control, chain-of-command, and other accoutrements that indicate positions of entitled privilege. In this world, empowerment reigns over entitlement. Responsible managers learn to build bridges between people in order to create a collaborative working climate and they learn to close gaps in performance areas by astutely applying the appropriate analytical tools of the quality movement to facilitate recognition, identification, definition, resolution, and elimination of problems.

Responsible managers know how to apply these words of a Biblical author, "You shall know the truth and the truth shall set you free." They recognize that, even when we know the truth, in a probabilistic way, about how work processes operate, it is not always absolute and this truth is typically complex. Pursuit of such organizational truth usually requires clarification for understanding, so once we gain the perspective of truth, we should follow the advice of the nineteenth-century British philosopher Alfred North Whitehead: "Seek simplicity, then distrust it."

For quality professionals, this future will unfold as long as we step forward and become the leaders who facilitate the transfer of knowledge to the masses. So, where is quality going? It is going in two directions simultaneously: it is broadening in its application to a universal method for problem solving and process management, and it is narrowing in its application as a technical tool to resolve truly knotty or chronic problems. What does the future hold?

Gaining Perspective: The Future of Quality in a Nutshell

The Rubicon of the Futures Study Team was the discovery that the future is a significant divergence from the past, and recognition that quality leaders have a responsibility to their profession to prepare it for a new future that will be driven by technology and the integration of quality methods into all business areas to the point where its tools will be ubiquitous—found everywhere and used by everybody.

As the Futures Study Team observed, "Every professional, in almost every field, will need to know advanced quality tools and approaches in order to succeed. In fact every organization will need to apply quality principles, or will be overrun by those that do so successfully. . . . Those who use quality must get involved in community improvement efforts. Looking into the future reveals how closely our destiny is linked to that of society as a whole. Our involvement is essential."

To achieve this degree of deployment of quality principles and methods will not require "ubiquitous competence"—the personal mastery of all quality skills and knowledge (process methods, statistics, accounting, teamwork, industrial engineering, etc.) by the masses—but, it means that the basic tools are everywhere in society. Basic quality competence has been deployed to a broad audience encompassing diverse applications to improve the quality of products, services, and life. What are these basic skills of quality management that will be deployed so universally? These skills include competence in areas such as problem solving, process analysis, the basic seven quality tools, the new seven quality management tools, process auditing, and team skills. In addition, professionals in other fields will annex some of the advanced quality tools to supplement their own tool kits, including design of experiments for exploratory data analysis, quality function deployment for translating customer needs into process features, and Failure Modes and Effects Analysis for risk management. How will this change happen and what will these transitions in the application of quality methods mean to current competence quality professionals and the need to enhance their competence?

One conclusion in the ASQ Futures Study was that "there will be fewer in number, in most areas, and will be more involved in strategy development. Communication, strategic thinking, information retrieval, and interpersonal skills will be essential to their work." You're probably thinking, "That's OK, until it comes down to me personally—here and now, at the place where I live." What does this mean to me? It means there are more opportunities to get out of the drudgery and make our careers more personally rewarding and challenging.

There is a parallel that can be drawn from another professional community: accountants were once seen as the green-eyeshade people, but have transitioned to a more strategic role working on business initiatives that the company values more highly than just bean counting.

This transition provides an opportunity to leverage our skills to a higher level and take responsibility for personal development that prepares us for higher-level and broader responsibilities. If we wait for it to happen to us, then we will only reinforce the prophecy that there will be less of us. Any quality professional who wants to be active in the future must take a leap in that direction and prepare today for what he or she needs to be successful tomorrow. Of necessity, we must change, but what form should that change take? We need to think better in terms of second- and third-order effects that this fundamental change (moving quality sciences to the masses and across the professions) will have on our profession and what effects our actions can have to facilitate the coming changes.

How do we learn to wield digital hammers and use electronic nails once the job of taking quality to the masses has been accomplished? We need to understand how to apply a variety of tools. As the saying goes, if the only tool we have is a hammer, then all of our problems will need to be nailed. This is the question that we must ask the morning after we have taken our mental "advance" into the future: What are the competencies that are going to be needed among the quality professionals of the future?

The Deployment: Making the Journey— One Logical Step at a Time

As a Chinese philosopher once said, "The journey of a thousand miles begins with a single step." The problem of translating a vision of the future into a pathway of concrete steps that leads to that destination reminds me of a story from China: A tutor once came to a wise man asking for advice on how to teach a man who has a depraved and murderous disposition. The answer: "The first thing that you must do is not to improve him, but to improve yourself." The journey of a thousand miles begins with self-preparation! Now, what does that mean for us?

Three transitions will have occurred based on this extrapolation: first, the transfer of knowledge from quality professionals to the public at large; second, the transfer of knowledge from quality professionals to all professionals; and third, the development of new competence among quality professionals. Most importantly for our profession, quality professionals will no longer be the "left-out" milquetoast of the management team, but will become the key problem solvers who attack those chronic issues that the organization must conquer in order to succeed. This means that the quality community must embrace two critical factors for sustained success: taking personal accountability for outcomes and technical competence.

The computational engines (electronic hammers) that take the drudgery away from analysis applications and help us to understand how to handle problems that used to require in-depth statistical training ("Dr. Quality" in our initial Quality Progress article), is here today in the form of the Six Sigma Navigator, which helps Six Sigma Black Belts to analyze and implement change projects. The key skill of the analyst is in selecting the tool and knowing when to use what tool. In addition, the digital nails are already present in the form of relational data bases (SAP/R3 and Oracle are two of the more prevalent; however, groupware such as Lotus Notes and Fujitsu's Teamware also contribute to these analytical capabilities).

The cross-pollination of quality skills is present in networks of professionals that also lay claim to our "body of knowledge," including industrial engineers (Institute for Industrial Engineering), the training and development community (American Society of Training and Development), reliability engineers (Institute of Electronics and Electrical Engineers), etc. Customer satisfaction is being measured and reported as an indicator of business performance through the American Customer Satisfaction Index and other countries are now following our approach. Quality skills are included in the curriculum offerings of graduate schools of business administration and teamwork is even recognized by the RIT/*USA Today* newspaper Quality Cup award.

Looking into a Crystal Ball

Once upon a future time, a new problem was presented to a competent young professional. He transmitted a broadcast e-mail to his network of colleagues around the company asking if anyone had encountered a similar situation. One colleague suggested that he activate Dr. Quality to see what she thought about the situation.

Dr. Quality is the name that has been given to the organization's chief quality agent, who inherited all the knowledge about past problems and appropriate problem-solving techniques from three generations of professionals—both quality staff and operational line experts. Dr. Quality actually has three related agent "heads:" Joe, Valerie, and Ed. This team specializes in resolving management, engineering, and statistical problems related to the organization's products (goods and services) and processes (work and business). Dr. Quality is invoked (perhaps prayerfully, as one would address the Oracle at Delphi) to identify the type of situation being experienced or, when a new situation is discovered, to categorize it into a problem type that may be addressed using the generic quality tool kit that was placed in the hands of Joe, Valerie, and Ed years ago by the wise ones of the organization.

Once invoked, Dr. Quality quickly evaluates the adequacy of the information that she has available on the descriptive event and categories the situation based on rules from her knowledge base. Analogous problem approaches are identified quickly, and potential solution methods are sorted for adequacy of information at the current time. When information to support a decision is either lacking or does not meet the criteria for use, Dr. Quality asks the host system to provide the missing or "underdeveloped" data and then analyzes the information to determine how to proceed with the analysis needed to provide a solution to the problem. Once a set of potential solutions is generated, Dr. Quality supervises pilot simulations of the alternatives to test the adequacy of each option. The best simulated solution is presented as the answer. Is this scenario a pipe dream? Well, maybe and maybe not. But, it is one future scenario that could answer the question of how to provide quality training for the masses.

Setting a Technology Action Agenda

If this future scenario is to be realized, then quality professionals and organizations must take some positive steps in this direction. They must sponsor or support research that seeks to establish the technological linkages described here. Many of the basic quality tools and methods can be taught through adaptive learning systems and distributed broadly via the Internet as a point solution to a particular learning requirement defined by a work situation. In addition, the means to characterize problems using standard logical criteria is another area where research is appropriate to determine similar types of problems and may be resolved by similar analytical approaches. A third area for involvement of quality professionals and organizations is in the development of expert systems. When experts retire from an organization, they take their expertise with them. Without this expertise, the system suffers and lessons that had been learned years ago may need to be relearned by the organization. If the future is to be supported by such smart systems as Dr. Quality, then quality organizations will need to sponsor or support research initiatives that capture this expertise.

We have not yet arrived at this Utopia. However, there is enough evidence to suggest that the transition is currently in progress. While ASQ will continue to encourage progress in this transition by providing suggestions as to how its members can accelerate these changes by participating in them more fully, what needs to happen on a broader front? What could each of us do in our national or regional quality organizations to anticipate this change? Can we share detailed success stories that describe technology integration? What organizational best practices will be the role models that influence the implementation of quality knowledge bases? What books and training topics will build our technological competence and thereby facilitate our personal transitions? Where can we go for mentoring and support in our personal development? How can we apply quality methods in our volunteer public and private sector networks to take advantage of the knowledge gained in our vocational applications? Perhaps we should build dedicated chat rooms on the Internet to share case studies and make knowledge transfer as practical as possible. There is so much that can be done, but first we must have the conviction that it needs to be done and that we are the people to do it.

Conclusion

The learned guru faces a tough decision: to sit on the hilltop and be the archetypical, iconoclastic guru of the "ivory tower" who is destined to eventually lose touch with the real world and watch the time pass by, or to be a true active learner who reflects on the past and the present and reaches out to discover the pathways to the future that will facilitate a personal journey of continued professional mastery by renewing competence in a way that better serves emerging expectations. Are we ready to take this journey?

I often wonder if any generation will see as great a revolution in the use of data and information as has been observed by mine. I remember the great advantage that I had in high school when I learned touch typing on an IBM Selectric typewriter. Now, the textbooks that I had throughout my entire school career can fit onto a single laptop computer. The pace of technology has accelerated over my 50 years at a blinding rate, with particular emphasis on the past 20 years. In order to keep up with this change it is inevitable that each of us must also change or be left on the sidelines as an anachronistic being who cannot metamorphose into the requirements of the future. Remember, it is not the fittest who will survive: Darwin said that it is the most adaptive who will survive. To adapt has become an imperative for the quality profession. However, change is not foreign to a quality professional, borne into the world of continuous improvement. We accept the fact that our work processes must change to improve, but what about the fact that we must change as people in order to improve? As Winston Churchill once remarked, "To improve is to change; to be perfect is to change often."

References

1. Davenport, T. H., and L. Prusak. 1998. *Working Knowledge: How Organizations Manage What They Know*. Boston: Harvard Business School Press.

2. Adams, S. 1996. *The Dilbert Principle*. New York: Harper Business.

3. *Ibid*.

4. Clarke, A. C. 1977. Quoted by Laurence J. Peter. *Peter's Quotations*. New York: Bantam Books.

5. Young, J. A. 1987. Speech to the Chevron Management Team. 6 March.

6. Negroponte, N. 1995. *Being Digital.* New York: Random House.

7. Bennis, W. G. 1992. Quoted by Louis E. Boone. *Quotable Business.* New York: Random House.

8. Barker, J. 1993. *Paradigms.* New York: Harper Collins.

9. Harry, M. J. 1995. *The Vision of Six Sigma.* Phoenix: Six Sigma Academy.

10. Gates, B. 1995. *The Road Ahead.* New York: Viking.

11. Watson, G. H. 1994. *Business Systems Engineering.* New York: John Wiley & Sons.

12. Zuboff, S. 1988. *In the Age of the Smart Machine.* New York: HarperCollins.

13. Wells, H. G. 1920, 1974. *Outline of History.* New York: Somerset Publishers.

14. Gates, B. 1995. *The Road Ahead.* New York: Viking.

15. Churchill, W. S. 1994. *Maxims and Reflections.* New York: Barnes and Noble Books.

16. Sinha, M. N. 1997. TQM in Voluntary, Non-profit Organisations. In *The Best on Quality*, vol. 8, chapter 19, edited by J. D. Hromi. Milwaukee, WI: ASQ Quality Press.

17. Sinha, M. N. 1997. Helping Those Who Help Others. *Quality Progress* (July):37.

Chapter 9

A Quality Management
Assessment Grid

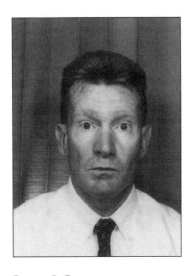

BARRIE G. DALE

Introduction

Managers and directors of the more progressive organizations are always keen to diagnose the state of their level of total quality management (TQM) development, continuous improvement, business excellence, or whatever they wish to call this type of intervention or progressive change management. The diagnosis is usually undertaken to identify the gaps between an ideal state or objective and the existing situation, assess the value of particular activities, determine the progress made, and decide the next steps that need to be taken. The interest and awareness in diagnosis activities underline the considerable impact that self-assessment against a recognized model, such as the European Foundation for Quality Management (EFQM) Model for Business Excellence or the Malcolm Baldrige National Quality Award (MBA) model, has had on managerial behavior and the understanding of TQM. There are, of course, other less-thorough methods of diagnosis than formal self-assessment against the EFQM or MBA models. One such method is the *Implementation Grid* described by Dale and Smith.[1] This grid outlines the organizational characteristics with respect to TQM of *unaware, uncommitted, initiators, drifters, improvers, award winners*, and *world class*.

This chapter examines how the grid was used in four different organizations. Each organization was briefed on how to use the grid and they applied it to suit their own situation to make best use of the opportunity. The main outcomes from the applications are explored together with the benefits to the organization.

Use of the Grid

The grid is shown in Table 9.1. It is for use by those individuals in an organization who can change things—usually senior site managers and directors. These individuals are typically bombarded with a bewildering amount of improvement data from a variety of sources, both internal and external to the organization. The authors claim that the grid offers a quick road map for plotting a path through this quagmire of data and provides effective guidance and advice to the development of TQM. It helps them first to discover, categorize, and prioritize problems and then to determine and apply solutions. By focusing attention on the immediate issues being faced, relevant to the current stage of TQM development as confirmed by observation of the typical behaviors specified by the grid, senior managers and directors can have a high degree of confidence that adoption of the effective transitional actions will in fact move their business forward in an effective manner.

To use the grid in the most effective manner, we suggest that directors and senior managers first carry out an assessment, independently of each other, of the position in which they perceive their organization to be on the grid with respect to *root causes of problems, issues being faced*, and *typical behaviors*. They must also make the point that it is useful to get a cross section of people from within the business unit to complete the same assessment. It is not unusual to find that management are more optimistic of the progress being made with TQM than staff from the operating level of the business. In going about this task it is suggested that typical root cause analysis methods (using the *five-why questioning approach*) should be used (the theory is that by the time you have asked *why* five times you will be at the root cause of the problem). This is then followed by a group meeting to pool thoughts and reach a consensus and to decide what steps to take, using the guidance provided in the *effective transitional action* column. The data contained in the grid also provide a check on the effectiveness of the solution to the identified problem. In addition to this semistructured use of the grid, it can also be used in a more informal manner. For example, a manager of a business unit could, by using the grid, pinpoint the causes of problems, issues being faced, and typical behaviors of people and from it decide a plan of improvement action.

Case Study 1

This case study was carried out by an organization involved in the manufacture of domestic appliances, employing 200 people at the site in question. The grid was distributed to 24 employees from different areas, representing shop floor to senior management. A total of 11 responses were received, mainly from middle and senior management. The discussion that follows relates to the four columns of the grid as shown in Table 9.1.

With respect to the root causals given in Table 9.1, the analysis reveals that the company is somewhere between *drifters* and *improvers*. There are indications that TQM principles and practices are becoming a way of life in all departments of the company. However, there is also evidence that some members of the senior management team do not have a good understanding of TQM principles and practices, and at times leadership is lacking. Current business reorganization has resulted in personnel changes in key positions, leading to insufficient commitment by senior management to TQM. Following an initial flurry of excitement with the introduction of a TQM training program, the motivation to continue the change process started to wane. There was lack of recognition for the need for training on the basics which underpin TQM. The participants

Stage (EFQM Score)	Root Causals	Issues Being Faced	Typical Behaviors	Effective Transitional Action
UNAWARE (0-300)	*Isolated Management Team *New Company *High staff attrition *Poor TQM awareness	*Sustaining improvement requires management focus *"Fire fighting" problems *Lack of clarity of purpose *"Death by Initiative"	*Performance root causals not known *Key managers over worked *Employees not clear of their role in delivering success	*Major internal or external threat *External accreditation required *New Management Team *Calibration against "Best in Class"
UNCOMMITTED (0-100)	*Inward looking *Poor TQM awareness *Lack of TQM success *"Comfortable" operating conditions	*Stakeholder imbalance *Inefficient operation *Inefficient operation *Declining or stagnant market share	*Few systematic processes *Management malaise *Lack of strategic thinking *Customer ignorance *"Functional silo's"	*Major internal or external threat *New Management Team *Strong leadership *Calibration against "Best in Class"
INITIATORS (0-300)	*Major external or internal threat/accreditation needed *New Management appointed *Calibration against "Best in Class"	*Misunderstanding of Quality approach *Overwhelmed by improvement activity *Badged as an initiative	*Quality/Improvement Circles *Communication campaign *Tools training initiated *Sporadic problem solving *Accreditation seeking	*Promote initial success *Implement strong infrastructure *Benchmarking to raise awareness of poor performance *Increased usage of Quality tools
DRIFTERS (100-300)	*Lack of initial success *Initial "turbulence" perceived as destructive *Change of key personnel *Loss of business confidence	*Quality approach discredited *Widespread cynicism *Improvement activity uncoordinated *New initiatives launched	*Tools abandoned *Disconnected business planning/appraisals *Accreditation fallen into disrepair	*Loss of accreditation *Major internal or external threat *Implement strong infrastructure *Calibration against "Best in Class"

IMPROVERS (300-650)	*Major external or internal threat recognized *New Management appointed *Calibration against "Best in Class"	*Internal vs External Customer confusion *Rise of bureaucracy *Key individuals over loaded *Process misunderstanding	*Endemic problem solving *Business planning/appraisal processes linked *Processes not fully deployed *Inconsistent results	*Introduction of High Performance Team Working *Introduction of Policy Deployment *Functional Benchmarking
AWARD WINNERS (650-750)	*Programme momentum *Improvement intensification required *External recognition sought/Strategic marketing need	*Process obsession *Functional disintegration *Key role of management recognized but inconsistent *In-process measurement	*In-process problem solving *Policy deployment in place *External recognition *Key processes identified *Customer loyalty	*Extensive use of Policy Deployment *Intense competition *Process re-organization *Competitive Benchmarking
WORLD CLASS (750 +)	*Intensely competitive market place *Programme momentum *Quality as a "Way of Life" seen as strategic differentiator	*Managing the acclaim *Inflexible data systems *Complacency *Career Development / Succession planning and Pay	*In-process problem avoidance *Strong process allegiance and organizational alignment *Management by leadership *Employee loyalty	*Flat organizational structure *Customer alliances *Strong leadership *Strategic Benchmarking *Academic collaboration

Table 9.1. Spectrum of quality implementation.

who completed the grid considered that a relaunch of the TQM training program, concentrating on specific areas of activity, would be beneficial.

The marketplace in which the product is predominantly sold at a premium price and on the back of a strong brand name poses a fundamental problem to the business. The previously competitive advantages offered (including performance) have been eroded due to increasing competition. However, this does not apply to service.

As was the case with root causals, the company is positioned between drifters and improvers with respect to the issues being faced. The company is currently undergoing an organizational transition with the intention to flatten the management structure. It is hoped that this will lead to increased employee responsibility and empowerment. However, there is a lack of cohesive managerial vision and divergence of beliefs. The impression is given that TQM is a "flavor of the month" rather than a fundamental change program, and this has resulted in poor coordination of initiatives, in particular JIT, cellular manufacturing, and Total Productive Maintenance Management (TPM). Adding to these difficulties was the fact that in the last two years there has been a rise in bureaucracy, resulting in issues with a business-wide focus not being correctly prioritized.

With respect to typical behaviors, the responses indicated that the organization was an improver. There was good business vision and a goal deployment system, but this is not fully understood by many employees and the fundamentals of empowerment are missing. The main processes were fully mapped; however, there were some systems and procedures which were not well understood by the majority of employees. Functional barriers were removed and cross-functional teams established, but high residual levels of functions remained and teamwork in some areas was poor.

With respect to effective transitional action, the responses indicated the characteristics of an improver. The organization was moving toward full process alignment, benchmarking had been undertaken for a number of core processes, and improvements had been made using this initiative. A number of key customers were aligned to the organization's processes via computer links and they were also included in project brief discussions. On a negative note, senior managers appeared to lack full understanding of effective transitional fundamentals.

Summary of Case Study 1

The information collected, using the grid, has provided a useful indication of the level of TQM the company has achieved, albeit subjective. The examination has indicated some clear trends and areas for improvement, outlined as follows. This suggests that the company is positioned within the improvers category. However, the results have to be considered with relation to the level and seniority of those involved in the exercise.

In general, the company has adopted some of the best practice principles and key elements that underpin improver status as described in the grid. However, there is need to embed current new practices throughout the company, particularly at the lower levels of the organizational hierarchy. Problems are based around a lack of clear ideas behind process mapping and the linking of objectives of employees to the wider company goals. There is a need to continue the investment in employee education and training, teams, and departments. This will help to increase the overall "buy-in" to TQM and provide the necessary motivation, whilst providing a catalyst for change. Within the new product development area, in particular, there is a need to achieve a balance in the functional/project organization matrix. The overlapping of roles and responsibilities within project teams and functional departments is not fully defined. Increased cooperation and trade-off is needed between functional excellence and product innovation. In summary, the company has adopted a good approach to technology development and the management of innovation.

There is potential to simplify and streamline the organization and develop current processes concurrently to improve effectiveness, which includes:

- Simpler communication and reporting systems
- Project management skills more widely distributed through the teams and organization
- Rotation of appropriate employees through functional and project roles

Increased and close collaboration with key suppliers and the use of benchmarking initiatives have helped to improve product reliability and quality to achieve a reduction in time to market. The combination of best practice principles in both the design and manufacturing capability, with a focus on the requirements of the customer, has lead to improved business performance, measured by customer satisfaction, market share growth, and a higher return on assets.

Case Study 2

This company employs over 500 people and is involved in the manufacture of automotive-related products. The grid was used by eight employees—two directors, two middle managers, three first-line managers, and a project officer. Table 9.2 summarizes the results, using the categories of *going well, going not*

Root Causals		
Going Well	Going Not So Well	Actions to Improve
Problems increasingly caused by external factors	Lack of "buy-in" by operators	Produce a robust plan, communicate it, and adhere to the plan
Personnel more confident in activities	"What's in it for me" approach	
Focus on departmental targets and goals	Management versus shop-floor	
Safety improvements		
	Teambuilding or efficiency improvement dilemma	
Understanding of competition		
Demonstrated commitment of senior management		
Issues Being Faced		
Going Well	Going Not So Well	Actions to Improve
Improvements have been made resulting in cost savings	Cynicism	Define clearly what is required and how it can be achieved
		(continued)

Table 9.2.   Results of analysis using the grid.

Going Well	Going Not So Well	Actions to Improve
Changes made to key processes	Outdated attitudes Poor documentation	Clarify the implications of failing to change Follow through the difficult actions
	Inadequate understanding of world class metrics	
	Lack of coordination of activities and functions resulting in duplication of activity	

Typical Behaviors

Going Well	Going Not So Well	Actions to Improve
Improvements made in the more traditional areas of the business	Buildings and environmental issues still significant	Produce the plan
Environment is conducive to improvement	Process team definition of objectives is unclear	Recruit suitable personnel
Success in changing culture, with a desire to be the best	Agreed actions not followed up	Brief the whole organization
	Individual projects not focused on company-wide objectives	Set and agree the time-scale and adhere to the timing
Competitive attitude of some individuals		
Focus on the process and people support		
	Duplications of some resource and insufficient maintenance staff	

Table 9.2—*continued.*

so well, and *actions to improve* the current status with respect to root causals, issues being faced, and typical behaviors.

Summary of Case Study 2

The responses varied from the managing director who believed the organization was an *improver* moving to *award winner*, to a first-line manager who considered it an *initiator.* Taking into account all responses, Table 9.2 summarizes the current status with respect to root causals, issues being faced, and typical behaviors. It is considered that the *drifters/improvers* category best describes the current position of this organization; however, in periods of stability, the emphasis switches to activities more in line with the characteristics of improvers.

Within the company, actions are taken and activities initiated that will improve performance. To make the quantum improvements required to be a world class business operating within a European context, the following have been identified as the types of actions which need to be put into place.

- Clearly defining the organization's key goals

- Developing a plan with all roles and responsibilities defined and objectives clearly aligned to the key goals (for example, policy deployment, see Lee and Dale[2] for details)

- Tackling and executing the difficult policies and decisions

- Supporting the process team concept and encouraging teamworking

The person facilitating the use of the grid in the organization commented:

The grid has enabled much thought-provoking debate on the position of the business, but also perhaps more importantly the direction in which it is going. A pleasing aspect was that within the range of comments and remarks both positive and negative, there were no real surprises. I found this very encouraging and will not hesitate to utilize the grid in the future to gain an indication of the progress being made.

Case Study 3

The organization of this case study manufactures components for domestic appliances and employs 750 people at the site. The grid was used to hold discussions with 20 individuals representing different functions and organizational levels. From this analysis it was concluded that the company is predominantly at the *drifters* stage, displaying hybrid characteristics and behaviors of *initiators* and *improvers*. From this analysis the following are the types of actions identified by the organization.

There is a pervading attitude of short-term planning coupled with the belief that TQM is carried out by a small number of middle management personnel, resulting in a lack of effective deployment of the concept. This problem could be solved by the introduction of an improvement framework as detailed by Dale and Boaden[3] to decide the priority actions within the business strategy and planning process.

With respect to company culture two issues were identified that need to be resolved: (1) development of a more open management style to address the blame culture and ensure that employees learn from their mistakes (it was recognized that this should start at the board level in order to foster team spirit) and (2) reducing the high level of staff turnover. The high levels of staff turnover could be addressed by the introduction of a personal development training program which would have a motivational effect on individuals and reduce the cost of recruiting new individuals into the organization.

It was considered that the current multifunctional teams employed in the new product introduction process could be more effective if they were more process-aligned with a common goal. Management personnel who only pay lip service to teams and members tend to feel isolated from their respective departments. The company is too flexible in agreeing to customer variants and is poor at transferring product concepts from the design stage to manufacturing. There is also evidence that attempts to reduce the time to market have tended to compromise design input. To stay in front of the competition, the company needs to introduce a number of new designs at a faster rate. This pressure has resulted in the sales function selling products before they are designed and without a clear product specification. There is also a lack of manufacturing input into the design and development processes; as a consequence, there are too many customer complaints.

The findings indicate that communications need to be improved, with goals being set and passed down through the organization, and teams and functions agreeing on individual targets and monitoring the results with appropriate feedback throughout the organization (or policy deployment, see Lee and Dale[2]).

Case Study 4

This company employs 1500 people and is involved in the manufacture of food products. A selection of 15 middle to executive management were selected from the manufacturing plants, supply chain, and service functions and requested to review the grid and indicate where they felt the company was positioned. In the evaluation they were also asked to indicate any good practices and areas which could be improved. The results were collated and reviewed to evaluate commonality and differences and to assess the stage of TQM development.

The findings clearly indicate there are a number of areas which suggest an organization that has aspirations to be *world class*. However, it is apparent from the responses that TQM is not part of the business strategy and improvement initiatives are started with a view to a quick fix. Overall, the organization is positioned between *initiator* and *drifter*. The organization gives the right signal to customers and suppliers, but a fire-fighting culture remains and TQM has not had any perceptible impact on the business results. The main reason for this is that it is not an integral part of the culture and managers are unable or unwilling to place it within a strategic business framework. In order to achieve world-class status, the following actions have been identified by the management who have used the grid.

- At senior executive level there is a need to increase the knowledge and understanding of TQM and agree on an approach appropriate for the company. A plan needs to be developed for deployment of the TQM philosophy throughout the organization and without this other actions in the move toward world class are unlikely to succeed.

- Organizational redesign is required to identify clear process owners and realign performance measures and objectives to fit the requirements of a process organization.

- A management training program to include TQM concepts is needed. All managers need to understand the importance of operating profit with respect to how the business is run and the means of communicating this to staff.

- Training should be introduced on the importance of customer–supplier relationships, with particular emphasis on internal customers, to reemphasise the business process approach rather than the traditional functional approach to management. Specific areas should be selected where problems have been highlighted and groups set up to work in these areas.

• A number of cross-functional teams need to be set-up to work in specific process improvement areas.

Conclusion

TQM is a strategy for continuous improvement and change in an environment where the accepted patterns of management are subject to constant challenges. The grid described in this chapter is intended to aid organizations in identifying their weaknesses and how to address them through a plan of improvement action using the guidance provided.

The extent to which organizations have adopted the values, principles, and practices of TQM are variable in the extreme. Many organizations have no clear idea of the progress they have made and what is needed to be done to increase the velocity of improvement. Self-assessment of progress against a recognized model such as the Malcolm Baldrige National Quality Award or the European Foundation for Quality Management Model can help with this. The grid outlined in this chapter can supplement the self-assessment process by providing a quick and easy-to-use method, in particular, at the department or business-unit level against seven levels of TQM adaption. In the early stages of TQM development, this form of simple assessment is perhaps more valuable than one conducted against one of the recognized models. By examining the characteristics of *award winners* and *world class*, motivation takes place in the next steps along the continuous improvement journey.

The four organizations using the grid have found it beneficial locating the current state of TQM adaption against the characteristics of unaware, uncommitted, initiators, drifters, improvers, award winners, and world class. In all cases, improvement actions have been identified which, if taken, will provide the appropriate guidance and spur to continuous improvement.

References

1. Dale, B. G., and M. A. Smith. 1997. Spectrum of Quality Management Implementation Grid: Development and Use. *Managing Service Quality* 7(6):307–311.

2. Lee, R., and B. G. Dale. 1998. Policy Deployment: Modelling the Process. *Quality Management Journal* (under review).

3. Dale B. G., and R. J. Boaden. 1993. Improvement Framework. *The TQM Magazine* 5(1):23-26.

Acknowledgments

The author acknowledges the contribution of Mark Smith to the grid described in this chapter. He also wishes to thank the people and the organizations involved in the four case studies described for carrying out the assessment using the grid and for making their data and deliberations available.

Chapter 10

New Quality Cost Model Used as a Management Tool*

RUNE M. MOEN

ASBJØRN AUNE

* This chapter was first published in *TQM Magazine,* vol. 10, no. 5, 1999. Reprinted with permission of the publisher.

Introduction

The need for a new approach to quality cost measurement arose due to difficulties in monitoring and documenting the effects of quality improvement activities in some Norwegian companies.[1] Top management was not willing to give their long-time support since they were unable to see the effect in their financial reports. It was also difficult to reveal the effect of the improvements on customer satisfaction and loyalty. Companies with an operational quality assurance system seemed able to prevent failures from leaving the production plant. Improvements usually embraced only internal processes that lead to reduced operating costs, and the quality of shipped products was not improved to the same degree. In general, customer needs are not adequately addressed because the current paradigm in many organizations is that marketing and sales groups have separate agendas, performance goals, vocabularies, and work processes than the product development and engineering group. They are out of touch with each other's business processes. Marketing has frequent contacts with the customer, while engineering is more technology-driven. Barriers between different parts of an organization have to be eliminated. The purpose of the research presented in this chapter is to develop a *customer-and-process focused top management tool* that enables a company to direct improvement efforts to yield maximum benefit for the customer and thereby ensure long-term relations and profit.

Problems with Traditional Quality Cost Measurement

Quality cost measurement has its origin from the early 1950s. Armand V. Feigenbaum's[2] classification of quality costs in the familiar categories of prevention, appraisal, and failure (PAF-model) has been almost universally accepted.[3] New cost elements have been added,[4] but the concept is still based on the same premises as in the early 1950s. There are several shortcomings in the traditional approach to quality cost measurement.[5] First, traditional quality cost systems are mainly internally company-focused and reactive by nature. Improvement activities are prioritized according to easily identifiable measures like failures and rework and negative feedback from the customer after problems have occurred. Customer requirements, needs, and expectations are not used proactively to direct quality improvement, and increased customer satisfaction and loyalty is not included in the measure. Performance measurement and top management decisions are usually based on traditional accounting information, which is inadequate to monitor and direct quality improvement. Standard cost systems usually institutionalize waste by relating it to a preestablished standard. A substantial amount of failure costs (including rework) is normally hidden in these figures. A certain percentage of rejects may be considered necessary in a production process, and as long as these figures are not exceeded, no failure cost is recorded. For administrative activities no discrimination is made between doing something and doing it over.[6] The validity of the original quality-cost categories has changed. *Failure costs* are eliminated according to the Pareto principle, where the most severe failures with the largest economic consequences (according to traditional accounting) are eliminated first. Minor problems are not addressed since they are isolated and are unprofitable to remove, but added up they become unacceptable to the customer. Failure costs are driven by defect rates, which are based on specification limits. These limits are often based on convenience, internal company opinions about customers' needs, and the performance of production equipment.[7] The most severe problem with *prevention costs* can be found in the underlying philosophy. It implies that it is necessary to distinguish between normal, error-prone activities and some extra effort to perform them error-free. Error-free design and work performance are normally the duty of everyone in an organization, and the extraction and definition of prevention activities is difficult, if not impossible.[8] The problem with *appraisal costs* is that they have no optimum value. A high figure may indicate badly performed production or an intrinsic necessity of the process. Understanding appraisal costs requires a thorough process understanding, and reporting an aggregated figure to top management serves no useful purpose. Appraisal costs that are a direct consequence of inadequate processes should be recorded as failure costs, and customer-ordered inspection and testing should be considered as separate processes.

New Customer- and Process-Focused Poor Quality Cost Model

A new proactive customer- and process-focused poor quality cost (PQC) model has been developed to overcome some of the problems in previous models.[2,4] The term *poor quality cost* has been used to stress that prevention and appraisal costs have been left out compared to Feigenbaum's PAF model, since they are difficult to measure and have limited application in the strategic decision process. *However, it is still important to measure these elements for internal operational use in each department.*

The model in Figure 10.1 divides PQCs into two main categories of direct and indirect costs. The direct element consists of cost categories that are monitored and perceived within the company, while the indirect element contains

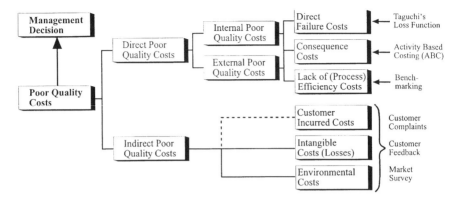

Figure 10.1.   New customer- and process-focused poor quality cost model.[5]

costs that are first perceived by the customer, but subsequently returned to the company as lost market shares. The basis for both elements is customer requirements, needs, and expectations. Both internal and external failure costs are made up by:

- Direct failure costs, which are the direct financial consequences of every failure that is discovered before shipment (internal) and all direct costs associated with claims, rejects, warranty administration, etc. as a result of problems discovered after shipment (external). Critical failures that have a direct influence on customer satisfaction are monitored by Taguchi's loss function.

- Consequence costs, which are additional costs such as administration, disturbances in current and related processes, additional planning, etc. These costs are assigned to direct failure costs through a simplified activity-based costing (ABC) approach.

- Lack of (process) efficiency costs, which are costs due to inadequate process performance compared to chief competitors or theoretical performance, determined through competitive or functional benchmarking.

Indirect PQCs consist of:

- Customer incurred costs, which are costs brought upon the customer as a result of unsatisfactory quality supplied by the producer. This element embraces much of the same costs as internal failure at the producer.

- Intangible costs, which cover customer dissatisfaction costs and loss-of-reputation costs. Customer dissatisfaction costs occur when a customer refrains from repurchasing a product as a result of dissatisfaction with the product's overall performance. Loss-of-reputation costs occur when the customer refrains from buying any products from the manufacturer, based on poor experience with one specific product. The latter reflects the customer's attitude toward the company rather than toward a specific product.

- Environmental costs, which are costs due to the short- and long-term environmental effects of the product.

The integration of the PQC model (Figure 10.1) is shown in Figure 10.2. The PQC system is based on tools and techniques that should be present in an organization that wishes to be a world class manufacturer. The dotted rectangle (1) represents the company with internal functions, where traditional quality cost systems are mainly based on allocating costs due to scrap, failures, and rework. The basis of the new system is instead customer requirements, needs, and expectations revealed through surveys of customers, customer complaints, and other kinds of customer feedback (2).

Customer requirements have been translated to key process parameters by using quality function deployment (QFD) (3). A key process parameter is a process parameter that directly influences the fulfillment of customer requirements. The QFD matrix has also been used to estimate intangible PQCs and lack of (process) efficiency costs.

PQCs for each cost element (4) (except intangible costs) have been measured through the Taguchi loss function (5), using the actual performance of each key process parameter and how the company meets customer requirements as input. This enables the company to predict PQCs at the present performance level, and also simulate how changes in performance due to quality improvement efforts will influence total PQCs.

Measuring Real Poor Quality Costs

Poor quality cost measures have normally been driven by defect rates, which are based on specification limits. These limits are often based on convenience, internal company opinions about customers' needs, and the performance of production equipment.[7] Another way of viewing costs and performance is by using Taguchi's loss function. Taguchi's loss function is based on the assumption

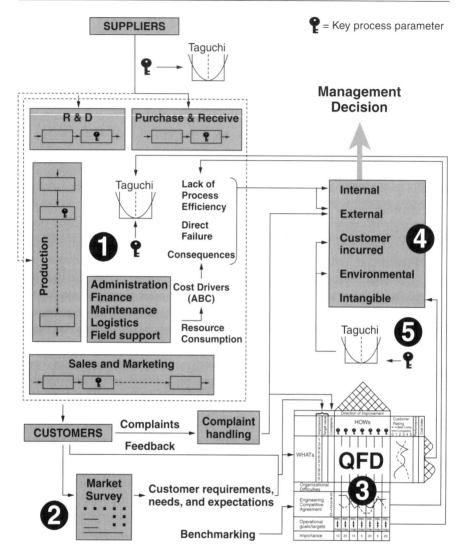

Figure 10.2.   Integrated poor quality cost system.[5]

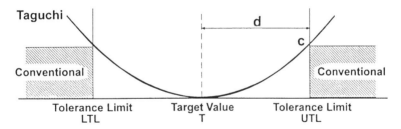

Figure 10.3.   Taguchi's loss function.

that any deviation from the target value of a characteristic will result in a loss to society. This loss is described by a symmetrical quadratic function:[9]

$$L(x) = k(x - T)^2 \text{ where } k = \frac{c}{d^2}$$

The function is described by the distance (d) from the target value (T) where the product becomes unfit for use, the cost to society at this point (c), and a proportionality constant (k). The function can also be used for a smaller-the-better and larger-the-better characteristic, which are only special cases of the target-the-best situation described in Figure 10.3. In recent years, the loss function has been proposed to be used to monitor external quality costs, including a primary component of lost sales[10] and intangible quality costs[11,12] like customers' dissatisfaction, loss because of bad reputation, and lost market shares. The ASQC Quality Cost Committee has also in general terms advocated the use of the loss function in *Principles of Quality Costs*.[13] However, little has been done to describe how to determine the magnitude of the loss at the tolerance limit (*c*) and the distance from the target value to this limit (*d*). These values are critical for determining the proportionality constant (*k*) and thereby the overall validity of the loss function. The literature emphasizes that these values have to be estimated, but a good methodology has not been provided. To overcome this problem, a simplified activity based costing (ABC) approach has been developed (see Figure 10.4).

The purpose is to break down the result of not meeting customer requirements into manageable and measurable activities, and subsequently add up the cost for each activity to an overall cost for each cost category. One standardized form is used to analyze each of the four cost categories for each customer requirement, except for internal failure costs where the analysis is based on key process

Customer requirement:	*Specified by the customer*
Cost category:	☐ Internal Failure ☐ External Failure ☐ Customer Incurred ☐ Environmental
Key process parameter:	*Translated customer requirements* (Only for Internal Failure Costs)
Type of characteristic:	☐ Smaller-the-better ☐ Target-the-best ☐ Larger-the-better
Performance; Satisfied: Shift: Shift; Dissatisfied:	*Satisfied indicates an adequate performance, improvement will not lead to additional customer satisfaction. A shift in performance indicates a situation leads to additional costs to resolve. Dissatisfied indicates when the product becomes completely unfit for use*
Failure/non-conformance:	*The problem as it is seen*
Cost driver:	*Activities that triggers costs (i.e. number of failures)*
CONSEQUENCES:	

ACTIVITIES	COST ELEMENTS										
	Labor		Material		Process		Facility		Total for
	Direct Who Time	Indirect Who Time	Direct What Vol.	Indirect What Vol.	Direct Which Time	Indirect Which Time	Direct Which Area	Indirect Which Area	Cost Dr.
1.									
2.									
3.									
4.									
etc.									

Labor Cost: Material Cost: Process Cost: Facility Cost:
Unit costs for each element like labor, materials, etc. These will differ with each type of failure.

Figure 10.4.   Process analysis based on a simplified activity-based costing (ABC) approach.

parameters. The consequence of inadequate performance is measured through activities that have to be undertaken to bring the performance back to an acceptable level. Each activity is divided into labor (time consumption), wasted material, process disturbances, and facility usage, both direct and indirect. Overhead costs are included. Shifts in performance indicate when additional activities, and by that additional costs, are necessary to regain acceptable performance.

One asymmetrical loss function with multiple intervals is used for each cost category where the shift in performance in Figure 10.4 gives shifts in the loss function (Figure 10.5). The cost at these shifts is the overall cost determined through the analysis in Figure 10.4. The expected loss for one customer requirement or key process parameter (for internal failure costs) can be illustrated as the shaded area under the loss function ($L_l(x)$) and the actual performance of the characteristic ($g_l(x)$) in Figure 10.5. The expected loss can be calculated as:

$$E[\bar{L}_1] = \int_{-\infty}^{\infty} L_1(x)g_1(x)dx, \; g_1(x) - N(\mu, \sigma^2)$$

A normal distribution has been assumed for a target-the-best characteristic, but for a characteristic with a smaller-the-better or larger-the-better loss function, a Weibul or exponential distribution would have been expected. For all

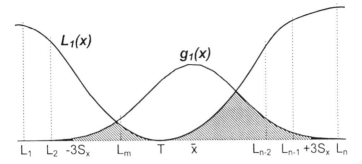

Figure 10.5. Calculated loss.

practical purposes the integration can be done between ±3σ. Necessary input to the loss calculation is the shifts in performance (L_i) and the cost at these shifts. In addition, the expected value of the process influencing the characteristic, and the standard deviation of this process, is required. These values can be used to simulate how changes in process performance, either the centering or the range of variation, will influence the loss for the characteristic.

Estimating Intangible Poor Quality Costs

Intangible costs have been described as the most important costs needed for management, but they are unknown and unknowable.[14] However, it is believed that by using the QFD matrix it is possible to make quite accurate estimates of these costs.[5] Intangible PQCs consist of customer dissatisfaction costs and loss-of-reputation costs, as previously described, and they are calculated as:

1. An estimate of the lost revenue of the current product or service because one existing customer is lost. This can be estimated as repurchase intention and the average number of repurchases during a given time frame.

2. An estimate of lost revenue from potential customers, which is lost because of dissatisfied customer advice against the current product.

3. Lost sales of other products provided by the manufacturer based on poor experience with one product. This element is strongly dependent on the product mix the company provides, and the similarity and coherence between each product.

The total cost of points 1, 2, and 3 has been denoted C_{tot}, which is an estimate of the potential intangible cost due to a dissatisfied customer who leaves the company. Actual intangible PQCs, based on the estimate of potential costs

(C_{tot}), has been determined by using the QFD matrix. The customers' rating of importance (2) of each requirement (1), along with the customers' perception of the company's performance for each requirement compared to chief competitors (3), has been used to calculate a cost index (4). This cost index is used as an estimator of the probability that poor product or service performance will result in an intangible cost (see Figure 10.6). If the importance of a customer requirement is low, the probability that a loss will occur is low, but if the importance is high, the probability of losing the customer is high. The performance of the company compared to competitors will also influence the probability of a loss. The difference between the company's and their chief competitor's performance has been denoted P_i, which is a performance index. A negative P_i indicates that the company's performance is better than its chief competitor, and it is assumed that a loss will most likely *not* occur even if the customer is dissatisfied and the requirement has a high importance attached to it. The customer has no alternative supplier and will not gain anything by leaving the company. If the company's performance is low compared to the chief competitor's, a loss will most likely occur.

In the worst case the difference in performance ($P_1, P_2, \ldots P_n$) can be 5 to the disadvantage of the company for every customer requirement (*Req 1, Req 2, . . . Req n*), which gives the maximum expected loss (C_{tot}). The cost index *CI* for each customer requirement can be expressed as: $CI_i = I_i \times P_i$

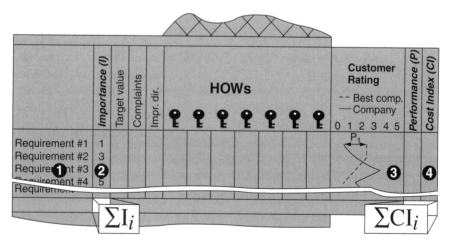

Figure 10.6. Estimating intangible poor quality costs.

Where: I_i = Importance attached to requirement i (2).

P_i = The company's performance for requirement i where a *negative* P_i indicates better performance than the chief competitor.

CI_i = Cost index for requirement i (4).

$CI_{i,max}$ = $I_i \times 5$, which equals worst case difference in performance ($P_i = 5$).

A loss factor (f_{loss}) can be described as the overall loss estimated in 1, 2, and 3 (C_{tot}), divided by the worst case cost index (Ci_{max}); that is, when the difference in performance is 5 for every requirement to the disadvantage of the company:

$$f_{loss} = \frac{C_{tot}}{CI_{max}} = \frac{C_{tot}}{5 \times \sum_{i=1}^{n} I_i}$$

The expected annual loss for one product can be expressed as the loss factor times the sum of cost indexes (the probability that not meeting each customer requirement will lead to an intangible loss):

$$E(L) = f_{loss} \times \sum_{i=1}^{n} CI_i$$

Where a positive P_i indicates that the performance of the chief competitor is better than the company, and a negative P_i indicates that the company performs better than the chief competitor. Negative values of P_i will per definition not result in a loss ($\div P_i \equiv 0$).

A product is described by the requirements in Figure 10.7 with their attached importance (I_i). The customer's evaluation of performance is given by P_i. The sum of the three cost elements is C_{tot} = \$400 (not calculated), which is the total estimated loss due to one dissatisfied customer who leaves the company as a result of poor product or service performance. The loss factor can then be described as:

$$f_{loss} = \frac{C_{tot}}{CI_{max}} = \frac{C_{tot}}{5 \times \sum_{i=1}^{n} I_i} = \frac{\$400}{5 \times 27.8} = 2.88$$

Example:

Customer requirement	Importance I_i	Customer rating 0 1 2 3 4 5	Performance P_i	Cost Index $CI_i=I_i \times P_i$
Fast delivery	3.3		2.1	6.93
Low cost	5.2		1.1	5.72
Reliable	7.8		-0.5	$-3.90 \Rightarrow 0$
Nice colour	2.0		1.5	3.00
Easy to use	8.0		-1.5	$-12.00 \Rightarrow 0$
Small	1.5		3.0	4.50
Sum	$\Sigma I_i = \mathbf{27.8}$	Manufacturer ——— Competitor − − − − −		$\Sigma CI_i = \mathbf{20.15}$

Figure 10.7.   Customer incurred costs: example.

which gives an expected *annual* intangible loss for the product:

$$E(L) = f_{loss} \times \sum_{i=1}^{n} CI_i = 2.88 \times 20.15 = \$57.99$$

By using this approach, the manufacturer can obtain a picture of the long-term consequences of not meeting customer requirements, and focus its improvement efforts on those elements that will lead to a reduction in intangible costs.

Conclusion

A new customer- and process-focused poor quality cost model has been developed to give a more accurate picture of the cost of poor quality and to enable management to make long-term strategic decisions concerning how to best satisfy customers. Areas for improvement are identified through first determining customer requirements and their importance and subsequently translating these requirements to key process parameters. The most important key process parameters, regarding how to meet customer requirements, are monitored through the loss function. The loss function describes how sensitive a characteristic is to process deviation from the target value, and when linked to actual process performance it becomes possible to predict expected PQCs for each characteristic. The model can also be used to simulate how changes in process performance will influence PQCs. Intangible costs have been made less intangible. By using the QFD matrix and a cost index based on the importance of each customer requirement, and the company's performance compared to competitors, it has become possible to estimate the expected intangible loss for each customer requirement. When this estimate is included in the overall cost picture, the priorities for quality improvement will most likely change dramatically. An allegation is that companies that rely exclusively on traditional quality cost models are suboptimizing their processes, and the results of quality improvement may at the worst antagonize customer satisfaction and loyalty.

References

1. Moen, R. M. 1995. Quality Improvement Based on Poor Quality Cost Measurement. Report from the Norwegian Institute of Wood Technology (in Norwegian).

2. Feigenbaum, A. V. 1956. Total Quality Control. *Harvard Business Review* 34(November–December):93–101.

3. Plunkett, J. J., and B. G. Dale. 1987. A Review of the Literature on Quality-Related Costs. *International Journal of Quality and Reliability Management. 4(1):40–52.*

4. Harrington, H. J. 1987. *Poor-Quality Costs.* Milwaukee, WI: ASQC Quality Press.

5. Moen, R. M. 1997. Customer and Process Focused Poor Quality Cost Model Used as a Strategic Decision-Making Tool. Ph.D. diss., Norwegian University of Science and Technology, Trondheim, Norway.

6. International Academy for Quality. 1995. Considerations Concerning Quality-Related Costs. Chap. 10 in *The Best on Quality Volume 6.* Ed. J. D. Hromi, Milwaukee, WI: ASQC Quality Press.

7. Diallo, A., Z. U. Khan, CMA, and C. F. Vail. 1995. Cost of Quality in the New Manufacturing Environment. *Management Accounting* 77(2):21–25.

8. Porter, L. J., and P. Rayner. 1992. Quality Costing for Total Quality Management. *International Journal of Production Economics* 27(1):69–81.

9. Taguchi, G., E. Elsayed, T. Hsiang. 1989. *Quality Engineering in Production Systems.* New York: McGraw-Hill.

10. Margavio, G. W., R. L. Fink, and T. M. Margavio. 1994. Quality Improvement Using Capital Budgeting and Taguchi's Function. *International Journal of Quality and Reliability Management* 11(6):10–20.

11. Kim, M. W., and W. M. Liao. 1994. Estimating Hidden Quality Costs with Quality Loss Functions. *Accounting Horizon* 8(1):8–17.

12. Albright, T. L., and H. P. Roth. 1992. The Measurement of Quality Costs: An Alternative Paradigm. *Accounting Horizon* 6(2):15–27.

13. ASQC Quality Cost Committee. 1990. *Principles of Quality Cost: Principles, Implementation, and Use.* 2d ed. Milwaukee, WI: ASQC Quality Press.

14. Deming, E. W. 1986. *Out of the Crisis.* Cambridge, MA: Massachusetts Institute of Technology.

Chapter 11

Statistical Tools and Techniques: Development of a Framework for Quality Improvement Strategies

T. N. GOH

Introduction

Quality practitioners in both management and technical functions today are inundated with a variety of statistical tools for quality improvement. To help develop a better appreciation of how such tools can be deployed in an effective manner, this chapter puts forth several frameworks for their roles and functions. First, a general framework of management, technology, and information is outlined. The statistical aspect of quality improvement is then highlighted, followed by a discussion of the stages through which the statistical competence and sophistication of a quality practitioner can be discerned. The actual approach to quality on an organizational basis is explained next, where distinctions are made between quality by inspection, monitoring, and design. Features of the Taguchi approach to quality, as well as the way they differ from those of conventional statistics, are then pointed out. Finally, the integration of all available tools is presented in the form of a *Seven-S* strategy, whereby statistical tools are used to *select* controls and performance indexes, *secure* valid measurements, *screen* design factors, *shift* performance levels, *shrink* variations, *search* for optimal settings, and *sustain* the resulting optimality. The goals of such a strategic deployment of statistical tools in a manufacturing environment are summarized in the concluding section.

Approaches to Quality Improvement

The importance of quality to the survival and growth of an operation or organization is well known. Regardless of how quality is defined, it is ultimately reflected by a universal set of criteria: on-target, least variation, least cost, and on-time performance. Factors that contribute to the attainment of superior quality are numerous and complex, but they fit into three broad dimensions. The most fundamental is a properly established *quality management* system, encompassing a wide spectrum of considerations ranging from corporate philosophy to policies, plans, procedures, and employee motivation, and supplier management and customer relations. Standards such as ISO 9000 or QS-9000, or the Malcolm Baldrige Award guidelines, reflect the range of requirements to be addressed in a quality management system.

A quality management system must have the strong backing of the requisite *quality technology* entailing engineering know-how and all the hardware and software resources commensurate with the technical performances required of the products or services to be generated. Beyond this, the full quality and productivity potential of an organization can be realized only with the presence of a third dimension; namely, a capability to handle *quality information*. Quality information utilization is statistical in nature; it is essential for intelligent decision making based on data on the behavior of processes or products in the face of natural variability. Generally, only an effective interplay of capabilities in management, technology, and information can maintain balanced and sustained advances in quality levels in an organization.

Development of Statistical Competence

Quality management and quality technology issues will not be addressed in this article, as their importance has been well recognized. The focus here is quality via data-based information utilization (in other words, statistics). Consider the fact that when one speaks about quality *improvement,* measurements must be taken so that one knows the performance of a process or product *before,* how it is *now,* and what target to set for the *future:* this can only be done via the quantitative vehicle for information—data. Inasmuch as statistics is related to the collection, analysis, and interpretation of data, a variety of tools based on mathematical statistics has been developed for applications aimed at quality excellence.

Descriptions of established statistical tools for quality abound in the literature.[1-5] It would be meaningful to examine the way in which these tools are acquired and used at the personal level by a nonprofessional statistician. Table 11.1 summarizes seven progressive stages in which applications of statistical concepts and techniques are realized.

Stage	Source of Information	Medium	Tools	Function	Result
1	Data of experience	Impressions of quantities	Judgment	Reference	Feeling
2	Available data	Measurements and counts	Tables	Storage	Numbers
3	Available data	Graphical analysis	f-D, π -C, RC, etc.	Summary	Information
4	Available data	Descriptive statistics	$\bar{x}$, s^2	Description	Knowledge
5	Sampled data	Descriptive statistics	$\hat{\mu}$, $\hat{\sigma}^2$, GRR, C_{pk}	Prediction	Foresight
6	Sampled data	Inferential statistics	TOH, SPC	Control	Action
7	Generated data	Statistical models	DOE, RSM	Optimization	Command

Table 11.1. Statistical applications: advances in seven stages.

The progression starts with the most common stage: namely, subjective reaction to quality issues. For example, if there is a customer complaint about quality, it may be taken seriously at once, or be dismissed as trivial "based on previous experience." Some impressions of quantitative information (such as frequency of past complaints) may come into play in such a situation, but there is usually little reference to actual data.

In a move toward more objective reasoning, data may start to be gathered on the subject of interest and exhibited in listings and tables. This is stage 2, in which raw data are stored unprocessed, but little insight is available regarding the properties or behavior of the physical entity or system from which the data are obtained.

Analysis-Oriented Studies

In stage 3, data is summarized graphically (for example, in the form of histograms and pie charts). A histogram (or frequency diagram, f-D) shows the central tendency, spread, and shape of the distribution of a collection of measurements; a pie chart (π-C) gives a breakdown of data categories. While histograms and pie charts provide a *static* summary of data characteristics, the *dynamic* nature of data variability can be exhibited in run charts (RC) which relate measurements to time. Stage 3 signifies the transition from mere possession of numbers to possession of information.

Information can next be crystallized and conveyed via descriptive statistics such as sample means ($\bar{x}$) and variances (s^2). Starting from stage 4, transformed rather than raw data values are routinely used for description and prediction of variability. The concept of distribution function for a large number of measurements is also formalized. This is necessitated by the fact that variability, being at the root of all quality and reliability problems, needs to be expressed quantitatively and accurately.

Another advance in statistical interpretation takes place when it is recognized that the available data are but a small portion of all possible data (a sample out of a population). Thus, for example, uncertainties due to sampling variability are recognized and accommodated in interval estimations of means (μ) and variances (σ^2); measurements are assessed and validated via gauge repeatability and reproducibility (GRR) analysis. For the first time, quality variations are judged against customer requirements through process capability indices such as C_{pk}. It is clear that such study, presentation, and management of uncertainties, which constitute stage 5, mark the beginning of a more formal and rigorous statistical reasoning process.

Action-Oriented Studies

Stage 6 now follows, touching on the theory and application of statistical process control (SPC) techniques.[1,2] Probability theory and statistical inference form the backbone of procedures for comparative studies via tests of hypothesis (TOH) as well as quality monitoring via statistical control charts.

In stage 7, statistical applications culminate in the deployment of design of experiments (DOE) to investigate quality variations in terms of parameter settings in a product or process.[3-5] Procedures such as response surface methodology (RSM)[6,7] help realize the optimal performance of a given operating physical system (in other words, ensure that the existing hardware functions at its full potential).

It is important for an individual to be able to appreciate at which of the seven stages of statistical reasoning outlined above he or she currently finds him- or herself. However, aside from the issue of personal competence, the actual nature of the statistical approach taken by the organization to improve quality is the most decisive factor in determining the results eventually attainable. Several possibilities will now be outlined.

Quality by Passive Monitoring

In chronological terms, the adoption of statistical techniques in industry went through three typical stages. The first is product inspection, where statistical sampling plans help determine the sample size and decision rules (for example, the maximum number of defects that can be tolerated in an inspected sample). Sampling inspection is, strictly speaking, not a quality improvement tool: all it does is attempt to detect products not conforming to quality requirements; what is defective will remain defective regardless of whether it is indeed detected. As a damage-control operation, its weakness is expressed in the oft-repeated saying, "Quality cannot be inspected into the product."

At the next stage, attention is paid "upstream" (to the process that generates the product in question), leading to techniques such as process capability studies and process control chart applications. The effectiveness of statistical process control (SPC), or more generally statistical quality control (SQC), lies in its ability to prevent the generation of unsatisfactory products; however, as in acceptance sampling, this is basically a negative and passive approach, since no attempt is made to *change* the process for the better. Even when a process is under control, as indicated by a *p*-chart (for product proportion defective), there is no evidence at all that the proportion defective reflected by the central line of the chart is the best that one can get out of the process (in other words, that the process has been fine-tuned to its optimal state). Product inspection and process control are thus mere monitoring activities: process capability indices, control charts, etc. all focus only on the *output end* of a process.

Quality by Active Intervention

It is clear that to fundamentally remove the possibility of occurrence of defective products, or to obtain the best performance of a given process, one has to pay attention to the *input end* of the process. It is necessary to manipulate and fine-tune the input variables—temperature, pressure, time, raw material property, etc.—in such a way that the output is optimized, where output refers to one or more measurable performance indexes such as yield, defective rate, or some specific quality characteristic such as length, amplification, or power. Such a rationale is straightforward, but adjustment of input variables in practice has long been based on experience, judgment, and even trial and error on the part of technical personnel. This is because there is usually a lack of knowledge concerning the linkage between the input $(x_1, x_2, \ldots x_k$ for k factors) and output (say two characteristics, y_I and y_{II}) in a given product or process (the P black box), as depicted in Figure 11.1 or, expressed mathematically, $y_I = f(x_1, x_2, \ldots, x_k)$, $y_{II} = f(x_1, x_2, \ldots, x_k)$.

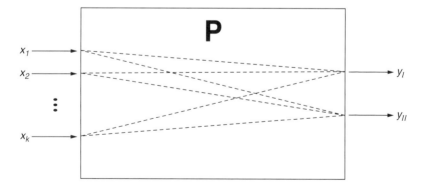

Figure 11.1.   Input-output linkage for a product or process "P."

While derivation of equations from first principles of physical sciences is all but impossible due to the complexity of most industrial processes, attempts to obtain them by empirical means could prove unproductive, since most technical personnel tend to conduct the study with the traditional "one variable at a time" experimentation procedure. Such a procedure not only entails a large number of observations, but would also fail to bring out interactions among the input variables.

The problem of empirically determining valid input-output relations was actually handled more than half a century ago by agricultural researchers with the solution provided by R. A. Fisher's work recognized as design of experiments.[8,9] The experimental design methodology discards the "one variable at a time" concept and enables the investigator to make use of only a small amount of experimental data to disentangle the effect of each input variable, identify the interactions that may exist, and explicitly assess the noise effects in the physical system. Understanding of complex input-output relations via empirical investigations and subsequent process and product optimization thus became feasible.[10]

The potential of design of experiments remained largely untapped by industry until after World War II. Subsequently, applied statisticians, represented notably by George E. P. Box, William G. Hunter, and J. Stuart Hunter, who also authored a seminal work,[3] started to educate engineers in statistical design of experiments, in addition to SQC/SPC, for quality improvement initiatives. They helped bring out the third stage of advancement in the industrial application of statistics: the objective now is to preempt the occurrence of defective products, not just detecting or preventing it; an active rather than passive approach is advocated in process management. Strategies such as response surface methodology[6,7] and evolutionary operation (EVOP)[11] then cap the effort to optimize the performance of black box systems.

Partly owing to the statistical language used in the presentation and teaching of techniques, industries in the West, except certain large chemical engineering companies such as ICI and DuPont, did not readily adopt design of experiments on a large scale before the 1980s. Table 11.2 summarizes the three broad stages that characterize the advances in statistical applications in industry. It may be noted, however, that the theoretical foundations for the various methodologies all date back to the 1920s. Table 11.3 further explains why strategies based on design of experiments should be introduced once SPC has reached the limit of its usefulness.

Stage	I	II	III
1. Philosophy	Quality by inspection	Quality by monitoring	Quality by design
2. Strategy	Passive	Defensive	Preemptive
3. Approach	Defect detection	Defect prevention	Defect elimination
4. Objective	Damage control	Status quo	Optimization
5. Technique	Sampling inspection	Process control	Robust design
6. Tools	Sampling plans	Indexes and charts	Design of experiments
7. Procedure	Data recording	Descriptive statistics	Statistical inference
8. Decisions	Number based	Information based	Knowledge based
9. Location	Check point	On-line	Off-line
10. Application	Product	Process	Product and process
11. Mode	Batch by batch	Line by line	Project by project
12. Adoption	1940s	1960s	1980s

Table 11.2. Advances in the application of statistics for quality improvement.

Statistical Process Control	vs	Statistical Experimental Design
1. Used for "on-line" quality control		1. Used for "off-line" quality engineering
2. Deals mainly with existing processes		2. Can be applied to process design and development stage
3. Meant for routine application		3. Has a problem-solving dimension
4. Aims to maintain status quo		4. Seeks improvements and best operating states
5. No new operational targets		5. Motivated by specific needs and seeks new results
6. Non-intervention of physical system		6. Purposeful probing of physical system
7. Based on passive observation of system output		7. Depends on active manipulation of system input-output linkages
8. Monitors known key parameters		8. Identifies key parameters
9. No forward planning element		9. Attempts to foresee and prevent problems
10. Awaits problems to happen		10. Identifies sources of problems and seeks their elimination
11. No obvious sense of urgency		11. Efficiency is important
12. Carried out continuously		12. Carried out project by project

Table 11.3. Design of experiments versus traditional statistical process control.

Taguchi Techniques

In the early 1980s Genichi Taguchi demonstrated at AT&T Bell Laboratories how certain adaptations of statistical design of experiments could enhance the efficiency of empirical investigations in industrial research and development, rationalize the product realization process, and improve the quality and reliability of manufactured products. Without delving into abstract mathematical concepts, Taguchi simplified design of experiments into a series of cookbook procedures that can be followed by those with little statistical background. Design of experiments is presented in the context of quality engineering, rather than something taken out of mathematical statistics.[5,12] It did not take long before a collection of ideas and techniques under the label *Taguchi methods* began to spread to other industrial organizations. Soon after, the concept and methods of *Robust Design* began to evolve from Taguchi's idea that variability in process or product performance may also be managed via experimental design and analysis. This has become a known approach for research and development activities today.[13]

It may be noted that certain aspects of Taguchi procedures have long met with criticisms and challenges from many veterans in the quality field as well as statisticians.[14-19] Some of the controversy surrounding Taguchi methods can be attributed to the difference in approaches taken by mainstream statisticians and Taguchi. Taguchi and his followers regard design of experiments as a means for studying engineering problems and developing new systems, whereas statisticians tend to handle design of experiments as a means for statistical inference; namely, using sampled data to draw general conclusions concerning an existing phenomenon. It is a general consensus today that routine Taguchi methods are useful for first-cut experimentation: they can be used for quickly screening a large number of parameters in an investigation and suggest directions for improvement for a given performance index. Since mathematical modeling is not emphasized in Taguchi procedures, the final solution is not necessarily the optimal. Thus Taguchi experiments could be supplemented, where necessary, by further design and optimization based on more in-depth analytical considerations (see, for example, Box and Draper[6] and Khuri and Cornell[7]). Table 11.4 summarizes some major differences in orientation between conventional experimental design and Taguchi methods.

The Seven-S Strategy

Regardless of the version of experimental design adopted, it is important to have a strategic sequence in the application of individual statistical tools. When

Mainstream Statistics	Taguchi Methods
1. How experiments can be conducted outside the laboratory for the study of an *operating system?*	1. How experiments can be used to improve the *design* of products and processes?
2. How to understand the true nature of the object of study via *inductive* reasoning?	2. How to translate data into engineering conclusions and hence *specific* actions?
3. How to secure valid *theoretical* foundations for the resulting conclusions and decisions?	3. How to reduce the entire methodology into *practical* procedures for non-statisticians?
4. How to represent significant cause-and-effect relationships in a product or process by mathematical models for performance *enhancement?*	4. How to insulate a product or process from both present and future external causes of performance *deterioration?*
5. How to obtain the *optimal*—not sub-optimal?	5. How to recommend a *better* solution?

Table 11.4. Approaches and concerns in experimental design applications.

the level of statistical expertise reaches stage 7 in Table 11.1, a plan of attack for quality excellence can be formulated with what may be conveniently referred to as the *Seven-S* strategy, summarized in Table 11.5. The discussion from this point on will be with reference to process optimization, although the ideas are equally applicable to product development and testing.

To begin, one must *select* the quality-related physical characteristic y that is to be improved or optimized. At the same time, appropriate controllable factors x_i that conceivably could influence the behavior of y must be identified. Quality function deployment (QFD) and failure mode and effects analysis (FMEA) are among techniques appropriate for this purpose. The linkage between x_i and y has already been depicted in Figure 11.1, where the process appears as a "black box" to the investigator.

Next, process capability studies are needed to judge the present performance of y with respect to customer requirements. This is best expressed by process capability indices such as C_{pk}. Benchmarking exercises may also be carried out to help set targets for the quality improvement effort. Gauge repeatability and reproducibility (GRR) studies are performed to ensure that measurement variability does not mask true variability in values of y. Thus, this step *secures* one's

Step	Tools	Object	Application
1. SELECT	QFD, FMEA	$x; y$	Identify which inputs and outputs should be studied
2. SECURE	C_{pk}, GRR studies	u	Validate measurement systems and understand customer requirements
3. SCREEN	Identification Expt	x	Focus on the vital few factors for adjustments
4. SHIFT	Characterization Expt	μ	Adjust inputs to improve levels of outputs
5. SHRINK	Robust Design	σ^2	Adjust inputs to enhance consistency of outputs
6. SEARCH	RSM, Tolerancing	x^*	Adjust inputs to obtain the best possible outputs
7. SUSTAIN	EVOP, SPC	y^*	Maintain performance over time

Table 11.5. The Seven-S strategy to quality excellence.

knowledge of the existing level and spread of quality characteristics and defines the quality improvement goal.

Design of experiments will now come into play in the rest of the steps. First, appropriate experiments must be designed and conducted to *screen* the multitude of x_i factors so that subsequent investigations can be focused on only those that have important influences on y; all conceivable factors are included in this critical step.

Characterization experiments are next conducted to determine the way in which factors already identified to be important should be adjusted in order to *shift* the long-term values (or μ) of y to the desired level. This is to be followed by Taguchi or Robust Design techniques to reduce variability in y (in other words, *to shrink*, variance σ^2). Finally, a *search* is needed to pinpoint the operating values of x_i that will lead to the best result for y: RSM is mandatory at this step for obtaining such optimal operating conditions (x^*, y^*), with the resulting contour plots serving as a basis for the tolerance setting for x_i values. Finally, techniques of EVOP and SPC can be applied on an ongoing basis to *sustain* the optimal conditions already attained.

Evidently, the steps in the Seven-S approach are meant to be carried out in a sequential manner. Any haphazard application of techniques (for example, searching for optimal x_i settings without first doing a screening study) might produce tentative improvements at best, but more likely would end up with inconclusive results, leading to uncertainty and a loss of confidence in the use of statistical tools.

An important feature of the Seven-S steps is that both passive and active statistical tools (process monitoring at the output end as well as process intervention at the input end, respectively), are applied in an integrated sequence. The main difference from the traditional approach is that SPC is meant to be applied to a process that has already been optimized, rather than one that happens to be operating. Particular emphasis is placed on both securing and maintaining system optimality.

Conclusion

The Seven-S strategy can be deployed not just to improve the performance of processes and products when they are first studied, but over their lifetimes as well. Generally, when performance over time is a subject of interest, quality matters start to evolve into issues of reliability. With statistical tools, a wide range of quality and reliability requirements can be addressed: Figure 11.2 summarizes the important goals to be achieved by statistical means, particularly when they are coupled with expertise in quality management and quality technology. In terms of product realization in the manufacturing industry, the role of statistical applications during the entire cycle is depicted in Figure 11.3.

For many individuals and organizations, quality improvement tools could sometimes be acquired at different stages in a disjointed manner. It is important to recognize that these tools are most effective when they are applied in an integrated fashion. For this purpose, several important frameworks for quality excellence have been presented in the previous sections. To summarize, the first is a fundamental framework comprising organizational capabilities in quality management, quality technology, and quality information utilization. The second entails seven stages in attaining statistical competence at the personal level; the progression through the seven stages is typical of what nonstatisticians would go through as their on-the-job exposure to applied statistics increases.

After an examination of the various passive and active statistical approaches to quality, accompanied by a discussion of the defect detection–prevention–elimination sequence, a Seven-S strategy is put forth, with which the performance of a given process or product can be systematically optimized. Such frameworks are useful to both management and operations personnel, as they could help formulate effective and focused approaches to solving quality prob-

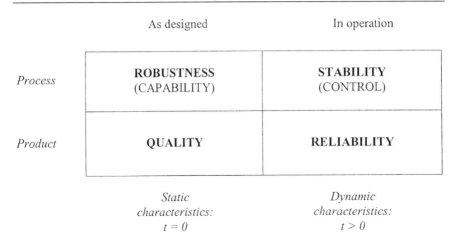

Figure 11.2. Goals of statistical approach to quality excellence.

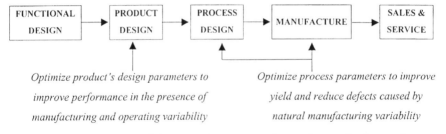

Figure 11.3. Application of the Seven-S strategy to the product realization cycle.

lems or elevating quality levels. With a clear understanding of such approaches and the availability of user-friendly software packages at the operational level, real and sustainable results can now be well within reach of many in industry.

References

1. Grant, E. L., and R. S. Leavenworth. 1996. *Statistical Quality Control.* 7th ed. New York: McGraw-Hill.

2. Quesenberry, C. P. 1997. *SPC Methods for Quality Improvement.* New York: Wiley.

3. Box, G. E. P., W. G. Hunter, and J. S. Hunter. 1978. *Statistics for Experimenters.* New York: Wiley.

4. Condra, L. W. 1995. *Value-Added Management with Design of Experiments*. London: Chapman and Hall.

5. Taguchi, G. 1986. *Introduction to Quality Engineering*. Tokyo: Asian Productivity Organization.

6. Box, G. E. P., and N. R. Draper. 1987. *Empirical Model-Building and Response Surfaces*. New York: Wiley.

7. Khuri, A. I., and I. A. Cornell. 1987. *Response Surfaces: Design and Analysis*. New York: Marcel Dekker.

8. Fisher, R. A. 1960. *The Design of Experiments*. 7th ed. Edinburgh: Oliver and Boyd.

9. Bisgaard, S. 1992. Industrial Use of Statistically Designed Experiments: Case Study References and Some Historical Anecdotes. *Quality Engineering* 4:547-562.

10. Box, G. E. P. and S. Bisgaard. 1987. The Scientific Context of Quality Improvement. *Quality Progress*. 20: 54-61.

11. Box, G. E. P., and N. R. Draper. 1969. *Evolutionary Operation*. New York: Wiley.

12. Kacker, R. N. 1986. Taguchi's Quality Philosophy: Analysis and Commentary. *Quality Progress* 19:21-29.

13. Phadke, M. S. 1989. *Quality Engineering Using Robust Design*. Englewood Cliffs, NJ: Prentice Hall.

14. Hunter, J. S. 1987. Signal-to-Noise Ratio Debated (letter to the editor). *Quality Progress* 20:7-9.

15. Ryan, T. P. 1988. Taguchi's Approach to Experimental Design: Some Concerns. *Quality Progress* 21:34-36.

16. Taylor, G. A. R. et al. 1988. Discussion on Taguchi. *Quality Assurance* 14:36-38.

17. Box, G. E. P., S. Bisgaard, and C. A. Fung. 1988. An Explanation and Critique of Taguchi's Contributions to Quality Engineering. *Quality and Reliability Engineering International* 4:123-131.

18. Pignatiello, J. J., and J. S. Ramberg. 1991. Top Ten Triumphs and Tragedies of Genichi Taguchi. *Quality Engineering* 4:211-225.

19. Levi, R. 1993. Cautions for Taguchi Lovers. *Manufacturing Engineering* 16 (March).

Chapter 12

Tools and Techniques: An Examination of Their Use

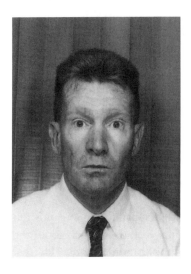

BARRIE G. DALE

Introduction

Tools and techniques are practical methods, like skills or mechanisms, that are applied to particular tasks. They come in many different forms, types, and levels of complexity. A tool may be described as a device with a clearly defined application. It is often narrow in focus and tends to be used on its own. Typical examples of tools are cause-and-effect diagrams, check sheets, check lists, Pareto analysis, and histograms. A technique, on the other hand, is something with a wider application than a tool. It usually requires more conceptual thought, knowledge, and skills to use it effectively. It may even be viewed as a collection of tools. For example, statistical process control (SPC) is a technique that employs a variety of charts, graphs, and analysis methods—all of which may be necessary for reaching effective conclusions.

There are many influences, internal and external to the organization, which impact on the successful use and application of tools and techniques. For example, training, support and coaching, use of a structured problem-solving approach, and a perceived need for tools and techniques can all be applied by an individual or a team. The various influences of these have been identified and described by McQuater, et al.[1] in detail as an education and training resource.

This chapter draws from the work of Dale and McQuater[2] and expands further on the methodology to assess the use and application of such tools and techniques. It summarizes the findings from its application in three different organizations. In each case study, the organization was given the details of the assessment methodology and used it in a variety of ways to suit its own specific needs and requirements.

Assessment Methodology

According to Dale and McQuater,[2] the objectives of the assessment methodology consist of a *recognition and use grid*, and an *application grid* designed for an all-inclusive purpose to:

- Establish the success or otherwise of the use of tools and techniques as perceived by the user

- Identify barriers to the implementation of tools and techniques

- Identify differences in the awareness, use, and perceived utility of the tools and techniques

- Highlight the degree of formality of use

- Identify which tools and techniques are used by each department and pinpoint the scale of usage

- Pinpoint training needs

- Establish the difficulties arising due to training

- Pinpoint areas which need more management commitment and support

- Assess available supporting mechanisms (for example, people, equipment)

- Identify misuse

- Pinpoint gaps between recognition and use

- Assess if the use and application of tools and techniques is fully appreciated and if their objectives and role are fully understood

- Examine the uses to which the tool or technique is put

- Identify further scope for the tools and techniques which are currently in use

- Highlight those tools and techniques which need greater usage in order to increase departmental and/or company efficiency

- Help raise the profile of the tools and techniques in common use

- Assess if the culture of the organization encourages the use of tools and techniques

The methodology is flexible, providing a framework for establishing both the negative and positive aspects associated with the application of tools and techniques. This is important, since by establishing the factors that provide for the effective use and application of tools and techniques in one area of the organization, it can be transferred to others, thereby building on best practices. The assessment can also provide a key input, in particular, to the processes and resources criteria of self-assessment undertaken against the criteria of, for example, the European Foundation for Quality Management (EFQM) model for business excellence or the Malcolm Baldrige National Quality Award (MBNQA).

The recognition and use grid is shown in Table 12.1 and the application grid in Table 12.2. In using these grids it is useful to give a sketch of each tool and technique by using a company's specific examples. This helps in eliminating the confusion regarding the title and content of each tool and technique and the description of the terminology that is employed therein.

Please indicate on the grid **ONLY** the techniques and tools you recognize. For those that you have recognized, if you use them for **ANY** purpose, not only for quality-related matters, please tick the box marked use.

Example	Recognize	Use
Seven basic tools		
Cause and effect	✓	
Check sheet/concentration diagrams		
Control charts		
Graphs/charts	✓	✓
Histograms	✓	✓
Pareto analysis	✓	✓
Scatter diagrams	✓	
	Recognize	Use
Seven basic tools		
Cause and effect		
Check sheet/concentration diagrams		
Control charts		
Graphs/charts		
Histograms		
Pareto analysis		
Scatter diagrams		
Seven new tools		
Affinity diagrams		
Arrow diagrams/critical path analysis		
Matrix data analysis methods		
Matrix diagrams		
Process Decision Program Chart (PDPC)		
Relation diagrams		
Systematic diagrams/tree diagrams		
Techniques		
Benchmarking		
Brainstorming/brainwriting		
Departmental Purpose Analysis (DPA)		

Table 12.1. Recognition and use grid.

	Recognize	Use
Design of Experiments (Taguchi, DOE)		
Failure Mode and Effect Analysis (FMEA)		
Flowcharts		
Forcefield analysis		
Problem solving methodology		
Quality costs		
Quality Function Deployment (QFD)		
Questionnaire		
Sampling		
Statistical Process Control (SPC)		
*		
*		
*		
*		
*		
*Add any company-specific techniques and tools not indicated on the list.		

Table 12.1—*continued.*

A plan must be developed by an organization regarding how the assessment is to be used. Initial decisions need to be made as to whether it will be company-wide or restricted to a sample of departments and, if the latter, which of the departments and functions are to be investigated. The number of people who are to complete the two grids needs to be decided and agreed upon. If the number of staff in a department to be examined is small, then everybody should complete the grids. On the other hand, if the department involves a large number of staff, then an appropriate sample needs to be selected.

First, the recognition and use grid should be completed by each person participating in the assessment. The person should indicate the tools and techniques they recognize. This recognition relates to the name, description, and/or visual picture of the tool or technique, without the person necessarily understanding how to construct or apply it. Once this has been done, the next step is to indicate which tools and techniques are used from those which have been recognized. The application grid should then be completed for the techniques and tools which have been indicated as being used by the participant in the

	Importance	Relevance	Use	Understand	Application	Resources	Management	Training	Benefit
For example: *Pareto Analysis*	5	4	2	3	3	2	1	1	4
	Importance	Relevance	Use	Understand	Application	Resources	Management	Training	Benefit
Seven Basic Tools									
Cause and effect									
Check sheet/ Concentration diagrams									
Control charts									
Graphs/Charts									
Histograms									
Pareto Analysis									
Scatter Diagrams									
Seven New Tools									
Affinity diagrams									
Arrow diagrams/ Critical path analysis									
Matrix data Analysis methods									
Matrix diagrams									
Process decision program chart (PDPC)									
Relation diagrams									

Table 12.2. Application grid.

(continued)

	Importance	Relevance	Use	Understand	Application	Resources	Management	Training	Benefit
Systematic diagrams/ Tree diagrams									
Techniques									
Benchmarking									
Brainstorming/ Brainwriting									
Departmental Purpose Analysis (DPA)									
Design of Experiments (Taguchi, DOE)									
Failure-Mode-Effect- Analysis (FMEA)									
Flow charts									
Forcefield analysis									
Problem solving methodology									
Quality Costs									
Quality Function Deployment (QFD)									
Questionnaire									
Sampling									

Table 12.2—*continued.*

	Importance	Relevance	Use	Understand	Application	Resources	Management	Training	Benefit
Statistical Process Control (SPC)									
Other techniques, tools, systems									
For Example									
ISO 9000 series									
QOS									
Other Awards (ie EQA)									

Table 12.2—*continued.*

A Note to the use of Table 12.2

Please complete the grid ONLY for the techniques or tools you indicated on the Recognition and use grid. Do not attempt to fill it in its entirety. There may be occasions that some of the categories cannot be allocated a score, in that case place insert, 9 (not applicable).

Score out of 5 in each of the categories where:

1 = No value

2 = Low value (ie, little used, not understood, little or poor training, etc)

3 = Some value (ie, basic understanding, small benefits, basic training, etc)

4 = High value (ie, good understanding, some benefits, reasonable training, etc)

5 = Very high value (ie, complete understanding, excellent benefits, effective training, etc)

9 = Not applicable or no training

- **Importance** to you in your job.
- **Relevance** to your job.
- How often you **use** it in your job.
- Your **understanding** of the technique, tool, or initiative.
- The degree to which you can **apply** it to your job.
- Availability of **resources** (ie, money, people, technology, facilities, equipment, time) necessary to apply the technique.
- **Organization and management**. The degree to which your manager or organization are committed to the use of techniques, shown by their support and encouragement and their willingness to act on the results.
- **Training**. The effectiveness of the training you received with regard to content, being able to apply the technique to your job or task, the method of delivery, time between training and using the technique or tool.
- **Benefits**. Do you see the tool or technique as being of benefit to you in doing your job.

recognition and use grid. The following are the categories that are assessed in the application grid:

- Importance to you in your job

- Relevance to your job

- How much you use it in your job

- Your understanding of the technique or tool

- The degree to which you can apply it to your job

- Availability of resources (money, people, technology, facilities, equipment, and time) necessary to apply the technique or tool

- Organization and management—the degree to which your manager is committed to the use of tools and techniques, indicated and demonstrated by his or her support and encouragement and willingness to act on the results

- Training—the effectiveness of the training you received with regard to content, being able to apply the technique or tool to your job or task, the method of delivery, and time between training and using the technique or tool

- Benefits—do you see the tool or technique as being of benefit to you in doing your job?

It is recommended that a score out of 5 should be attributed to each of the nine categories, using the following scoring system as a guide.

1 = No value

2 = Low value (little used, not understood, little or poor training, etc.)

3 = Some value (basic understanding, small benefits, basic training, etc.)

4 = High value (good understanding, some benefits, reasonable training, etc.)

5 = Very high value (complete understanding, excellent benefits, effective training, etc.)

9 = Not applicable or no training

Application of the Methodology

This section details the main outcomes from three organizations that have applied the methodology. A different degree of detail is presented in each case, which reflects each organization's use of the methodology, their employees' degree of knowledge of tools and techniques, and the commitment and leadership of the senior management team to continuous improvement.

Case Study A

This company is involved in the manufacture of gas-pipeline-related products. The two grids were distributed to 30 out of the 40 current number of employees, representing a selection of the organizational hierarchy. Twenty-three grids were completed and a summary of their details are given in Tables 12.3 and 12.4. The classification used in codifying the responses was senior management, middle management, and others.

There is some degree of knowledge of the tools and techniques (employees know of or have heard of some of them) but there are clear indications that they are not understood in any detail and their use and application is extremely patchy. The five tools and techniques most recognized are: questionnaire (22 out of 23 responses), graphs and charts (21 responses), brainstorming (19 responses), and workflow mapping (15 responses). At the opposite end of the spectrum the seven management tools were barely recognized and this was also the case with SPC and departmental purpose analysis. In general, the simpler the tool and technique the more likely it is to be recognized, the exception being benchmarking (13 responses). However, it is suspected that this was understood by the respondents in terms of product, equipment, and competitive analysis and not as detailed by Camp[3] with respect to the benchmarking of processes using the 10-step methodology.

Analyzing Table 12.3, the difference between recognition and use pinpoints the lack of use and application of tools and techniques in this company; this is confirmed in the application grid. For example, the questionnaire was only perceived to be used by four respondents, compared to 22 who recognized it. Graphs and charts, brainstorming, histograms, and workflow mapping show similar low trends of usage.

Turning to the application grid in Table 12.4, it can be seen that across all the categories of importance, relevance, use, understanding, application, resources, management, training, and benefit there is a relationship between recognition and use (in other words if a respondent recognizes and uses a tool and technique the larger the score given to each of these nine categories, in particular, importance, relevance, use, application, and benefit).

The major reason for this inadequate use of tools and techniques is that five years ago a substantial amount of work was undertaken by the organization to

Tools and Methods	SM	MM	O	Total Recogn.	Use SM	MM	O	Total Use
Seven Basic Tools								
Cause and effect	4	3	3	10	1	2	2	5
Check sheet/ Concentration diagrams	2	1	0	3	1	0	0	1
Control charts	1	0	0	1	0	0	0	0
Graphs/charts	4	5	12	21	2	4	8	14
Histograms	4	5	10	19	3	3	3	9
Pareto analysis	3	2	1	6	1	1	0	2
Scatter diagrams	2	1	0	3	0	0	0	0
Seven New Tools								
Affinity diagrams	1	0	0	1	0	0	0	0
Arrow diagrams/ Critical path analysis	2	1	0	3	1	0	0	1
Matrix Data Analysis Methods	1	0	0	1	0	0	0	0
Matrix diagrams	1	0	0	1	0	0	0	0
Process decision program chart (PDPC)	1	0	0	1	0	0	0	0
Relation diagrams	1	0	0	1	0	0	0	0
Systematic diagrams/ Tree diagrams	1	0	0	1	0	0	0	0
Techniques								
Benchmarking	4	5	4	13	3	2	0	5
Brainstorming/ Brainwriting	4	5	10	19	4	2	2	8
Departmental Purpose Analysis (DPA)	1	0	0	1	0	0	0	0
Design of Experiments (Taguchi, DOE)	2	1	0	3	0	0	0	0
Failure-Mode- Effects-Analysis (FMEA)	1	1	0	2	0	0	0	0
Flowcharts	4	4	6	14	3	2	5	10
Forcefield analysis	0	0	0	0	0	0	0	0
Problem solving methodology	2	1	0	3	0	0	0	0
Quality costs	2	2	0	4	0	0	0	0

Table 12.3. Recognition and use grid (n=23).

Tools and Methods	SM	MM	O	Total Recogn.	SM	Use MM	O	Total Use
Quality Function Deployment (QFD)	1	0	0	1	0	0	0	0
Questionnaire	4	5	13	22	2	2	0	4
Sampling	1	3	3	7	0	0	0	0
Statistical Process Control (SPC)	1	1	0	2	0	0	0	0
Workflow mapping	4	5	6	15	2	5	4	11

KEY: Management = SM
   ** *Middle Management = MM*
** *Other = O*

Table 12.3—*continued.*

achieve ISO 9001 registration. The development of the quality management system was intended as a subsequent base for the development of total quality management (TQM). At the time of this initiative, the organization consisted of 135 people; however, a downturn in market conditions culminating in poor financial results resulted in considerable organizational restructuring. Most of the people who subsequently left the organization were those who had participated in the ISO 9001 registration process and the application of the fundamentals for the introduction of TQM.

Within the organization there is a lack of senior management commitment to TQM, and this typically surfaces in the view that it takes too much time from activities associated with project work. At the present time some effort is being devoted to putting in place the basics of TQM. This is starting with the creation of standard work process maps, and as part of this activity the more simpler tools and techniques, such as the seven quality control tools, are starting to be used.

Case Study B

This company is involved in the design and manufacture of prefabricated cabins and units and employs 200 people. The recognition and use and application grids were completed by 40 people from the functional areas of sales and projects, engineering, procurement, production, and quality control.

Tools and Methods	Importance	Relevance	Use	Understanding	Application	Resources	Management	Training	Benefit
Seven basic tools									
Cause and effect	2.7	2.9	1.9	2.9	2.4	2.3	2.9	1.9	2.9
Check sheet/ Concentration diagrams	1.6	1.6	0.9	1.7	1.6	1.6	1.6	1.0	1.6
Control charts	1.4	1.4	1.4	1.4	1.4	1.4	1.4	1.4	1.4
Graphs/charts	3.9	3.9	3.1	3.3	3.4	2.9	2.9	2.6	3.1
Histograms	3.1	3.1	2.7	3.1	2.7	2.7	1.9	2.7	2.7
Pareto analysis	2.1	2.1	1.4	2.1	1.6	1.9	1.9	1.9	1.9
Scatter diagrams	1.9	1.7	1.1	1.9	1.6	1.6	1.4	1.6	1.6
Seven New Tools									
Affinity diagrams	1.0	1.0	1.0	1.0	1.0	1.0	1.0	1.0	1.0
Arrow diagrams/ Critical Path Analysis	1.9	1.9	1.6	1.9	1.6	1.6	1.6	1.6	1.6
Matrix Data Analysis Methods	1.0	1.0	1.0	1.0	1.0	1.0	1.0	1.0	1.0
Matrix diagrams	1.0	1.0	1.0	1.0	1.0	1.0	1.0	1.0	1.0
Process decision program chart (PDPC)	1.7	1.7	1.3	1.7	1.4	1.3	1.3	1.3	1.6
Relation diagrams	1.0	1.0	1.0	1.0	1.0	1.0	1.0	1.0	1.0
Systematic diagrams/ Tree diagrams	1.0	1.0	1.0	1.0	1.0	1.0	1.0	1.0	1.0
Techniques									
Benchmarking	3.1	3.3	2.4	3.4	2.9	2.9	3.1	2.3	3.3

Table 12.4. Application grid (n=23).

(continued)

Tools and Methods	Importance	Relevance	Use	Understanding	Application	Resources	Management	Training	Benefit
Brainstorming/ Brainwriting	3.0	3.1	2.6	3.0	3.0	1.7	3.0	3.0	3.0
Departmental Purpose Analysis (DPA)	1.0	1.0	1.0	1.0	1.0	1.0	1.0	1.0	1.0
Design of Experiments (Taguchi, DOE)	1.0	1.0	1.0	1.0	1.0	1.0	1.0	1.0	1.0
Failure-Mode-Effects-Analysis (FMEA)	1.0	1.0	1.0	1.0	1.0	1.0	1.0	1.0	1.0
Flowcharts	3.3	3.3	3.1	2.9	2.9	2.9	3.4	2.9	3.3
Forcefield analysis	1.0	1.0	1.0	1.0	1.0	1.0	1.0	1.0	1.0
Problem solving methodology	1.1	1.1	1.1	1.1	1.1	1.1	1.1	1.1	1.1
Quality costs	2.4	2.4	1.6	2.1	2.4	2.3	2.1	2.0	2.6
Quality Function Deployment (QFD)	1.0	1.0	1.0	1.0	1.0	1.0	1.0	1.0	1.0
Questionnaire	3.4	3.6	2.1	3.6	3.0	3.0	2.6	1.9	2.7
Sampling	1.0	1.0	1.0	1.0	1.0	1.0	1.0	1.0	1.0
Statistical Process Control (SPC)	1.0	1.0	1.0	1.0	1.0	1.0	1.0	1.0	1.0
Workflow Mapping	4.0	3.6	3.1	3.4	3.4	3.9	3.9	2.4	4.0

The numbers represent the averages of the scores received. Any number 9 has been set to = 1

Table 12.4—*continued.*

This analysis was undertaken in the same manner as with Case A and revealed a similar profile. It is clear that tools and techniques are not widely used within this organization. The main reason for this appears to be that employees believe they have too much to do to consider the use, in a formal manner, of tools and techniques and their use and application high on their agenda. However, it is clear that in their daily work some of the tools and techniques detailed in the recognition and use grid are used without people necessarily recognizing them. The tools and techniques which are claimed to be in use are limited and, in the main, centered around the use of competitive benchmarking in the sales and projects department, brainstorming in engineering, and SPC in purchasing.

The main difficulty identified was that tools and techniques are not used in any organized or structured way and there was considerable lack of awareness of what specific tools and techniques can achieve. Employees rarely spent time together trying to improve their activities and methods of working, and information sharing is lacking. In addition, little in terms of processes and procedures was documented. Some of this situation is due to the project nature of the business, which leads to problems of resource allocation and sharing.

Case Study C

This organization is involved in the manufacture of energy equipment and employs 250. Discussions were held with respect to the two grids with four employees from the engineering, logistics, production, quality control, procurement, and planning functions. No attempt was made to quantify the responses as with Case A: instead, Table 12.5 was compiled, which shows the tools and techniques recognized or used within the company. The analysis reveals that the engineering and production functions recognize and make more use of tools and techniques than in the other functions. It may have been expected that the quality function would have recognized and made more use of tools and techniques than was the actual case. The main reason for this is that the function operates in an inspection role and lacks the strategic perspective, as described by Bertsch, et al.[4]

As with Cases A and B, the simpler the tool and technique the more chance it will have of being recognized and used, particularly within the logistics, quality control, procurement, and planning functions.

The assessment grid was used with the same 24 employees from the six areas to examine the status of each of the tools and techniques, where they are employed, the extent of use, for what purpose, and what problems in use have been identified. Table 12.6 is an example of this analysis.

Tools and Techniques	Engineering	Logistics	Production	QC	Procurement	Planning
Cause and effect	R/U		R/U	R/U		
Check sheet	R/U	R/U	R/U	R/U	R/U	R/U
Control charts	R/U	R/U	R/U	R/U	R/U	R/U
Graphs/charts	R/U	R/U	R/U	R/U	R/U	R/U
Histograms	R/U	R/U	R/U	R/U	R/U	R/U
Pareto analysis						
Scatter diagrams	R/U	R	R/U	R		
Affinity diagrams						
Critical Path Analysis	R/U		R		R	R/U
Matrix Data Analysis	R/U				R/U	
Matrix diagrams	R/U	R/U	R/U	R/U	R/U	
Process Decision Program Chart						
Relation Diagrams			R/U			R/U
Tree Diagrams	R/U	R/U	R/U			R/U
Benchmarking	R		R/U			R/U
Brainstorming	R/U		R/U		R/U	
Departmental Purpose Analysis						
Design of Experiments	R/U		R/U			
Failure-Mode-Effects-Analysis	R/U	R/U				
Problem solving methodology	R/U		R/U	R/U		
Quality costs	R	R/U	R	R	R	R
Quality Function Deployment						
Questionnaire	R/U	R/U	R/U		R/U	
Sampling		R/U	R/U			
Statistical Process Control	R	R/U	R			
ISO9000	R/U	R/U	R/U	R/U	R/U	R/U
FS-7610 31110 (AQAP 110)	R/U	R/U	R/U	R/U	R/U	R/U
Configuration Management	R/U	R/U	R/U	R/U	R/U	R/U
Notation	*R = Recognized*					
	U = Used					

Table 12.5. Recognition and use grid.

Tool & Technique	Perceived Purpose	Comment
Cause and effect diagram	Used to determine the causes for deficiencies in the quality of engineering documents and drawings. Used by the QC Department to determine the consequences of production.	Used in an active manner when determining production deviations and possible corrective action. Used by the engineering department when production deviations appear to be caused by engineering documents/drawings. The QC Department assists departments with the use of this tool.
Check sheet	Used to verify that certain controls are actually performed.	All departments are familiar with the use of this tool. Typically used to verify that routines and procedures within the quality management system are being followed.
Control charts	Used for visualizing the flow of information and work.	All departments claim they are familiar with this technique.
Critical path analysis	Used in determining the critical activities to fulfill project milestones.	This is not fully employed as a key tool within the company's planning process.
Quality costs	Used only by the QC Department for verifying the cost of failure.	Used in determining corrective actions of nonconforming processes. Quality costing is not fully recognized as a technique for reducing cost.
Sampling	Used as a method for collecting data from production.	Used on important key values of a technical character. A considerable amount of information is collected, but not analyzed to any degree.
Brainstorming	Used when processes/routines are in serious trouble.	The method is not used in a routine manner.

Table 12.6. An example to summarize the use of tools

A number of the tools and techniques are recognized and to a certain extent are in use, but there is a lack of structure in utilizing them actively to facilitate continuous improvement. The tools and techniques are not subject to any specific training across the organization and there is a need to devise and launch a training program. This should start with the seven basic quality control tools with a focus on how to use them with a problem-solving methodology to improve product and service quality.

There is a lack of network analysis, including critical path analysis, within the company and this often results in an out-of-control state with respect to a number of its projects. There also exists an overlap between sequential tasks, which results in information arriving too late with respect to tasks which have already started. Consequently, a considerable amount of work is not completed within the scheduled duration and there is an overspend on both labor-hours and materials due to modifications or changes.

Statistical process control is not employed to any great extent. The responses indicate a lack of understanding of the fundamental purpose of SPC, despite good recognition and claimed use of control charts. Although a considerable amount of information is collected, the analysis of this is slow or even not performed. This means that the possibility for tracking out-of-control processes is limited and trends are identified and noted much too late in the process.

Conclusion

This chapter has briefly outlined the means by which the use and application of tools and techniques can be assessed within an organization. It has been shown that the methodology described can help an organization to identify gaps between (1) perceived importance and relevance, (2) benefits and usage, and (3) application and training. It also provides the basis for a diagnostic analysis along the lines indicated in the three case studies.

The main issues that have surfaced in the three organizations are: a lack of commitment by management to the use of tools and techniques, no evidence of a framework guiding their use, and inadequate training.

The use of the assessment methodology in the three organizations has confirmed the following as key issues.

- A planned approach for the application of tools and techniques is essential. The temptation to single out one tool or technique for special attention should be resisted, and to get maximum benefit it is important to use tools and techniques in combination.

- The application of tools and techniques should be encouraged as part of daily work activities.

- It is important to understand the limitations of how and when tools and techniques can best be used.

- At the operative and first-line supervisor level, tools and techniques are likely to be seen as a means of measuring performance and consequently they may not be given the attention they deserve. The need to use tools and techniques can also be considered by these staff members as obstacles in meeting production schedules.

- Tools and techniques on their own are not enough—they need an environment which is conducive to improvement and their use.

References

1. McQuater, R. E., B. G. Dale, R. J. Boaden, and M. Wilcox. 1996. The Effectiveness of Quality Management Tools and Techniques: An Examination of the Key Influences in Five Plants. *Proceedings of the Institution of Mechanical Engineers* 210(B4):329–339.

2. Dale, B. G., and R. E. McQuater. 1998. *Managing Business Improvement and Quality: Implementing Key Tools and Techniques*. Oxford: Blackwell Business.

3. Camp, R. C. 1989. *Benchmarking: The Search for Industry Best Practice That Leads to Superior Performance*. Milwaukee, WI: ASQC Quality Press.

4. Bertsch, B., A. R. T. Williams, T. van der Wiele, and B. G. Dale. 1998. The Changing Role of the Quality Manager: A Critical Examination. (A research report in process of development.)

Acknowledgments

The author acknowledges the contribution of Ruth McQuater to the assessment methodology described in this article. He also wishes to thank the people in the three case studies for administering the tool and technique assessment methodology and for making the data available for this presentation.

Section III

ISO 9000 and Total Quality

Chapter 13

ISO 9000 and Total Quality*

KENNETH S. STEPHENS

*This chapter was first published in *Quality Management Journal*, fall 1994, 57–71. Reprinted with permission of the publisher.

Introduction

With the 1994 revisions of the ISO 9000 Series, including their widespread adoption and implementation, these international standards continue to generate much attention. This is deserving, but needs understanding as to what the ISO 9000 Series is and what it is not. Such an understanding will contribute significantly to the correct implementation and use of these standards and guidelines on quality systems and management—to meet customer demands for a quality system and to establish a *total quality* system that has direct and long-term beneficial results for the enterprise itself.

Quality Systems—Not Invented by ISO 9000

First, it is important to realize that quality systems or even standards for quality systems were not invented by ISO 9000. Inputs to the evolution of the ISO 9000 Series are reflected in Figure 13.1, which portrays the historical and widespread influences in the development of ISO 9000. An historical perspective of this development, with dates associated with the inputs, is given in Appendix A for greater detail.

ISO 9000—Not Invented in Japan

Many terms (with related concepts, methodology, and techniques) of the modern disciplines of quality have been borrowed from innovative and successful

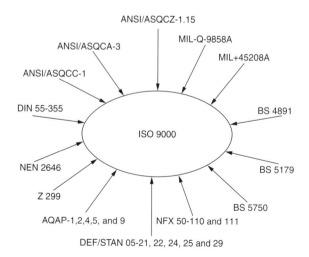

Figure 13.1.   Historical influences in the development of ISO 9000.

Japanese applications. Examples of such terms are *Kaizen* (improvement), *Hoshin-Kanri* (management by policy), *Kanban* (visible record or order ticket—as an integral part of the Kanban System of management by policy and Just-In-Time [JIT] production management), *Jishu Kanri* (self-management), *Poka-yoke* (foolproofing/prevention), *Seiri* (organization), *Seiton* (neatness), *Seiso* (cleaning), *Seiketsu* (standardization), and *Shitsuke* (discipline)—the latter five being referred to as the 5Ss (see Osada[1]). In addition to these, as further examples, additional terms (also with related concepts, methodology, and techniques) that took on English references directly include *QCC* (quality control circles), *CWQC* (company-wide quality control), *QFD* (quality function deployment), *CE* (cause & effect) *Diagrams, TPM* (total productive maintenance), etc. To these must be added Deming's 14 Points for Management.

It is instructive to note that most of these concepts are not an integral part of the ISO 9000 Series and that none of these terms, concepts, and techniques represent quality system assessment, certification, registration, and/or accreditation—especially as third-party programs. The system, so successful in achieving quality in Japanese products (including innovative breakthroughs in design quality, low maintenance quality, competitive pricing via economic measures such as scrap, rework, and waste elimination and avoidance; variation reduction; employee participation and involvement via quality improvement teams; planning and control for prevention; direct top management involvement and leadership; customer satisfaction; and continual improvement), was not based on quality system certification, registration, and/or accreditation! And this is the system that has attracted the attention of corporate management and the quality profession in the Western world—often with provocative exhortations by Western consultants such as Deming and Juran, in particular. It is also the system that has been assimilated and implemented with equally beneficial results by many of the world's leading corporations and enterprises. It has gone under many names, some of which are mentioned later in this article. The inputs to the evolution and development of quality systems are reflected in Figure 13.2.

It is a quality system that has evolved with early principles and techniques transferred to Japan from the West and with many successful additions and innovations introduced by Japan for transfer back to the West. But it has not involved third-party quality system certification, registration, and accreditation—as presently being promoted with national and international fervor in conjunction with the ISO 9000 Series. And while we will address certain positive aspects of international standardization of quality systems as per ISO 9000 below, one must pause and reflect whether we would not be better off promoting, teaching, and

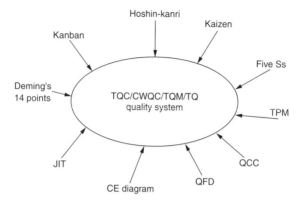

Figure 13.2. Inputs to the evolution and development of quality systems.

implementing the evolved quality system that includes the Japanese innovations rather than so much emphasis on third-party certification/registration of quality systems. In fact, enterprises and corporations implementing such quality systems would not need certification or registration—the results would speak for themselves—as is presently the case with well-recognized (by consumers) world class producers.

As a further historical perspective the Japanese showed little or no interest in the early developments and implementation of the ISO 9000 Series, per se—they simply didn't need it—their quality systems were equal, and in most cases far superior (and recognized as such) to ISO 9000. One must recall or take note that the numerous tables showing national adoptions (in growing numbers) of ISO 9000 either as "identical" or "equivalent" did not include Japan. In fact, the ISO 9000 Series was only adopted as the JIS Z 9900 Series in the Japanese national standards system in October 1991. The motivation for this was not based primarily on introducing and/or improving quality systems in enterprises and corporations (though they recognize this as one benefit for those enterprises lagging earlier developments—note the discussion later in this article), but more on reasons dictated by international harmony, trade, cooperation, and the sheer business opportunities related to third-party registration under ISO 9000 (and its expected improved successors).

In an interim *Report of Special Committee on JIS Marking Systems*, by the Japanese Industrial Standards Committee (JISC[2]), the following items are mentioned as factors for consideration of adopting ISO 9000:

- Acceptance of the results of certification (registration) based on the ISO 9000 Series abroad in the JIS marking system (for product certification).

- Adoption of the ISO 9000 Series as JIS to start the private certification (registration) scheme by third-party bodies (in Japan).

- Internationalization of the JIS factory examination (for product certification) and active utilization of both domestic and foreign private inspection (assessment) bodies in response to the ISO 9000 Series movements.

- Japanese companies are beginning to recognize the merits of the ISO 9000 Series, such as the clear positioning of responsibility for quality control, by introducing the Series in their companies.

- Requests for establishment of a new scheme conforming with global movements are increasing for export to European Union countries, which are establishing unified criteria based on the ISO 9000 Series; or coping with the procurement policies of the governments and companies in foreign countries which are based on the Series.

- Necessity of adoption of the Series as JIS has been indicated, from a viewpoint of equalizing the bases of many existing certification, assessment, and registration schemes.

- Japanese companies wishing to receive factory assessment and registration based on the ISO 9000 Series (at the present time) have no alternative than to receive it from assessment bodies in foreign countries either directly or through the private assessment bodies (being proliferated in Japan without uniform national accreditation).

- Taking into consideration international trends and domestic companies' demands, it is considered necessary to establish an accreditation body as soon as possible and to start the assessment and registration scheme based on the ISO 9000 Series.

- It is, therefore, essential for our country, too, to harmonize the ISO 9000 Series assessment and registration scheme from an international perspective, and to create the criteria for auditors according to international standards and guidelines.

- For accreditation of foreign accreditation bodies it is desirable that the results of accreditation are to be respected between the two governments according to their mutual accreditation agreement.

• The JIS marking examination involves an examination of quality control for designated products, and does not examine quality control and quality assurance concerning products other than the designated ones; therefore, it is not considered that JIS-marked factories will easily be internationally regarded as factories registered under the basis of the ISO 9000 Series (this is perhaps more an example of Japanese humility).

• However, *since the ISO 9000 Series text is not considered the best in our country* and the ISO/TC 176 is proceeding with review work of the ISO 9000 Series, proposals should be actively made to ISO/TC 176 from the Japanese Industrial Standards Committee concerning any parts of which it considers revision to be desirable.

Other papers that should be considered in this respect are by Hayashi,[3] Morita,[4] and Gomi.[5] Hayashi points out three merits of the ISO 9000 Series:

1. Manufacturers are given specific targets of their quality control activities, leading to improvement of the quality of their products.

2. The state of quality control activities can be assessed and registered fairly, impartially, and neutrally by the third-party assessment body in line with objective check items common to the world.

3. The result of the assessment and registration becomes a "common passport to international markets," and there is a possibility that such schemes will grow up to be a measure to avoid unnecessary repetitive examination conducted in different countries.

Hayashi also presents some points (which he refers to as three traps) to be avoided when introducing the ISO 9000 Series: (1) lack of unity in implementing the ISO 9000 Series, and a lack of harmonization of assessment by assessment bodies, (2) perfunctory/bureaucratic examinations with assessment bodies requesting submissions of massive volumes of papers useless to the manufacturer, thus diminishing the meaning of the assessment of their quality systems, and (3) overconfidence of manufacturers in having passed the examination—the feeling that TQC is no longer necessary.

ISO 9000: Strengths and Weaknesses

In terms of application, the ISO 9000 Series of standards is well illustrated by the diagram presented in the pamphlet *Quality 9000* by ISO and shown in Figure 13.3. A brief description of each of the basic documents is presented in Appendix B for reference and completeness.

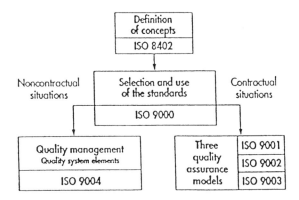

Figure 13.3. Structure of the new quality standards.

The ISO 9000 Series is a set of standards. Thus, it has both the advantages and disadvantages of standards in general. As a standard it is subject to periodic review and revision. The first cycle of that process has just been realized with the 1994 revisions, referred to as "Phase I." More extensive ("Phase II") revisions are already under consideration.[6] The standards need to be understood adequately in order to assure correct and beneficial implementation, together with other elements of a total quality system that are not a part of the Series. It is extremely important for enterprise/corporate managers to understand that the ISO 9000 Series is not intended as a standard on total quality. A total quality system must go beyond ISO 9000. This is discussed subsequently in greater detail.

On the positive side, its strengths lie in the structure that puts forth a uniform, consistent set of procedures, elements, and requirements that can be applied universally, albeit within limitations of interpretation and individual implementation. It provides a basis for designing, implementing, evaluating (assessing), specifying, and certifying (registering) a quality assurance system. With widespread adoption (now a reality) it provides a common language for international trade with respect to the quality assurance disciplines. It requires a sound, well-documented contractual relationship between customer and supplier. Hence, it aims to establish a common understanding between these parties based on agreed requirements.[7]

For further understanding, the ISO 9000 Series is generic—and in two significant aspects. It is not product or process specific: the quality assurance system (including the related quality manual, now a requirement) will, of necessity, have to contain specific subsystems related directly to the processes and the products to which it is being applied.

It is not even quality-system specific in that it does not specify a fixed system (beyond the requirements enumerated) for every enterprise (this, of course, is not a criticism). It provides considerable flexibility to the enterprise to design and specify (document) its own system within the framework of the requirements and then directs attention to evaluating conformance to that system. It places considerable attention on documentation (perhaps with too much emphasis on conformance rather than on adequacy and/or effectiveness).

On the negative side, as for many standards passing through debate, review, negotiation, and consensus, ISO 9000 represents a "least-common denominator" in its coverage of the quality management/assurance/system disciplines. It would be well for everyone to understand this clearly, together with the understanding that it is not a standard on total quality, and realize that the actual quality system that is optimum for a given enterprise or corporation may go well beyond the requirements, elements, and procedures of the ISO 9000 Series. Note the remarks of Hayashi[3] with respect "that no TQC is anymore necessary." Many authors voice this caution (some as direct criticism). A number are included in the reference section.[8-11] It is encouraging that many companies implementing quality systems do, in fact, go beyond the requirements of the particular standard used and incorporate other elements of a total quality system.

As mentioned previously, there is too much emphasis on conformance rather than on adequacy and/or effectiveness. Meeting the requirements is the principal concern. Short-term corrective action is emphasized rather than long term improvement. Sayle[10] addresses these and other concerns with respect to ISO 9000. The Series is also believed by many to contain a weak quality audit program. Sayle[11] also discusses this aspect while drawing contrasts with management audits.

Returning to the previous discussion (ISO 9000—Not Invented in Japan), there are many aspects of total quality systems not incorporated in ISO 9000. And, incidentally, the name one gives to these systems is not as important as the content. We see references to TQC, TQM,[12,13] IQM[14] (integrated quality management), SQM (strategic quality management), TQ,[9] reengineering, whole system architecture, etc.

At this juncture we pause from the dialogue to enter an historical note. The quality sciences have always been plagued by problems of semantics and the NIH (not invented here) syndrome. Young (and/or new) proponents of total quality management (TQM), for example, often are ignorant of, or ignore, the fact that programs and systems with previous names as simple as quality control or total quality control (and in existence as much as 25–35 years ago—including those developed in Japan) included such concepts and methodologies as project-by-project continuous improvement *and with a prevention orientation and with quality teams,* customer needs assessments and satisfaction programs, quality as a strategic business component including its contribution to costs and cost reduction, design quality and innovation, etc. This is not to say that important strides in refining and exposing these concepts to a wider audience have not been made in recent years; they have. But overzealous proponents of certain concepts have shown tendencies to idealize and ignore the conditions and necessities calling for a full range of tools (including statistical and others) for the total job of achieving quality and its related benefits.

Now with respect to understanding that ISO 9000 is not a standard for total quality, in ISO 9000, where are quality cost analysis and applications (other than as elements in ISO 9004-1)? Where is top management involvement and leadership—top-management-driven quality councils and quality as a business strategy encompassing planning, control, and improvement? Where is project-by-project improvement, pursued with revolutionary rates of improvement? Where is joy and pride in work and employee participation, involvement, and empowerment via project teams and quality circles? Where is variation reduction, statistical process control, and process capability (other than as very generic references)? Where are production/inventory management systems such as JIT? Where is the concept of single sourcing, long-term cooperative supplier product and quality system assistance (rather than mere assessment) based on trust and experience? Where is innovation? Where is customer satisfaction? Where are Deming's 14 Points for Management?

Juran[15] lists the following exclusions from ISO 9000 as essentials to attain world-class quality: (1) personal leadership by the upper managers, (2) training the hierarchy in managing for quality, (3) quality goals in the business plan, (4) a revolutionary rate of quality improvement, and (5) participation and empowerment of the workforce.

Now what has been said here must be properly interpreted and/or understood. It is not so much a criticism of ISO 9000 as it is an exhortation not to limit one's quality program/system to that of ISO 9000 alone. ISO 9000 is intended as a set of standards on quality assurance systems, not for total quality systems.

In fact, alternative (or additional) resources for total quality/management systems assessments and criteria for designing and implementing such systems are the various quality awards. Among these are the Deming Prize, the Malcolm

Figure 13.4. ISO 9000 as a basic foundation, with additional elements of a total quality system.

Baldrige Award, and the European Quality Award. The latter, in particular, encourages self-appraisal and assigns 50 percent of the criteria to results in terms of people satisfaction (9 percent), customer satisfaction (20 percent), impact on society (6 percent), and business results (15 percent).[16,17]

With consideration of these additional resources, the resultant system should be better, more dynamic, more comprehensive, more effective, and more economical than that of ISO 9000 alone in its present form. This is illustrated in Figure 13.4 with ISO 9000 shown only as a basic foundation for a total quality system that for completeness includes other techniques and procedures as shown. Future revisions to the ISO 9000 Series, within the framework of its intended purpose, will address many of its inherent weaknesses. For example, the weaknesses of the "life-cycle model" versus a "process model" are being addressed by the phase II developments. With respect to its role within a total quality system, the phase II design specification prepared by the U.S. delegates to the ISO/TC 176 working group should be consulted, as given by Tsiakals.[6] The research paper by Peach[18] and Puri[19] should also be studied.

ISO 9000 Assessment, Certification, and Registration

As explained in ISO 9000-1, in the Scope of ISO 9001 to 9003, and as illustrated in Figure 13.3, major parts of the ISO 9000 Series are intended for contractual use. This has its roots in the documents leading up to ISO 9000, including MIL-Q-9858A. ISO 9004-1 is intended to assist in developing and implementing total quality management systems.

Associated with these two major parts of the ISO 9000 Series are various assessment and certification/registration programs. It should be apparent from the above that the ISO 9000 Series is intended to facilitate two-party contractual arrangements for assurances of quality. The customer will want to have assurance that the supplier is, in fact, carrying out a comprehensive program of quality assurance in compliance with one of the ISO 9000 Series quality assurance models as specified in the contract. To gain that assurance the customer will arrange and carry out an external audit (assessment) of the supplier's quality assurance system. Such an assessment is referred to as a *second-party audit or assessment*. The ISO 9000 Series may also be used on a first-party basis (self-assessment, design, and implementation of systems) to provide in-house management with assurances of quality. These were the original intentions of the standards including their predecessors.

Additionally, extensive programs and efforts are now underway to use the ISO 9000 Series on a third-party basis for assessment (on behalf of either of two parties) and eventual certification. These programs include the certification (and registration) of assessors and lead assessors for carrying out the assessment and certification activities.[13,20-22] They also include the accreditation of bodies qualified to carry out third-party certification. As with the quality system standards themselves these programs of certification and registration also have both positive and negative aspects.

Positively, third-party programs have as a basis the minimization of multiple audits carried out on given suppliers by multiple customers, which otherwise may involve considerable outlay of time, effort, manpower, and cost. The principle is that if a qualified, competent, reputable, and reliable auditing organization (registrar) carries out a thorough audit leading to approval (certification and registration) of a supplier's quality system, then this approval can serve all potential customers of this supplier's products and/or services for which the approved quality system applies. Hence, the initiation for the audit/assessment may come from the supplier itself as part of its marketing strategy.

On the negative side, certification, registration, and accreditation programs must be watched very carefully and influenced by the international community to the extent that they do not become barriers to trade or even to a lesser degree economic barriers (with exorbitant fees for assessment/certification/accreditation). Small businesses have unique problems with these programs and have expressed concern. Developing countries, in particular, have also voiced their concern that they not be held ransom by demands to meet ISO 9000 when no infrastructure exists locally to be assessed and certified. Certain aspects of third-party certification (registration) are being viewed as "technical colonization." Additionally, the certification and accreditation process must be implemented very carefully to diminish or avoid "business opportunists" with no long-term interests in quality. Sayles[11] mentions a deplorable practice of issuance of "conditional certificates."

Much of the earlier reference to the JISC report with factors relating to adoption of ISO 9000 by the Japanese, has to do with assessment and certification (or registration). Hayashi[3] mentions merits (his second and third) and traps (his first and second) associated with assessment and certification. Hutchins[9] is especially critical with respect to the practice of third-party certification diluting the effectiveness of quality systems. He opines that, "third party accreditation has probably cost the United Kingdom ten years of leadership in quality."

Reliance on third-party assessment and certification often represents an irresponsible delegation of responsibility (and leadership) on the part of top management. Hutchins[9] refers to it as "one of the worst examples of delegation equals abdication."

A particular "bad scenario" is when companies feel forced to comply, which can lead to minimum attention being paid to the quality system that is implemented. This is often in response to initial or several assessment failures— simply plugging holes or filling gaps to satisfy the assessment body, perhaps with hostility and a desire to fake or cheat the system—resulting in a fragmented quality system that no one is devoted to maintaining or even using, relegating quality to a police role rather than as a significant aid to business strategy and results.

Another U.K. quality professional has spoken out concerning third-party quality system certification. Burgess[23] relates the following (with parenthetical additions for clarification).

Academicians (of the International Academy of Quality, IAQ, to whom he was writing) will know that the initiation of this new phenomenon (quality system certification), using the systems given in the ISO 9000 series, can be levelled at the United Kingdom. What they may not know is that since the first assessment of quality systems by third parties almost 20 years ago, the issue has now gotten out of hand. Many U.K. companies have developed quality systems for certification purposes only and, equally, many purchasers call up system certification as a condition of contract. Whilst this seems quite logical at first, it has led, in the United Kingdom and other countries, to the development of quality management for the wrong reasons. Commercialism is now leading to a lack of credibility for many of the activities associated with such quality systems and with registration.[24]

At the World Quality Congress in Helsinki, I was able at the IAQ seminar to give some statistics relating to the U.K. situation. For example, there are now well over 20,000 companies registered to ISO 9000 (or its U.K. equivalent). There are 4,300 registered assessors (auditors) and you can imagine the variables that this produces. Further, I identified some 40 registration bodies, of which 27 are accredited quite properly by our accreditation body, the NACCB. Of course, the consultant community has grown in parallel, encouraged by government funding schemes. Academicians can imagine the different interpretations put upon the subject of quality in so many hands, not least the supplier himself!

All this (sometimes misguided) activity has led to concerns about value, short-term rather than long-term improvement, unfairness, different levels of achievement, and sometimes about the whole concept of system certification.

To many, certification has become an end in itself! Originally intended as a mark of distinction, it is in danger of becoming a shallow approach to quality achievement.

Conclusion

No single standard (or set of standards) has had more universal or worldwide results in increasing the awareness of quality than has the ISO 9000 Series, with its direct linkage to the unified market of the European Union, though mandatory compliance as a requirement of the EU is not an expected reality (see, for example, Zuckerman[24]). But one has to wonder what portion of the awareness created corresponds to the "bad scenario" mentioned previously.

The national and international communities of quality professionals and related organizations have a serious responsibility (with related opportunity) to see that the ISO 9000 Series is properly used and promoted to create the correct and beneficial awareness and improvement of quality in its broadest sense.

Every country, trade association, corporation, and enterprise that wishes to compete in international trade must give serious consideration to the use of the

ISO 9000 Series on a first-party, second-party, and/or third-party basis for establishing and demonstrating assurances of quality of their products or services based on their quality management and systems, at least as a minimum program that may be extended to a more comprehensive system of total quality.

The publication of the ISO 9000 Series in 1987, together with the accompanying terminology standard (ISO-8402), has brought harmonization on an international scale, and has supported the growing impact of quality as a factor in international trade. The ISO 9000 Series has quickly been adopted by many nations and regional bodies and is rapidly supplanting prior national and industry-based standards (and otherwise filling existing gaps in quality assurance system standards). It is a basis for promoting and disseminating quality management/assurance/systems globally. But, as mentioned, its promotion and implementation must be done on a sound business and quality basis—with understanding, fairness, equality, encouragement, and benevolence—and with technical assistance where needed.

References

1. Osada, T. 1991. The 5S's, Five Keys to a Total Quality Environment. Tokyo: Asian Productivity Organization.

2. JISC. 1991. *Report of Special Committee on JIS Marking Systems.* 17 May, Tokyo: Japanese Industrial Standards Committee.

3. Hayashi, A. 1991. Japan's Policy Toward International Assessment and Registration System Using ISO Quality Assurance Standards. Transactions, Seminar on Achieving Competitive Quality Through Standardization and Quality Control, 29–31 October, MITI, JSA, UNIDO, SIRIM, Kuala Lumpur, Malaysia.

4. Morita, C. 1991. Implementation of Quality Assurance Activities (ISO 9000) in Factories. Transactions, Seminar on Achieving Competitive Quality Through Standardization and Quality Control, 29–31 October, MITI, JSA, UNIDO, SIRIM, Kuala Lumpur, Malaysia.

5. Gomi, Y. 1991. Voluntary Third Party System for Electronic Components Based on ISO 9000 Series. Transactions, Seminar on Achieving Competitive Quality Through Standardization and Quality Control, 29–31 October, MITI, JSA, UNIDO, SIRIM, Kuala Lumpur, Malaysia.

6. Tsiakals, L. J. 1994. Revision of the ISO 9000 Standards. *ASQC Quality Congress Transactions*, Milwaukee, WI: ASQC Quality Press.

7. Eicher, L. D. 1992. The ISO 9000 Standards—An International Phenomenon. *ISO Bulletin* 23(7):3.

8. Kalinosky, I. S. 1990. The Total Quality System—Going Beyond ISO 9000. *Quality Progress* 23(6):50-54.

9. Hutchins, D. 1992. *Achieve Total Quality*. Cambridge, England: Director Books.

10. Sayle, A. J. 1988. ISO 9000—Progression or Regression? *EOQC Quality* 1:9-13.

11. Sayle, A. J. 1992. Audits—The Key to the Future. 1st Annual Quality Audit Conference, February 27-28, ASQC, St. Louis, MO.

12. Searstone, K. 1991. Total Quality Management: BS 5750 (ISO 9000, EN 29000). *Total Quality Management* 2(3):249-253.

13. Stephenson, A. R. 1991. Management Systems for Quality—A Bonus for TQM? Proceedings, 3rd Conference of Asia Pacific Quality Control Organization, 18-22 March, Auckland, New Zealand, vol. 2; Stephenson, A. R. 1991. Auditor Registration and the Accreditation of Certification Bodies in the U.K. Proceedings, 3rd Conference of Asia Pacific Quality Control Organization, 18-22 March, Auckland, New Zealand, Vol. 4.

14. Asian Productivity Organization. 1990. New Waves in Quality Management—An Integrated Approach for Product, Process and Human Quality. Workshop on Quality Management—An Integrated Approach. Tokyo: APO.

15. Juran, J. M. 1994. The Upcoming Century of Quality. Key-note Address to the ASQC Quality Congress, ASQC, Milwaukee, WI.

16. Conti, T. 1991. Company Quality Assessments. *Total Quality Management* (June) 167-172; (August) 227-233.

17. European Foundation for Quality Management. 1992. *The European Quality Award*; *Total Quality Management—The European Model for Self-Appraisal 1992*; *Guidelines for Identifying and Addressing Total Quality Issues*. Eindhoven, The Netherlands: European Foundation for Quality Management.

18. Peach, R. W. 1994. Planning the Journey from ISO 9000 to TQM. *ASQC Quality Congress Transactions*. Milwaukee, WI: ASQC Quality Press.

19. Puri, S. C. 1991. Deming + ISO/9000, A Deadly Combination for Quality Revolution. *ASQC Quality Congress Transactions*. Milwaukee, WI: ASQC Quality Press.

20. Craig, R. J. 1991. Road Map to ISO 9000 Registration. *ASQC Quality Congress Transactions*. Milwaukee, WI: ASQC Quality Press.

21. Sawin, S. D., and S. Hutchens, Jr. 1991. ISO-9000 in Operation. *ASQC Quality Congress Transactions*. Milwaukee, WI: ASQC Quality Press.

22. Puri, S. C. 1992. The ABC's of Implementing ISO/9000. *ASQC Quality Congress Transactions*. Milwaukee, WI: ASQC Quality Press.

23. Burgess, N. 1993. Burgess Addresses Quality Management Certification. *CONTACT* (Newsletter of the International Academy for Quality) 53 (December):5-6.

24. Zuckerman, A. 1994. EC Drops Ticking Time Bomb—It Could Prove Lethal to the ISO 9000 Community. *Industry Week*. (16 May):44-51.

25. MacDonald, B. A. 1976a. British Standard 4891: A Guide to Quality Assurance, British Standard 5179: (Parts 1, 2, & 3) Guide to the Operation and Evaluation of Quality Assurance Systems. *Journal of Quality Technology* 8(3); MacDonald, B. A. 1976b. List of Quality Standards, Specifications and Related Documents. *Quality Progress* IX(9):30-35; MacDonald, B. A. 1977. British Standard 4891: A Guide to Quality Assurance, British Standard 5179: (Parts 1, 2, & 3) Guide to the Operation and Evaluation of Quality Assurance Systems. *Quality Assurance* (1):21-24.

26. Wadsworth, H. M., K. S. Stephens, and A. B. Godfrey. 1986. *Modern Methods for Quality Control and Improvement*. New York: John Wiley & Sons, Inc.

27. Sjoberg, A. 1987. 1985 revision of Z 299, Quality Assurance Program Standards—Impact on Effectiveness. 1-5 June. Proceedings of the EOQC Annual Quality Conference, Munich, Germany.

28. Marquardt, D., J. Chove, and K. E. Jensen, et al. 1991. Vision 2000: The Strategy for the ISO 9000 Series Standards in the '90s. *Quality Progress* 24(5):25-31. (See also *EOQ Quality*, vol. 2, 1991).

Appendix A

Historical Perspective of ISO 9000

As with many of the principles and methodologies of the quality sciences, quality systems and standards thereof have evolved. Early in the development was *MIL-Q-9858*, issued on April 9, 1959, and *MIL-I-45208* of October 12, 1961. These were further developed as a companion two-part multilevel set of standards with the revision of December 16, 1963, as *MIL-Q-9858A, Quality Program Requirements* and *MIL-I-45208A, Inspection System Requirements.* Complementing these were *MIL-C-45662A, Calibration System Requirements,* February 9, 1962; *H-50, Evaluation of a Contractor's Quality Program,* April 23, 1965; *H-51, Evaluation of a Contractor's Inspection System,* January 3, 1967; and *H-52, Evaluation of a Contractor's Calibration System,* July 7, 1964.

An early nonmilitary standard was *ASQC Standard C1-1968, Specification of General Requirements for a Quality Program.* It was subsequently adopted as *ANSI Standard Z1.8-1971,* approved on November 18, 1971. It served a very useful purpose in procurement quality specifications. While not adopted as a standard, the *Aid, A Tested System for Achieving Quality Control, Technical Aids No. 91* for small manufacturers, small business administration, provided a fairly comprehensive set of essential elements of quality control. It was issued in January 1969.

MacDonald[25] provides a list of quality system standards and discusses in some detail the British Standards *4891, 5179 (Parts 1, 2 & 3),* the NATO Documents *AQAP-1, 2, 4, 5, & 9,* and the British Defence Documents *DEF/STAN 05-21, 22, 24, 25, & 29.* He traces the development of these standards as an evolution from *MIL-Q-9858A.* Following misgivings in many sectors of industry about the issuance of defense standards, covering quality management systems, as British standards, BSI developed *BS 4891:A Guide to Quality Assurance* that was issued in 1972. Following that, *BS 5179: Guide to the Operation and Evaluation of Quality Assurance Systems* was published in December 1974 and represented a three-part multilevel set of standards. It was the forerunner of *BS 5750.* At the time (1972–1974) there were no comparable ASQC/ANSI standards for quality systems. The ANSI Committee Z1 on Quality Assurance was established in 1974 with ASQC as its secretariat. It was not until 1979 that ASQC was appointed secretariat to the US TAG for ISO/TC 176 on Quality Management and Quality Assurance, shortly after the establishment of TC 176.

Further developments in the evolution of quality system standards took place over the period 1978–1979, in particular. *ASQC's Standard A-3* (1971), *Glossary of General Terms Used in Quality Control* was revised extensively in 1978 with the change of title to *Quality Systems Terminology* with associated terms—eliminating other terms previously common to *A-1* and *A-2* (ASQC Standards).

A multilevel set of quality assurance program standards, *Z 299 Series,* was issued by Canada in 1978. Then in 1979, *BS 5750, Quality Systems,* was issued by the British Standards Institution. It consisted of a three-part multilevel set of standards, and as mentioned was based on *BS 5179*. The major changes were that (1) recommendations were changed to requirements, (2) parts 1 and 3 of *BS 5179* were changed to parts 3 and 1 of *BS 5750*, respectively, (3) references were made, where relevant, to *BS 5781, Specification for Measurement and Calibration Systems*, and (4) clauses dealing with *review, evaluation guidance*, and *significant questions* were excluded, with *BS 5179* and *BS 4891* still available for guidance purposes. *BS 5750 (1979)* was intended primarily for contractual purposes for a broad range of industries. It was a relatively brief document with less than three pages devoted to level 1 (design, manufacture, and installation) and less than one page devoted to level 3 (final inspection and test).

The American National Standard, *Generic Guidelines for Quality Systems, ANSI/ASQC Z-1.15-1979*, was issued on December 19, 1979, providing "guidelines for establishing, structuring or evaluating product quality systems." It was intended to "encompass the quality functions at all stages and levels of the total product life cycle, from a product's conception through its development, manufacture, delivery, installation and extended application by the ultimate user." It was not, therefore, a multilevel standard. It provided basic elements for structuring a quality system. An expanded set of basic elements based on *Z-1.15* is given in Wadsworth, Stephens, and Godfrey.[26] *ANSI/ASQC Z-1.15-1979* with 17 pages contained considerably more detail than *BS 5750* (1979). It was particularly useful in the development of ISO 9004.

ISOTC 176 was formed in 1979 and began work on standards for quality management, quality assurance, and quality systems. The next major, and significant, phase in the evolutionary development of standards on quality systems was over the period of 1985–1987. In 1985 Canada revised its standard *Z 299 Series*, representing a four-part multilevel set of standards on quality assurance programs. A discussion of these changes is provided by Sjoberg.[27] These standards are essentially contractual in nature but can also be used in a noncontractual situation as a guide to establish, evaluate, and improve quality assurance programs. These standards remain in effect today (see the following comment on Canada's adoption of ISO 9000).

On June 15, 1986, ISO/TC 176 published a standard on quality: Vocabulary, *ISO 8402*. It is comparable to *ANSI/ASQC A3-1987* on *Quality Systems Terminology*, presenting definitions and related discussion (via notes) for 22 items.

In March of 1987 the International Standards Organization (ISO) issued the ISO 9000 Series, prepared by ISO/TC 176. This was followed in June 1987 by the issuance of a revised set of BS 5750 standards identical to ISO 9000. In November 1987 CEN's adoption of the Series was completed with the EN 29000 Series. This set in motion the rapid dissemination and adoption of the standards worldwide. The ISO 9000 NEWS (the ISO newsletter on Quality Management Standards), March 1992 issue, lists 45 countries with identical adoptions and three countries (China, Jamaica and Venezuela) with equivalent adoptions. Canada's adoption, however, is limited to ISO 9004 (as *CSA Q420-87*) on *Quality Management and Quality System Elements—Guidelines*. They continue to use their *Z 299 Series* for the other (principally contractual) levels of application. The Russian Federation has adopted only levels 9001 to 9003.

National standards that contributed to the development and were studied and used by the committee to write ISO 9000 included *BS 5750* (the 1979 and 1987 versions), *BS 5179* and *BS 4891*, ANSI/ASQC Z-1.15, *MIL-Q-9858A*, *ANSI/ASQC C-1*, Canada's *Z 299*, as discussed previously, and, in addition, *ANSI/ASME NQA-1*, France's *AFNOR NFX 50-110 and 111*, Germany's *DIN 55-355*, and Netherland's *NEN 2646*.

These inputs to the evolution of ISO 9000 are reflected in Figure 13.1, which portrays the historical and widespread influences in the development of ISO 9000.

The work of TC 176 continues. New standards in the 9000 Series have been developed. These include: (1) *ISO 9000-2* (1993), *Quality Management and Quality Assurance Standards—Part 2: Generic Guidelines for the Application of ISO 9001, ISO 9002, and ISO 9003*, (2) *ISO 9000-3* (1991, reissued in 1993), *Quality Management and Quality Assurance Standards—Part 3: Guidelines for the Application of ISO 9001 to the Development, Supply and Maintenance of Software*, (3) *ISO 9004-2* (1991, reissued in 1993), *Quality Management and Quality System Elements—Part 2: Guidelines for Services*, (4) *ISO 9004-3* (1993), *Quality Management and Quality System Elements—Part 3: Guidelines for Processed Materials*, and (5) *ISO 9004-4* (1993), *Quality Management and Quality System Elements—Part 4: Guidelines for Quality Improvement*.

ISO/TC 176 has also started a new series for auditing. Standards completed include: *ISO 10011-1* (1990, reissued in 1993), *Guidelines for Auditing Quality Systems—Part 1: Auditing; ISO 10011-2* (1991, reissued in 1993), *Part 2: Qualification Criteria for Quality System Auditors*; and *ISO 10011-3* (1991, reissued in 1993), *Part 3: Management of Audit Programs*. A further standard is *ISO 10012-1* (1992), *Quality Assurance Requirements for Measuring Equipment—Part 1: Management of Measuring Equipment*.

Revision of the basic 9000 Series is now complete, including a draft revision of ISO 8402. This includes: (1) *ISO 9000-1*, (2) *ISO 9001*, (3) *ISO 9002*, (4) *ISO 9003*, and (5) *ISO 9004-1*.

ISO has published *Vision 2000, A Strategy for International Standards' Implementation in the Quality Arena During the 1990s*, a report of an ad hoc task force. This is further described by Marquardt, et al.[28] Four generic product categories are identified to help direct future standards development. These are: (1) hardware, (2) software, (3) processed materials, and (4) services. Four strategic goals have been set for further development: (1) universal acceptance, (2) current compatibility (with parent documents and part supplements), (3) forward compatibility (minimize revisions and with acceptance in existing documents), and (4) forward flexibility (combined supplements for the needs of industry/product categories and incorporation of useful supplements in revisions of parent documents).

Appendix B
ISO 9000 in Brief

In terms of application the ISO 9000 Series of standards is well illustrated by the diagram presented in the pamphlet *Quality 9000* by ISO and shown in Figure 13.3. As mentioned, ISO 8402 presents vocabulary or terms for quality systems. It thus serves as a reference base for terminology.

ISO 9000 is a series of five international standards (but with respect to new work completed and yet underway, various parts are being developed under these five basic standards) on quality management, quality assurance, and quality systems. They deal with the structure, procedures, requirements, and the elements of quality management/assurance/systems.

The following individual standards make up the principal Series:

ISO 9000-1: Quality Management and Quality Assurance Standards—Guidelines for Selection and Use

This standard consists of a general introduction, a set of definitions (referencing ISO 8402 Quality-Vocabulary), the contractual and noncontractual situation, types of standards (9001 through 9004), selection of a quality assurance model (9001 through 9003), precontract assessment, tailoring and reviewing a contract, and a cross-reference list of quality system elements (between 9001 through 9004).

This standard provides the essentials of putting a management and quality assurance policy into action. It clarifies the relationship between different quality concepts and specifies the rules for using the three models given in ISO 9001, ISO 9002, and ISO 9003. The standard introduces the notion of *degrees of demonstration* which is associated with the proof any client may require concerning the adequacy of the quality system and the conformity of the product with the specified requirements.

The three ISO Quality 9000 Models represent three distinct forms of functional or organizational capability suitable for two-party contractual purposes.

ISO 9001: Quality Systems—Model for Quality Assurance in Design/Development, Production, Installation, and Servicing

Model 1 is for use when conformance to specified needs is to be assured by the supplier throughout the whole cycle from design to servicing. It is used when the contract (between supplier and purchaser, for example) specifically requires design effort and the product requirements are stated (or need to be stated) principally in performance terms. Model 1 represents the fullest requirements, involving 20 quality system elements at their most stringent level.

ISO 9002: Quality Systems—Model for Quality Assurance in Production, Installation, and Servicing

Model 2 is more compact. It is for use when the specified requirements for products are stated in terms of an already-established design or specification. Only the supplier's capabilities in production, installation, and servicing are to be demonstrated. All the quality system elements listed in ISO 9001 are present at the same level, except for design control. All requirement clauses are now harmonized between the three QA models, with "place-keepers" in the clauses that do not apply. This is the case for "4.4 Design control" in ISO 9002.

ISO 9003: Quality Systems—Model for Quality Assurance in Final Inspection and Test

Model 3 applies to situations where only the supplier's capabilities for inspection and tests (conducted on the product as supplied) can be (or must be) satisfactorily demonstrated. In this model a reduced number of the quality system elements of ISO 9001 are required. Four requirements, in particular, are given "place-keeper" clauses to align common requirement clauses between all of the

QA models. For ISO 9003 these nonapplicable clauses are design control, purchasing, process control, and servicing.

ISO 9004-1: Quality Management and Quality System Elements—Guidelines

This standard consists of a set of more than 90 quality system elements that should be considered when designing and implementing a quality system. It provides additional details for each of the broader categories of the 20 quality system elements referenced in ISO 9001 and the other system (model) standards. A manufacturer needs to understand an operation in sufficient detail so that only the appropriate elements are selected for each step of the operation. The object is to minimize the cost of the quality system while maximizing the benefits. ISO 9004 is intended to serve as a guideline for this task.

Chapter 14

Effective Use of ISO 9000 in Quality Management

HITOSHI KUME

Introduction

The system of certification to the ISO 9000 series of standards has come into widespread use throughout the world. Whether or not this actually turns out to be useful to the development of quality management depends on how the standards and the system are utilized and applied. The system for certifying suppliers' quality systems to ISO 9000 in reality is halfway from both the purchaser's and the supplier's standpoint, and quality cannot be totally assured by this means alone. This very incompleteness hinders the purchaser and supplier flexibility in the way they use the system. It could be argued that the effectiveness of the system depends largely on the way it is used. The ISO 9000 series standards are formulated in general terms and are therefore unlikely to completely satisfy the requirements of individual purchasers.[1-4]

Certification is based on an assessment of conformance to standards and does not involve any evaluation of performance. The amount of information available to the auditor in a third-party audit is limited, and this in turn restricts the scope of the audit.

In this chapter, the capability of the ISO 9000 standards in relation to quality management is examined, with particular reference to the potential of a certification system based on utilization of third-party auditing.

Utilization of ISO 9000 by Purchasers

Quality System and Product Quality

From the purchaser's viewpoint, the problem with the ISO standards and the associated certification system is as follows. The ISO 9000 standards relate to quality systems and are not directly concerned with product quality. However, the purchaser is interested in the product, not in the supplier's quality system. The fact that the supplier's quality system matches that specified in the ISO standard does not necessarily mean much to the purchaser.

If a product standard is appropriately defined, and if the product in question meets this standard, that means the product's quality is satisfactory. However, the fact that a quality system meets the ISO standards does not, as things currently stand, convey much information about the quality of the product. It is clear that product quality cannot be assured 100 percent by the ISO 9000 standards alone. The quality activities that must be performed by purchasers themselves in order to assure total quality, and the elements that can be left to the ISO-standards-based third-party certification system, must now be defined.

Those certain aspects of product quality that cannot be assured by the ISO standards must be taken care of by the purchaser.

Technical Capabilities of Suppliers

When a purchaser approaches a supplier for the first time, the supplier's quality system is not the purchaser's only concern. The first thing the purchaser wants to know is whether the supplier has the technical capability to make products satisfying the purchaser's quality, price requirements, and the production capacity to make the products in the quantities required. The purchaser's initial quality assessment will therefore focus mainly on the supplier's technical capability and production capacity rather than on its quality system. Although, from the purchaser's standpoint, it is desirable for the supplier's quality system to conform to ISO 9000 series, the purchaser is unlikely to start dealing with the supplier on the strength of standards utilization alone.

Requirements Specific to the Purchaser

The "Big Three" American automobile manufacturers have formulated a set of quality system requirements known as QS-9000, common to all three companies. These requirements consist of the following three categories.

S1. ISO 9000-based requirements

S2. Sector-specific requirements

S3. Customer-specific requirements

S1 quotes ISO 9001 verbatim. S2 includes requirements shared by all three car manufacturers but are not included in the ISO standards, such as engineering change validation, quality and productivity improvement, and facilities, equipment, and process planning and effectiveness. S3 gives the requirements specific to each company.

The ISO standards are formulated in general terms and can be used widely in many industries. On the other hand, because they are generic, individual companies cannot easily use them as they stand. Purchasers naturally expect to have to work out their own mutually agreeable quality system requirements by augmenting the ISO standards with standards specific to their own industry. This "tailoring" is recognized and admitted under the ISO 9000 standards. Modified standards analogous to the QS-9000 series will no doubt arise in other industries in the future. The significance of general certification based on the ISO 9000 series and the form that this certification should take will remain likely to be called into question.

Utilization of ISO 9000 by Suppliers

Conformance and Performance

From the supplier's standpoint, although the ISO 9000 standards are necessary conditions relating to corporate quality management activities, they cannot in themselves be regarded as sufficient to obtain quality economically. This is because the concept of performance of quality activities is completely absent from the current standards. This is why organizations must carefully consider the role of ISO 9000 in quality management, find the best way to utilize the system of quality-system certification, and use the full potential of these standards and the certification system to make their quality management activities even more effective.

Furthermore, activities based on standards require:

1. That some sort of standards exist (the *what*)

2. That the standards are appropriate to the purpose of the activity (the *how*)

3. That the work is carried out in accordance with the standards (conformance)

The ISO 9000 series makes pronouncement concerning the first, but does not deal with the matters on the second requirement.

Suppose the following two situations of welding processes in the example of the construction of a plant.

1. The welding defect rate is 8 percent, and the defect rate is kept to an acceptable level by strict inspections and repairs or reworks of the defectives.

2. There is no welding defect at all, and the welding processes are only monitored as required to confirm the quality.

From the standpoint of conformance to the requirement for the quality level of outgoing products, there is no difference between these two situations. However, from the standpoint of performance of the welding process, there is a big difference.

The ISO 9000 series specifies what must be done to manage quality, but not how to do it. This is because the *how* depends on factors such as the type of product, the organization's size, and cultural background. It is therefore sensible for the ISO organization to refrain from addressing the *how* matters. From the viewpoint of performance, however, the really difficult question is in fact the *how*, not the *what*. Although it is important to say what needs to be done in order to manage quality, it is often more important to explain how to do it.

For example, section 4.4.7 (Design Verification) of ISO 9001 states, "At appropriate stages of design, formal documented reviews of the design results shall be planned and conducted. Participants at each design review shall include representatives of all functions concerned with the design stage being reviewed, as well as other special personnel, as required. Record of such reviews shall be maintained." More important things in a design review, however, are the level of knowledge and experience of reviewers, appropriateness of the materials and documents prepared for the review, and the hours spent for it than the records of it.

Section 4.9a stipulates, as a requirement of process control, "documented procedures defining the manner of production, installation and servicing, where the absence of such procedures could adversely affect quality." Such documented procedures should certainly exist. Their existence is undoubtedly important and their contents are also equally important. These will vary according to the products and processes concerned, and the number and skill levels of the employees in the workplace. The ideal contents of the documented procedures for a company with a few highly experienced and hand-picked staff will be different from those for a company with a large number of untrained workers and a high turnover of employees. Situations may also arise in which it is necessary to stipulate how people should be trained and checked. Standards cannot help when it comes to deciding when something "could adversely affect quality."

External Audit and Internal Audit

Companies audited by the certifying bodies and accepted as complying with the standards are certified, and their certifications are made public. From the supplier's viewpoint, certification is a form of advertising and publicity. But, more significantly, it allows purchasers to find companies excelling in quality by scanning the list of certified companies, so it helps purchasers by reducing the amount of vetting involved in product procurement.

From the supplier's viewpoint, however, the primary aim of the certification system has to be to ensure that its quality is kept up to mark, and to exert a beneficial effect on the management of the company through quality assurance.

For the supplier, the current ISO 9000 standards are quality system standards, and the purpose of third-party auditing is to find out whether the supplier conforms to those standards. The audits are not concerned with improving the performance of the supplier's quality management activities or with improving quality. Conforming to ISO 9000 is only a part of the quality management activities required by the company. A quality system certified under ISO 9000 may not necessarily be satisfactory for the supplier's own purposes. Where ISO 9000 certification leaves off, internal auditing must take over. In fact, it would be better to place internal auditing in the central position and augment it with external auditing.

However, since an internal audit is carried out by the company's own people, the departments being audited sometimes find it difficult to treat the audit with the respect it deserves. Examinations are apt to be left undone due to pressure of routine work, and recommended corrective measures are often not thoroughly implemented. Institutionalized third-party audits have the advantages of being objective and reliably performed owing to their mandatory nature within the system, and can therefore be an effective means of ensuring that a quality system is faithfully maintained.

Audits, like school examinations, are something of an ordeal. Nevertheless, it cannot be denied that the prospect of examination is what motivates many pupils to study. Quality systems can be effectively maintained and improved by judiciously combining the compulsory element of the certification system with the autonomous element of the internal audit. The quality systems stipulated in the ISO standards are defined in general terms and need to be tailored and supplemented to fit individual companies.

ISO 9000 and TQM

Quality Assurance System and Quality Improvement System

The difference between quality management in the West and quality management in Japan is that in the West quality management focuses on *controlling* quality, while in Japan it is aimed more at *improving* quality. This difference arises from contrasting views of the proper role of quality management, which arose in the early days of this discipline.

Many improvement methods have been developed in Japan in the name of quality management, but many of them are also useful for improving other areas such as production volume, cost, marketing, administration, and other activities. This is because these methods are not specific to quality: they take a given process or system, analyze its capability, and improve it. Although they were developed for the purpose of improving quality, they are essentially *improvement methods*, not specifically tied to quality or quality systems, and can be used to improve other activities and systems as well. Statistical methods and the Plan-Do-Check-Act loop are classic examples, but there are also many others.

This is not to say that every company in Japan has built itself a good quality system. Many Japanese companies tend to regard quality management as the piecemeal patching up of weaknesses, but this is no more than ad hoc improvement and does not constitute a true quality system. Some people believe that if an organization amasses enough improvements, it will eventually end up with an ideal quality system, but this is a misconception. If the starting level is low, considerable improvement will be needed to reach the required level, and management resources will have to be invested to this end. If the organization fails to accumulate its improvements because it has not built a coherent system, the returns on its investment will be no more than temporary, and it will end up going on for years without being able to raise its quality level.

Any activity can be improved, but this requires an investment of management resources and time. Moreover, managers capable of handling this sort of task are not always there for the taking. Rather than starting out with an imperfect quality system requiring many improvements, it makes far better business sense to start out with a reasonably well-developed quality system, applying recognized and generally accepted standards that do not need too much improvement.

When a company uses ISO to establish its first-ever quality system, and then uses TQM to carry out methodical improvements, its improvement activities are implemented systematically and the quality level rises faster. This effect is not confined to quality systems, but also occurs in other activities where standards are applied in general.

Standardization and Improvement

Japanese TQM systems incorporate feedback mechanisms for improving the systems themselves. This contrasts with quality systems based on the existing ISO 9000 standards where, although the quality system is explicitly defined, the concept of using feedback to improve the system is weak.

Once a technology has been perfected, the main job of quality control is *maintenance*. In other words, standards are defined for the purpose of maintaining the current quality level, and the emphasis must be placed on ensuring that operations are carried out in accordance with those standards. But, if standards based on the erroneous assumption of a perfect technology are used without modification, then inconsistencies are bound to arise. If we ignore the discrepancy between reality and the conditions assumed by the standards and behave as though the reality is the same as the standards, we will be engaging in self-deception. If the technology is immature, the level of the technology must be raised. It is more important to analyze and improve the processes than to draw up useless standards documents. Before setting a standard, we must ask whether it is worth setting standards at all, and consider how we could set a better standard instead. If defects occur even when a standard is followed, it is pointless to require that the standard be obeyed and dishonest to ascribe any virtue to operations carried out in accordance with the standard. This is the danger in the superficial application of the current ISO 9000 standards merely for the sake of compliance.

Conclusion

From the viewpoint of both the purchaser and the supplier, the certification of suppliers' quality systems to ISO 9000 does not go far enough. This is due to the generic nature of the ISO standards and the limitations of third-party audits. However, the very generality of the standards gives the purchaser and the supplier some leeway in how they use the certification system, and the way in which the system is used is the key to its effectiveness.

The economic advantage of an audit performed by a certification body depends on how much of the auditing work is performed by the purchaser. The present certification system deals with the supplier's quality system and cannot completely substitute for the quality audit required by the purchaser. However, if the purchaser already has a clear idea of the supplier's quality expertise and only needs to periodically confirm that the supplier's quality system is being properly maintained, the audit can be carried out by a third party. Before the ISO certification scheme was introduced, a supplier's quality system had to satisfy a different set of requirements for each purchaser. However, because the certification scheme provides a basic template for these requirements, the supplier at least only needs to provide one basic quality manual for them, even though there will still be some duplication of the audits carried out by purchasers. The author believes that the quality systems offered by suppliers will increasingly be based on those specified in the ISO standards.

The ISO 9000-based certification system works best when used in conjunction with internal auditing. Quality management systems and quality assurance systems are not easy to maintain properly. Standards and procedures rendered obsolete by organizational changes, alterations in processes, personnel transfers, and other factors are often overlooked, and quality systems consequently cease to function properly. There are limits to what can be achieved by third-party audits, but since these audits are carried out compulsorily and objectively within the certification scheme, they help to keep quality systems updated and functional and to nip potential quality problems in the bud. By combining third-party audits with internal audits, it is possible to build a detailed and thorough assessment system that benefits the organization considerably.

The ISO 9000 series of standards is concerned with quality systems, whereas quality management in Japan has tended to focus on improvement of quality. However, the Japanese approach only works if the management resources are available for it. To raise a level of quality management to an acceptable level in a short space of time, it is best to introduce a set of quality system standards and manage quality scrupulously on this basis.

Conversely, the current ISO 9000 series lacks the concept of quality improvement. To make quality management activities based on these standards more effective, Japanese-style quality improvement activities should be introduced. Viewed from this perspective, the shortcoming of quality systems based on the ISO 9000 standards is that they have no feedback loop for the purpose of improvement. Future amendments to the ISO standards should include provisions for such a feedback loop. This is where ISO-based quality management and total quality management (TQM) can complement one another.

The ISO 9000 standards are the *what* of quality systems, not the *how*. Before they can be applied to individual operations, they must be made more specific. However, standards devised by people who are out of touch with shop-floor realities will never become living standards. Good standards must incorporate the wisdom of the people in the workplace and must be open to improvement by them. When it comes to the *how* of applying standards in real situations, quality management could be made more systematic and more complete by introducing the Plan-Do-Check-Act improvement loop in order to make quality systems more intelligent.

References

1. Kume, H. 1995. *Management by Quality*. Tokyo: 3A Corporation. (*Hinshitusni ni Yoru Keiei*. Nikka Giren Shuppansha [in Japanese]).

2. Kume, H. 1993. Quality Management by ISO 9000 and by TQC. Proceedings of EOQ Annual Congress, Helsinki, Finland.

3. Kume, H. 1993. ISO 9000 Tokuhon (An ISO 9000 Reader). JUSE Management Seminar Special Handout (in Japanese).

4. Kume, H. ed. 1994. *Hinshitsu Hosho no Kokusai Kukaku, dai-2han (International Quality Assurance Standards, 2d. ed.).* Tokyo: Japanese Standards Association.

Chapter 15

Quality Systems: The Evolution from ISO 9000 to TQM

DIETMAR MANGELSDORF

Introduction

The beginning of the implementation of formal quality systems in the late 1980s was mainly a market-driven event. Only a few companies recognized the real added values given by the philosophy of a comprehensive quality management system and its key quality elements. In the first approach for implementation, people focused on documentation of processes and on writing of quality manuals. It was recognized more or less as an operational process and the responsibility of the quality managers, apart from real business management. Even in the certification and registration procedures, the formal hold of certain quality elements prevailed.

Meanwhile, companies recognized the essentials and learned to introduce the quality elements step by step in the factories, in development and engineering, as well as in sales and marketing. The focus changed from documentation and formalities toward managing for process control and improvements in products, processes, and business management. The decisive factor was the will and the engagement of the management and the establishment of a long-term training program for all employees to practice the essentials of quality management day by day in all levels of the organization.

The main influences for the breakthrough of this idea were the difficult business situations at the beginning of the 1990s in all traditional European industries, with the growing complexity of businesses and technology. Globalization, with loss of market shares, higher productivity in standardized processes, the introduction of new and in many cases more powerful modern products (due to advanced technologies), as well as lower labor costs in Eastern Europe and other regions, had as a consequence a continuous growth of unemployment and a far-reaching effect of changes of types of jobs within the European Community. All of these aspects needed a new approach in business management for a turnaround.

In search of competitiveness and business excellence, many ambitious programs for productivity and innovation have been set up by management, mainly supported by business schools or consultants, to face the challenges of the dramatic changes in the marketplace. The main aspects of these programs are process reengineering and improved process control in all functions of the company. Continuous improvement, together with the culture change program combined with a new approach for business management by people empowerment, started taking shape. At the beginning, these programs managed as separate projects under labels such as "Re-engineering," "Change Management,"

"6 Sigma," "*top*," etc., and have incorporated all essential elements of a quality system, but people hardly recognized them as such a system. In many companies today we still observe that quality systems, mainly under the banner of ISO 9000 programs, are being operated as something separate.

The Integration of Quality Management into Business Management

Parallel with the ISO system, additional management aspects based on customers' and markets' requirements (for instance, environmental protection, occupational health and safety, and risk management) have been integrated into one management system based on the fundamental requirements of ISO 9000 managing elements (see Figure 15.1). In this situation, companies often adopt maturity models, such as that of the European Foundation for Quality Management (EFQM), as tools of higher value, using the criteria of the European Quality Award (EQA) for a regular self-assessment of improvements.

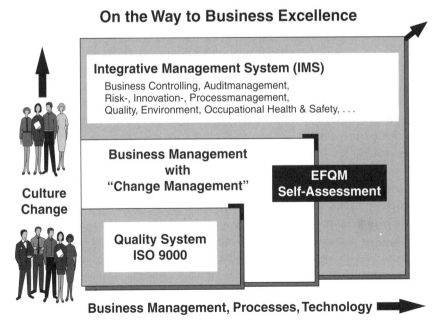

Figure 15.1.   The evolution from quality management toward an integrative management system.

World-class companies are now in a "post-ISO era." Their point of interest is how to evaluate, optimize, and practice a solid quality-related *integrative management system* (IMS) for the successful business management of tomorrow, based on total quality management (TQM) philosophies.

The international standards are following this evolution slowly. Classified quality system standards (for instance, the automotive industry follows QS 9000 standards and the telecom industry follows TL 9000 standards) are being proposed to be set up with additional branch- specific requirements. In parallel, the added value of a traditional system certification procedure is under discussion. Figures given in the literature show that 60 percent to 80 percent of the certified companies are only interested in the certificate as a key to enter the market, thus wasting money for a formal quality system without any real added value for internal process control and improvements.

Alternative methods for maintaining certification and registration are under investigation and are discussed as proposals at the International Accreditation Forum (IAF). In Germany, quality professionals have started an assessment and verification procedure for advanced management systems, named *Supervised Management System* (SMS), based on a supplier's declaration. If required, it is supposed to be used as an alternative method for certification and registration of management aspects of quality (in conjunction with the ISO 9000 certificate or the Environmental Protection ISO 17000 certificate).

ISO 9000 Quality Systems: Some General Comments

For many years, quality control, quality assurance, and quality management have been viewed as technical and operational aspects in companies, and even today quality systems are frequently operated separately from business management. It is also well known that many quality systems that have been documented, certified, and sometimes in operation for many years do not produce good results for various reasons. Lessons learned by experience and by observing the situations in many companies are that the quality systems must be totally integrated into business management to be successful. If so, in consequence, we cannot talk about "quality systems" anymore. Nevertheless, for many companies, at least in Europe, a quality system based on ISO 9000 standards has been the beginning of a never-ending TQM journey. These companies learned, often by hard trial and error, to design, control, and improve processes not only on the factory floors but also in all other functions, such as development and engineering, sales, marketing, customer service, and administration.

In the early days the third-party certification procedures, supposedly performed by qualified and well-trained auditors, supported this process. However, quality systems based only on ISO 9000 standards did not give enough input for the way business excellence was managed. Furthermore, companies willing to use TQM philosophies as a management platform do not necessarily need the traditional certification procedures any more. Certification bodies and industry are looking for a new approach to cooperation in search of business excellence.

Integration of Quality Vision into Business Management

With the changing business situation at the beginning of the 1990s, and in search of a new approach to meet the challenges of globalization, companies started reengineering programs for productivity and competitiveness. Key elements of those programs are:

- To give the company a new vision/mission and to implement a process for the deployment of goals and objectives through the entire organization, combined with programs for improvements and related controlling systems (see Figures 15.2 and 15.3)

Vision, Mission, Goals & Objectives

Figure 15.2. Deployment of a company's goals and objectives.

Business Unit Controlling Activities

Level 1: Company/ Group
           Overall Strategy

Level 2: Business Unit (BU)
           Business Activities

Level 3: BU
           managerial

Level 4/5: BU
            operational

B'- Strategy

Strategy Review
Business Review
Business Data Balancing

Management Review
EQA- Selfassessment
Project-Controll-System (PCS)

Project-Management-Meeting (PMM)
Project/ Product-Status-Reviews
in Sales, Development, Factory, Service etc.

Culture Change Programmes
Audit (product, process, business)
Re- engineering and Improvement- Projects

Figure 15.3.   Controlling system harmonized and effective over the whole organization.

- A dedicated customer focus, supported by the training of people to understand and to meet customers' needs, including the *internal customer*

- Empowerment and a culture change program to systematically mobilize all people

- A redesign of traditional processes for effectiveness and efficiency; in terms of cycle time, first-pass yield, costs as well as failure costs, etc.

- Product redesign for objectives and design for costs to manufacturing to serviceability optimization, as well as programs for innovations based on new technologies

- A new approach for business management combining the soft facts and traditional hard facts; for instance, by coaching and delegation of responsibility with authority, and by reorganization into smaller business units for globalization and growth to help establish additional local companies in a new marketplace through cooperations and joint ventures and acquisitions

Under the pressure of the changing marketplace, these revolutionary programs are managed strictly by the top management and at best are supported by their quality officials. A company's organization, however, needs time to adapt to all of these elements and many training activities need to be held at all levels to get people to understand the essentials and believe in the new approach in order to act effectively and efficiently within the new concepts.

Until now, these programs have needed many resources and investments, but for many companies it has paid off. These companies have succeeded in a turnaround for profitability and a better standing in the highly competitive global marketplace.

The process of deployment of goals and objectives and the systematic deduction of improvement activities has been a sensitive task (see Figure 15.2). Frequently, there is a gap between vision, mission, and business objectives and the deployment of goals and objectives to the operational level (the level of groups and employees). The managers in all levels of the organization have to learn to adjust with the priorities of productivity versus improvement activities and programs consistently with the short- or medium-term business objectives. In Siemens, Germany (the place of the author's employment), the yearly self-assessments based on the European Quality Award criteria have been very helpful to support this process.

To assess the results in soft and hard facts and to assure the effectiveness of the complete system, a dedicated controlling system considering all activities had to be installed (see Figure 15.3). For this purpose, management reviews, as already established in quality management, have to be harmonized and integrated into the traditional activities for operational project control as well as for business controls.

Within the various culture change programs, the communication of the company's vision, mission, goals, and objectives as well as of the results achieved, has to be installed. Even the interworking of the different activities and events needs to be explained so that people can understand the various relationships. To support the various improvement programs and activities, a broad training program in coaching and the specific tooling for this purpose are needed for employees as well as for managers.

Business Planning Based on the Maturity Model of the European Foundation for Quality Management

The reengineering programs are initialized generally through various improvement projects in soft and hard facts within all levels of the organization. In search of an overall assessment method for improvements, the maturity models given by national or international quality award criteria seem to be helpful.

The introduction of self-assessments based, for instance, on the European Quality Award (EQA), a maturity model for business excellence elaborated by the European Foundation for Quality Management (EFQM), should start again with an extensive training program to understand the model and to qualify a company's own assessors. Step by step the management, willing to use this assessment tool, will learn to handle the maturity model with its criteria and will recognize the benefits and added values. In the author's own organization, business units started with regular self-assessments year by year. The objective was to assess the improvements of all activities within the company's extensive reengineering program, named "Siemens-ÖN *top*," at the senior management level. After two to four years of experience, many units were convinced of the advantages, recognizing the added values given by this holistic approach for business management. As a result, the self-assessments have been synchronized with the regular business planning process in a way that the improvement goals and objectives derived from the achieved assessment results are integrated in the yearly business plan, committed by the top management and deployed through the organization (see Figure 15.4).

Figure 15.4 shows the relationship between the nine criteria of the European Quality Award, the estimated range achievable by only fulfilling the ISO standards, and the goals and objectives of the reengineering program "Siemens-ÖN *top*" for Public Telecommunication Networks ÖN within the Siemens company.

The self-assessment is now part of and fully integrated into the controlling and reporting of these business units.

Supervised Management System (SMS): An Alternative Method

In many businesses, as in public telecommunications, the certificates are needed even if the customers do not rely on the documents. It is assumed as a prerequisite for the acceptance of tenders. The added values of standard certification audits remain extremely low because the processes in modern global businesses are too complex and their innovations too rapid for the third-party auditors to penetrate and understand. These certification audits thus end in formalism only. For this reason the German Electrical & Electronic Manufacturers Association ZVEI, the German Registrar for Certification of Management Systems DQS, and the German accreditation body TGA created an alternative method for certification and registration, based on a manufacturer's declaration, and a complementary procedure for the product certification process, well-known under module A within

ISO 9001—ÖN *top*-Program—EQA-Criteria

EQA: European Quality Award

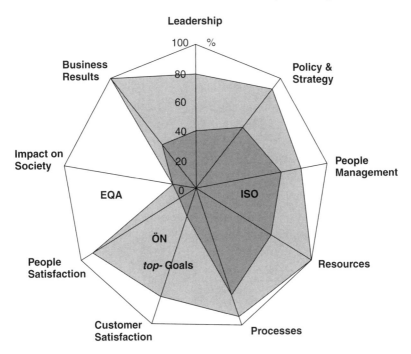

Figure 15.4. The goals and objectives of an ambitious reengineering program within Siemens Telecommunication Networks Group ÖN, fit into the European Quality Award criteria.

the European Community Directive for Testing and Certification. This method is known as the Supervised Management System (SMS).

The SMS procedure is especially suitable for supporting high-level integrative management systems. Key elements of this model are:

- To support a company's specific strength by utilizing and supporting the responsibility of the company and its management for the individual, quality-related management system implemented.

- To enable a better utilization of a successfully implemented and practiced management system with its own effective controlling procedures, and to pool well-trained and highly qualified auditors in the audit procedures established for such a system.

- To enable the inclusion of several management aspects into one integrative management system, thus opening the door for future market requirements (for instance, quality, environmental protection, risk, security, and so on).

- To strengthen the confidence in the company's ability to provide quality, by giving prospective customers more detailed information about its management system and the results achieved.

- To lead to an improved cost–benefit relation in favor of the internal controlling performance and to add value for the company through the certification evaluation process. Internal and external auditors jointly learn to control processes in a rapidly changing environment and to handle new aspects, thus deepening the knowledge and the basis for trust on a regular basis and in a company-specific manner.

The general conditions and prerequisites that follow apply to the pilot project of the SMS procedure for validation and verification of the manufacturer's declaration and for the certification of management systems on the basis of recognized and certifiable standards.

General Conditions and Prerequisites for Entering the SMS Procedure

As a basic prerequisite, the company has to maintain a quality management system that has been certified by an authorized and accredited certifier for at least three years. No open noncompliances shall exist. The company should have a management representative for quality who is sufficiently independent of the units subjected to auditing. Qualified and approved auditors conduct internal audits under the direction of a lead auditor, who is sufficiently independent of the section subjected to auditing. In an audit the lead auditor must not be a direct subordinate to the manager(s) of the unit(s) subject to audit.

Thus, the company regularly conducts internal audits, self-assessments, and management reviews within the scope of verification and the certificate. It implements scheduled and controlled improvements based on the audit results and findings and management reviews firmly grounded in adequate assessment procedures. The company prepares a manufacturer's declaration for its management system. This declaration is primarily directed to its customers and briefly describes its strength and achievements (for example, recognized supply quality, environmental declaration, awards, specific customer benefits, and so on). The company has proof of the facts and figures given in the declaration (documents, data, actual/objective results).

Description of the Procedure

The steps are as follows. The certifier checks the application documents. If these are accepted and the certifier has gained confidence in the management system demonstrated, a SMS project plan is elaborated. At the beginning of the next step the certifier checks whether the company's internal audit process is appropriate and effective by conducting a confidence audit. For this purpose the certifier samples the company's regular audit planning. Additionally, the certifier annually participates in a regular management review at the top management level. During the annual surveillance, evidence shall be submitted, including reports on results of conducted audits and management reviews as well as records covering the planned measures and results and their effectiveness. Further, the certifier conducts assessment interviews with the audit team leaders.

As part of the surveillance, the certifier reviews the statements made in the valid manufacturer's declaration on the basis of the presented facts and data as well as their conformity with relevant standards, if certificates are applied for. If there is a reasonable lack of confidence, the certifier may conduct an in-depth review of the relevant items.

The certifier annually prepares a written assessment report of the manufacturer's declaration and the obtained validation results. The company takes into account the results of the verification within its declaration. If requested, a certificate for the scope of the declaration and for fulfilling relevant standards (ISO 9001, ISO 14001, and others) shall be prepared. The certificates issued shall be valid for a period of three years, with surveillance conducted annually. If the surveillance proves to be successful on a regular basis, the surveillance frequency may be reduced to a two-year sequence.

Self-evaluation procedures (for example, quality award assessments) are envisioned as an expansion of or an alternative to internal audits. It is possible to extend the validated manufacturer's declaration by substantially new and generally recognized certification procedures. New procedures could be occupational health and safety management, risk management, or industry-specific management systems such as QS 9000 or TL 9000. The application of new procedures requires a statement of conformity issued by an accredited and recognized certifier. In borderline cases the rules of the current certification based on EAC and TGA definitions shall apply. Based on the current practice, the certifier's procedure shall be adjusted to these rules.

The SMS procedure takes into account the full responsibility of a company for all activities in its business. If the performance of the company is good to excellent, nobody is interested in certificates anymore because the aim of the company is business excellence. Those in industry should foster the acceptance of suppliers' declarations. The certification industry has recognized this evolution and is looking for a new role to support its customers in their search for an individual optimized way to excellence. The first results of the SMS procedure, started in 1997, are very encouraging.

Conclusion

Quality systems, as given in the ISO 9000 series, have paved the way for a quality-related business management. World-class companies are, however, in a post-ISO era, in search of business excellence to meet the challenges of the globalization in all market segments. Only the total integration of quality-system elements into business management will bring the breakthrough needed. We are on the way from a quality management system to a quality-related, integrative management system.

Section IV

Quality's Worldwide Trends and Projections

Chapter 16

Some Experiences of Implementing TQM in Higher Education in Denmark

JENS J. DAHLGAARD

OLE N. MADSEN

Introduction

The research activities at the Aarhus School of Business on quality management in education were started in 1993 with an international seminar held in Aarhus and funded by the Commission of the European Union. One of the most clear and outstanding conclusions from the seminar was that the European Model for Business Excellence, based on the European Foundation for Quality Management (EFQM), has a lot of potential for use in education. It was a conclusion agreed upon by even non-European academics.

Cases from all over the world were put forward to document the applicability of total quality management (TQM) in educational institutions. These experiences looked very inspiring and promising, whether dealing with quality performed by service staff, quality performed by faculty staff, or both. Selected papers from the seminar have been published in *Total Quality Management.*[1]

A result of the international seminar was the next step in the research: establishing a project to implement TQM in educational institutions. This project was funded by the Danish Ministry of Education with the aim of developing a general implementation model based upon the case of implementing TQM at the Aarhus Technical College.

In that project, the EFQM model was used for three purposes: (1) as a framework for an organizational culture analysis of the whole educational institution, (2) for prioritizing and planning quality development initiatives, and (3) for evaluating quality effects of those initiatives. The EFQM model turned out to be the core element of the model suggested for implementing TQM at educational institutions.

While the project aimed at quality at the institutional level, another project was carried out by the Aarhus Technical College and the Aarhus School of Business to figure out how to improve quality, particularly in teaching. The Danish Ministry of Education also funded the project. A part of the project focused on how to transform the EFQM model into a tool for teachers' self-assessment of quality in classroom. Looking upon education from a management point of view, an *educational paradigm* was developed, comparing learning as a classroom activity to a service provision (meaning production) that involved students as employees and teachers as managers or leaders. A conclusion from the project was that "quality in classroom" might be validly assessed, but with small modifications, in a way similar to any other service producer dealing with the assessment of normal products and processes.

There are two main aims of this chapter. The first aim is to discuss the applicability of the EFQM Model for Business Excellence, referring to the initial case from the Aarhus Technical College. The second aim is to discuss the problems that are usually inherent when higher educational institutions try to implement TQM principles. We use the experiences from the Aarhus School of Business as a reference.

Development of TQM in Educational Institutions

The implementation of TQM at the Aarhus Technical College was based upon the European Model for Business Excellence. The model was used by the top management team of the institution for an organizational assessment of the whole organization (see Figure 16.1).

The European model, which is divided into *enablers* and *results,* has a structure that turned out to be very useful at the Aarhus Technical College, and it might certainly hold true for other educational institutions as well. Because both enablers and results of an organization are in the same model, it was possible for the leaders to evaluate and plan for the whole organization and business. It also made it possible to find out which enablers (leadership, policy and strategy, people management, resources, processes) had to be taken into account for leaders wishing for outstanding results.

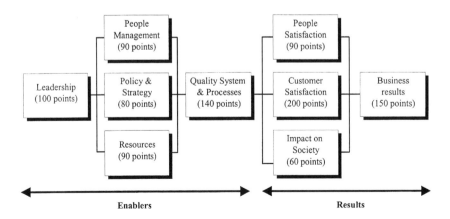

Figure 16.1. The European model for business excellence.

The model has several strengths:

- It takes into account both enablers and results.

- It makes it possible for the leaders to plan in a structured way what to do to achieve the particular results they want.

- It makes it possible for leaders to make priorities in an organization, assuring that resources will be used properly.

The European model also proved to be a well-suited framework for the implementation process, since an initial quality diagnosis of the institution was elaborated on, referring to the model criteria. Furthermore, the model was helpful to the leader's decisions on how to carry out the implementation process, how to improve quality, and how to train people for quality. Improving quality was an integral part of the implementation process. The European model was later used to measure progress compared to the quality diagnosis.

The Concept of Customers

When an educational institution begins to work with quality management principles and concepts, problems accrue because of the difficulties of copying successful companies in other fields (for example, manufacturing industries). Misunderstandings and resistance arise, and the intended "quality journey" soon stops. In order to have a reasonably high chance for success with quality improvement initiatives, quality management principles and concepts, within the group of leaders in the first step of the quality journey, must be discussed. The authors agree with Myron Tribus[2] that

1. The school is not a factory.

2. The students are not the product.

3. Education is the product.

4. The customers for the product are several:

    a. The students themselves

    b. The students' parents

    c. The students' future employers

    d. Society at large

5. Students need to be "co-managers" of their own education.

6. There are no opportunities for recalls.

The previous statements should carefully be discussed and jointly under-stood as part of the discussion of one of the most important concepts of qual-ity management[3]—that one must understand who the customers are, what wants have to be satisfied, and what vital areas of customers' needs, expecta-tions, experiences, and problems are to be discovered.

It is important to understand that the student is one of many customers, but discussing and understanding are not enough. The authors believe that one has to define customers in education as in any other service organization. One has to think of customers as being both internal and external customers, and one also has to understand that a customer may in one situation be regarded as a supplier and in another situation as a customer (internal or external).

As soon as leaders realize that one of the serious challenges when imple-menting TQM is to think of customers as being both internal and external, they are in fact on the road to creating a very powerful cultural change in their organization. When leaders start to think of the meaning of internal customers and how to treat employees—their colleagues—as customers, and when they also start to focus more on external customers, and especially on students, they soon realize that detailed specifications of the internal and external cus-tomers' are needed. In this process, there can be some discussion on what kind of customer the students are. Should the students be treated as external customers, where *the customer is the king,* or should we treat students as internal customers (like employees)? In some situations it seems reasonable to treat students as external customers, but in other situations it seems more reasonable to treat students as internal customers (as employees). Accord-ingly, it may be a reasonable conclusion that achieving student satisfaction is a combination of both; that is, treating students as employees as well as exter-nal customers. This combination of employee and customer in one person has been developed into a model (by research assistant Ricci Carlsson), as shown in Figure 16.2.

In Figure 16.2, both internal and external customers are divided into pri-mary and secondary customers. *Primary customers* are the internal or external customers who should be delighted and made loyal to the institution through total satisfaction. *Secondary customers* are to be satisfied as well, but their sat-isfaction depends on the capability of the institution to satisfy its primary cus-tomers, whether external or internal. The educational institution may, for exam-ple, find it worthwhile to care about employers of their graduated students, but they should do so from a customer's perspective, where the students are the primary customer. Likewise, management (leaders and teachers) should care

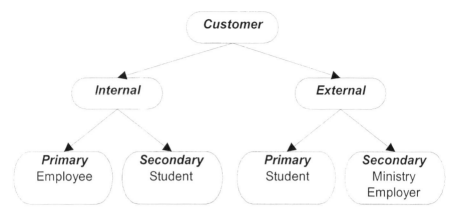

Figure 16.2. Customer concepts in educational institutions.

about students as employees, in the sense that a satisfied student will learn more than a dissatisfied student.

The reason for defining students as both internal and external customers can be found in the fact that learning implies the students' own studying, reading, understanding, and taking a critical stand on what the study subject is all about. In education, one should not graduate without making a contribution to the lessons. One of the most critical parts in any kind of education system is to make the students capable of learning by themselves. Making students capable of learning by themselves means that teachers must have requirements for the students, and that they should be involved in learning and not just in listening. Students must be treated as employees when they are in the classroom. They have to learn what it means to be an employee and what it means to fulfill the teachers' expectations (and specifications).

Planning for Continuous Improvement in the Classroom

In a learning situation, treating students as employees means that the teacher sets out the framework in which students are to work. It is the teacher who decides on the curriculum and knows the expectations from outside the educational institution (from the external customers' perspective). It is the teacher again who sets out the agenda for the semester and the specific lessons. But in doing so, the teacher must remember that he or she is obliged as being a leader, at least in the classroom, to help students produce their own learning.

The teacher as a leader and the student as an employee make a whole new set of meanings for expectations in education, which must be taken into account when referring to customers and customer satisfaction as the most important criteria in the EFQM model.

Looking at students both as employees and customers also means that students have different expectations for various kinds of delivery programs from their educational institutions, even though the students are not specifying their expectations. Most importantly, the teacher makes assumptions of what the students expect in different situations, and he or she makes decisions on how to satisfy these expectations and how to influence students' expectations (for example, by making materials to inform students what it means to be graduating from a specific educational institution and what the educational institution expects of the students following the graduation).

It is also important that the institutions make a program of education and training for the teachers so that they become aware of the differentiation between students as employees and external customers.

The authors have found that a program for education and training of the teachers must make special efforts to divide customer expectations into what the customers expect unconsciously and what they are able to require. In that way, it is possible to decide how to fulfill students' needs. It is also possible to decide what kind of information students need before coming to the educational institution.

Treating Students as Employees: An Example

The following example is a bottom-up strategy, which proved to be very efficient seen through the eyes of the external stakeholders.

The example is about a newly established Department of Quality Management at the Aarhus School of Business. The department was formally established in the last part of 1991, and from the beginning it has been very small; one professor and one associate professor (the authors of this article), plus a Ph.D. student and a secretary. The most important aim for this small group of people was to develop a new two-year MSc. program in quality management—the first and still the only program of its kind in Denmark. Because we were so few, we felt that partnership was a necessity, and therefore the program was developed in close cooperation with the Department of Information Science. Later, other internal partners were chosen, especially partners from the Department of Organization and Management. We also established a close contact with external partners from abroad. Most important were Professor Bo Bergman and his staff at Linköping University in Sweden and Professor Yoshio Kondo of Kyoto University, Japan. We learned much from both of them.

The most unique thing in our process has been the way we have worked with our students. As mentioned, we were the smallest department at the business school, but we always felt that there was so much to do, both within research and teaching. We discussed intensively how we could increase our capacity so that we could do what we felt was necessary. The solution to our problem was obvious. We decided to involve our students in our teaching as well as in our research. With this solution, we grew from being the smallest department to the biggest department at the Aarhus School of Business. The first year we had 16 students who chose to follow the whole MSc. program. Then we had 50 students who followed part of the program. In September 1997, we received 25 students who decided to follow the full two-year program, 75 students who followed an introductory program, and 42 students who chose to follow a new introductory course in our Bachelor program (this number increased to 66 in 1998). Several students came from abroad to follow our advanced courses delivered in English as part of a European master program in TQM.

It is easy to think of involving students in teaching and research, but it may not be easy practice. Our approach was the following.

From the very beginning we declared to our students that we regarded them primarily as employees, and secondarily as students (or external customers). We told them that this declaration had many meaningful consequences. The main consequence was that they had the primary responsibility for their results. We, the teachers, were regarded as coaches. The teachers' job was to give them the aims and guidelines for their study and to guide them. It was their job to listen to them and try to understand what kinds of problems they experienced in their learning process. It was the main job to change students' traditional study behavior from that of relative passive listeners when listening to traditional university lectures to being active in the classroom and proactive between the lectures and other formalized study activities.

From the beginning there were a few courses which were almost totally delegated to the students. One of these courses was "Quality Tools and Techniques." A lecture plan was designed by the responsible professors—one from the Department of Quality Management and one from the Department of Information Science. In that lecture plan, different groups of students (two to three students) had the responsibility of preparing a short lecture and deciding on the exercises to be used in group work. The professors' responsibility was to inform the students of the literature they should study and to help them with understanding, if they experienced problems during their study.

This method of guidance was a huge success from the start. Many students said that it was the first time during their studies that they had met professors who had time to listen to them. They also felt that they had a great responsibility for their own progress.

In other courses, it was not possible to involve the students in the same way. We had to find a balance between lectures delivered by the professors, with a focus on class discussions and group presentations prepared and delivered by the students. If we relied too much on group presentations the students felt that they did not get the maximum knowledge from the professors. We found that the most critical success factor with group presentations was the group feedback. The idea balance between group presentations and professors' lectures, including professors' feedback, was found when the students' learning was optimized. For example, if we had too many group presentations the professors did not have time to give feedback in the classroom, and feedback could only be given after the class had finished. This was not regarded as satisfactory as seen from most students' points of view. If, on the other hand, we had too many professor-given lectures, the students became passive and the learning process was not as effective.

A special course was designed to run intensively for three days, from morning until night, at a remote conference center. The title of the course was "Quality Motivation," and the course was inspired by a so-called "Japanese Training Package on Human Motivation" developed by a group of professors and managers in the Kansai district (the Osaka, Kyoto, and Kobe areas) of Japan.[4] The basic idea of this course was that no lectures were given. The participants in the course worked in groups with different study material. They read and discussed in their groups. After discussion they presented their findings in plenum for discussion with other groups. In this way they gradually understood how difficult the subjects of human motivation and team building were. They also understood through practice. If someone wants to motivate others, the point is to start with oneself. This is the foundation for quality motivation. We have taught that course every year since 1992, when Professor Yoshio Kondo came to Denmark to guide us. In 1998, the students' average satisfaction rating with the course was 4.5 on a scale from 1 to 5. This was the only course in our master program with an average score above 4. This shows clearly that we have much to do in the involvement of students in the other courses. We have learned that students' involvement is a precondition for student satisfaction and student learning. We wish to go further in that direction in the future.

With respect to students' involvement in research, the main strategy has been to be very attentive when students start their work on their master thesis. If the professors are proactive during the students' process of problem definition, there are many opportunities for combining the students' master thesis work with their own research. Most professors may be characterized by having a few research projects running and many potential research projects not running, either because they are new and not mature ideas, and/or the professor cannot find enough resources to start and fulfill the research project. If such a professor is proactive in involving his or her students, there are huge benefits for both the professor and the students. Because our staff was so small we had to think in this way and we tried to follow such a strategy.

The results of this strategy were excellent. For three years in a row (from 1994 to 1997), our students have won the European Award for best master thesis in total quality management established by EFQM (European Foundation for Quality Management). The students also got a very good reputation in industry (all the theses were written with relations to a private or a public company). Gradually, the demand for our students has increased, and we had difficulties supplying enough students to meet this demand.

Self-Assessment of Quality in the Classroom

Looking upon education from a management perspective, this educational paradigm compares classroom activities to service production, involving students as employees and the teachers as leaders. This means that education can be assessed for continuous improvement ideas within the framework of the entire educational institution. The teacher, of course, responsible for this assessment and for making decisions and taking actions for improvement and development.

Figure 16.3 contains suggestions for the necessary transformation of the EFQM Model for Business Excellence into a teacher's self-assessment model, to be used by teachers within an educational institution for improving quality in the classroom or quality of learning produced by students (with guidance from their teachers).

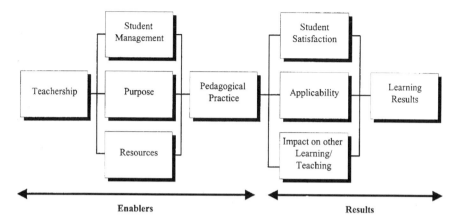

Figure 16.3. The EFQM model transformed into a teacher's self-assessment model.

The definitions of the five enabling criteria and four results criteria are:

- *Teachership:* Teachers' efforts (approaches) to lead students' learning. The aim is to make sure that students improve learning continuously by using TQM principles and tools.

- *Purpose:* Planning and deploying educational policies, pedagogical aims, and considerations about how to teach and what to learn.

- *Student management:* Teachers' involvement of students in learning processes and making use of students' joint potential for continuous improvement of learning according to purposes.

- *Resources:* Teachers' control and maintenance of means provided for teaching to fulfill learning purposes.

- *Pedagogical practices:* Teachers' management of value-adding learning activities and how these activities are identified, evaluated, and improved.

- *Applicability:* The satisfaction by the educational program of external demands and expectations, including how teachers identify, evaluate, and make use of measurements of external customers' satisfaction, and how these results are progressing.

- *Student satisfaction:* The measurement of students' evaluation of teaching and how teachers succeed by teaching according to students' expectations and needs, including how teachers identify, evaluate, and make use of measurements of students' satisfaction, and how these results are developing.

- *Impact on learning and teaching:* The general image of the teaching as seen by other parts of students' educational programs as a whole and how the teaching is affecting the parts involved.

- *Learning results:* The effects of teaching according to institutional aims and how teachers make sure that these effects are provided in accordance with expectations and wants of the educational institution.

The quality for classroom assessment should not invalidate management of the educational institution of which the teacher is a part. The EFQM model is very well suited for teachers' self-assessment and planning as well as for managing educational institutions. This is due to the fact that students' learning paradigm, based upon a comparison of teaching against management, is similar provided the students do the job of learning, lead by their teachers as managers or leaders.

When assessing quality in the classroom, the authors suggest the generic approach for organizational self-assessment as suggested by Conti.[5] One has to start with the results (the right part of the EFQM model) and then move left in order to understand the cause-and-effect relationships which generate the results. Having understood the causes for the results is a necessary condition for setting up an effective quality improvement program, since one is focusing on the right things to change (the causes). Using self-assessment in this way the scientific approach is utilized, where causes are regarded as hypotheses which have to be tested through a cycle of data collection and data analysis. Without measurements (data), profound understanding of the results of quality improvement programs will be hard to obtain and efforts will not be very efficient when trying to set up and implement new and better quality improvement programs based on the causes. Effective and efficient quality-improvement programs are characterized by the scientific approach, where continuous changes between inductive approaches and deductive approaches are taking place. The models presented in Figures 16.1 and 16.3 support the application of this type of scientific approach. Focusing on this scientific approach of TQM helps a great deal when trying to implement TQM in a higher educational institution.

Another important measurement to establish when assessing quality in the classroom is a student satisfaction measurement. But, according to the model in Figure 16.3, it should not be the only one that has to be established. The *right-*

left approach of Conti underlines the very important need of analyzing a student satisfaction measurement for *causes* of students' satisfaction to be maintained and improved, and causes for students' dissatisfaction to be eliminated.

The teacher shall certainly not register student satisfaction just for his or her pleasure or for some controller's convenience. Student satisfaction measurements, without proper analyses, have produced not only costs, but fear as well, which may invalidate classroom quality work.

An example from the Aarhus School of Business will illustrate some of the problems likely to accrue when an educational institution decides to set up a student satisfaction measurement system. Then, another example from the Aarhus School of Business will be presented. The last example will discuss the process of setting up a new mission statement.

An Example of Preparing a Student Satisfaction Measurement

In 1992, at the Faculty of Modern Languages, the Aarhus School of Business, it was decided to evaluate the quality of teaching by using questionnaires.[6] The result was that it was very tedious work to make the necessary data analysis, and it was also difficult to decide on standardized guidelines for the manner in which the students' evaluations should be put to use. The students were not always serious when they filled in the questionnaire, and the evaluations created much fear within the faculty. Some experienced and stable external lecturers decided to quit their jobs at the Aarhus School of Business. That was not the intention when student satisfaction measurements were started. It was obvious that the whole process was not very well planned.

In order to design a better evaluation procedure, a working group consisting of five teachers and five students was established to design a questionnaire that could be used in all courses at the faculty. The new questionnaire was used in a few courses in the fall term of 1995 and in other courses in the spring term of 1996. After this pilot test, the questionnaire and its related procedures were evaluated again in the fall of 1996.

The working group was asked to finalize its work within two months. It actually took them a year and a half. There were many unexpected reasons for the delay. The first reason was that nobody in the working group had knowledge about how to design a questionnaire. The second reason was that many teachers became nervous about the work. Typical questions were, *What is the idea about this sort of measurement?* and *For what are the measurements to be used?,* which the working group had to ask and discuss with their colleagues.

The answers to these questions should have been communicated to all faculty staff and to the students before the working group was established. The third reason for the delay was that the students rarely participated after the first months. They were disappointed with the slow progress of the work.

The teachers' resistance against evaluations was traced back to several causes. First, most teachers had been employed to teach and do research. Until now, all "the carrots" had been tied to research output in their activities. The main criteria for promotion from assistant professor, to associate professor, and to full professor are the research-output-related criteria. With such a system it becomes obvious that teaching for many is considered a "side activity" and not as a "main activity." Another reason for the teachers' resistance against evaluations of the teaching activities is that many teachers were nervous about being evaluated on areas for which they personally were not responsible. The third reason was that many teachers felt that there was a risk that the students' main focus would become the teachers rather than the teaching and learning processes.

During the second meeting of the working group a brainstorm session for the design of an affinity diagram was done during three to four hours. The issue was to identify the factors that had an influence on the teaching and learning process. This session was recommended by a representative of the research group on quality management from the Faculty of Business Administration who was willing to share his know-how on measurement issues of students' satisfaction.

The affinity diagram was analyzed and discussed by the members of the working group, and it became evident that the affinities comprised three main groups of ideas. One group comprised ideas related to the departments, the teachers, and the students. Another group comprised ideas related to general study rules and study guidance. The third group comprised ideas related to all other instances with an effect on the teaching and learning situation. As a result of this observation, it was recommended that the faculty should use three different questionnaires for the evaluation of the teaching and learning process:

1. A questionnaire covering areas related to the departments, the teachers, and the students. This questionnaire should be used in all courses delivered every term.

2. A questionnaire covering areas related to the general study rules and study guidance. This questionnaire should be used once a year.

3. A questionnaire covering all other areas with an effect on the teaching and learning situation. This questionnaire should be used after a whole study program has been finalized by a student.

In their work, the working group concentrated on the first questionnaire only. After several meetings which took place over a year and a half, the working group came up with a machine-readable questionnaire covering 20 areas which the students were asked to evaluate. The students were asked to evaluate both the satisfaction and the importance of those 20 areas on a scale from 1 to 5, where 5 means very important or very satisfied.

The idea of asking the students to evaluate both satisfaction and importance is that if the students evaluate an area as very important, it is also very important that they have a high satisfaction within this area. If, on the contrary, the students evaluate an area to have a minor importance, it is also acceptable if the satisfaction is not very high. In fact, the optimum state is characterized by having satisfaction equal to importance of all areas.[3,7]

The 20 areas evaluated by the students are listed as follows:

1. The description of the course in the study guide

2. The relevance of the course

3. The suitability of the lecture form for the course

4. Number of group works/reports

5. Number of individual exercises/reports

6. The overall planning and preparation

7. The practical capabilities which the course has given to the student

8. The theoretical insight which the course has given to the student

9. The working form in relation to group work

10. The suitability of the teaching and study material

11. The degree of difficulty of the course

12. The conformance between the course description and the actual course deliverance

13. The teacher's communication of the aims of the individual course elements

14. The teacher's planning and preparation of the individual course elements

15. The teacher's pedagogical capabilities

16. The teacher's inspirational capabilities

17. The teacher as a coach

18. The student's possibilities to give feedback on the teaching

19. The student's own contribution

20. The student's total benefit from the course

Figures 16.4 and 16.5 show the results of using the questionnaire in one of the courses delivered in the fall of 1996. Figure 16.4 shows the results in the same order for the 20 areas covered. The solid bars show the average student satisfaction of the 20 areas and the shaded bars show the average importance evaluated by the students on the same 20 areas included in the questionnaire. In Figure 16.5, the areas have been ranked in order of the gaps between satisfaction and importance. By doing this it is very easy to identify the "vital few" areas which should be improved first. According to the theory of measuring and improving customer satisfaction, the areas with the greatest gaps need to be improved first. These areas are very easily identifiable in Figure 16.5.

Without having done any scientific research, it was the experience that fear disappeared gradually when it was realized that the measurements could be

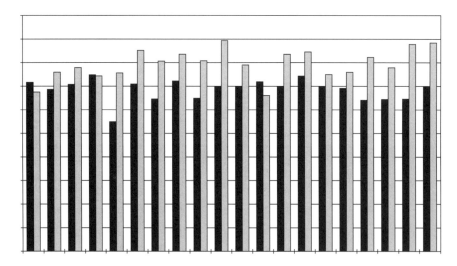

Figure 16.4.   Satisfaction and importance of the 20 areas measured by the questionnaire. (solid = importance, shaded = satisfaction)

used positively as a tool to identify areas with the highest priority for improvement. The teachers understood that the measurements were not established with the purpose to punish them. Yet, there were many teachers who were neutral or passive toward the measurement and there are still a few teachers who are active in criticizing the measurement process. There has been much progress; however, a lack of understanding and support from the faculty staff still prevails. What is needed for many teachers seems to be the link to an overall mission statement with a focused strategic planning process, which will make it obvious as to why the measurement system of students' satisfaction is so important for an institution of higher education.

While "teachership" is the very fundamental part of the model in Figure 16.3, the leadership according to the right–left approach is the root cause of the original EFQM model at the institutional level. Proper leadership is a necessity for establishing a clear policy and strategy to guide all activities in fulfilling the demands according to the criteria of the model. Experiences show that it is difficult to implement improvement methods for a whole university or a whole faculty because it is difficult to get full understanding and support, especially from the academic staff. Skepticism and resistance are normal occurrences. The main reason is that every university consists of many small "kingdoms" (the different departments), where professors act as the kings. They have a long

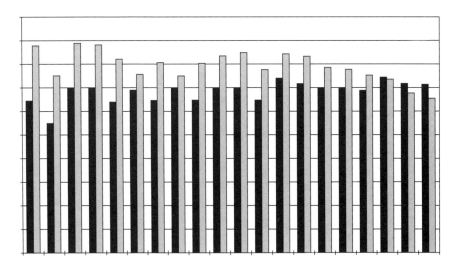

Figure 16.5. Ranking of the 20 areas measured by the questionnaire.
(solid = importance, shaded = satisfaction)

tradition of sovereignty and independence and nobody is supposed to tell them what quality and quality improvements in relation to their subject areas ought to be. A traditional top-down process for initiating quality improvements is very difficult and may be an impossible process to implement in the educational institutions. This may be the reason why there are so few success stories about the implementation of TQM in institutions of higher education.

From the previous discussion, it may be concluded that the most intelligent process for quality improvements in a university setting should be based on a bottom-up strategy instead of a top-down strategy. This conclusion is only valid if the institution has made a decision and agreed on a common mission statement with a clear vision or long-term goal. There must also be a decision on clear *core values* or *principles,* with an overall agreement and total support to follow (an example will be presented at the end of this article). If these conditions are not met, then all the kingdoms may decide to follow different directions and there will be a high risk that the bottom-up strategy will create competition and not cooperation between the different kingdoms. If the students' study programs consist of courses delivered from different departments they will suffer tremendously from this situation. The quality of teaching and learning will not be good enough, and there will be a risk that the quality of research will also suffer. Interdepartmental cooperation based on the freedom to choose partners seems to be one of the most critical preconditions for excellence in research and in teaching. Having decided on a common mission statement, there should be maximum freedom on how the different departments would decide on individual goals and how they would assure that the goals are met.

An Example of Preparing a Mission Statement

In the spring of 1997, the Academic Council of the Aarhus School of Business decided to establish a working group to come up with a suggestion for a new mission statement related to core values, to be regarded as important for achieving the vision and the yearly strategic goals of the business school as a whole. The reasons for this decision were many, but one of them was that an external member of the Academic Council, coming from a famous Danish industrial company, criticized the school for not having an up-to-date mission statement. Criticism from such an external member was accepted more easily than if the same criticism had come from one of the faculty members or from the inside administration.

The working group consisted of three professors from the two faculties of the Business School, together with a few members of the administration and the library. One of the professors in the group happened to be one of the authors of this chapter. The group worked very effectively, with joy and enthusiasm, and in November 1997 came up with a suggestion for a new mission statement related to core values. The results are shown in Figures 16.6 and 16.7.

The background for identifying and presenting the core values in this way gave the following clarification of a definition of business excellence:

- Excellent *people* who continuously adapt.

- Excellent *partnerships* with internal and external suppliers, internal and external customers, and society at large.

- Excellent *processes*. People who work in the different processes understand why they are working and what they have to do in order to satisfy their internal as well as external customers. They understand that continuous change is a necessity for satisfying their customers. Only through continuous improvements is it possible to produce excellent products.

- Excellent *products* which will not only satisfy the users but also delight them.

The Mission of
The Aarhus School of Business

● It is the purpose of The Aarhus School of Business to contribute to the welfare of society by increasing competences in connection with the solving of tasks within modern languages and business administration

● It is our vision to become recognized as a research and educational institution on a high international level

Figure 16.6. The mission of the Aarhus School of Business.

The Values of
The Aarhus School of Business

The Mission of The Aarhus School of Business is based on a range of mutually dependent Core Values within the following areas:

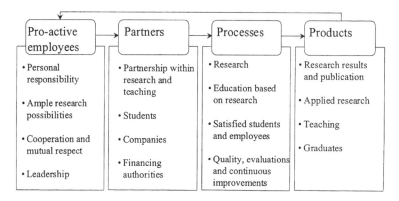

Figure 16.7.   The values of the Aarhus School of Business.

For anyone who has worked in a university it is not difficult to understand the meaning and importance of the *"4 Ps."* Neither is it difficult to use the *"4 Ps"* as a reference in the process of identifying the core values important to achieving the vision (the long-term overall goal) of the organization. This was what the working group did when they discussed and identified the most important core values for the Aarhus School of Business. Since there is a logical relationship between the *"4 Ps,"* it is natural to work with the same relationship when the core values are identified. This is the reason why the work group chose the presentation form for the core values as shown in Figure 16.7.

The suggested mission statement with related values was communicated to all employees—not to the students. At the beginning of 1998, with an invitation to come up with comments and suggestions for improvements, the members of the working group had suggested a communication process where members were given the opportunity to explain the details of the suggestions (for example, what and why they had come up with the suggestions of Figures 16.6 and 16.7, together with clarifying explanations). This was not accepted and the communication process was done in the traditional way—through written communication.

The feedback was varied. The feedback from the faculty of Modern Languages was more positive than the feedback from the faculty of Business Administration. The most negative feedback came from faculty staff who were quantitative-oriented. It was obvious for the working group that much of the negative feedback was caused by misunderstandings as to why a mission statement with related core values was important in the first place. There were also more negative styles of feedback, because the suggestions did not have explanations about the required measurements. So, it was very difficult to understand how the suggested mission statement with related core values could be tied to the yearly strategic planning process. In fact, it was pointed out by the Academic Council that the working group should not bother with the relations to the strategic planning process. What was requested was "only" a suggestion for a new mission statement with related core values and nothing else.

As a result of the feedback it was decided to establish an enlarged working group, so that the original group could be complemented with the business school's two deans—the dean of the faculty of Modern Languages and the dean of the faculty of Business Administration. This new working group now has half a year to come up with a new suggestion based on the previous group's suggestions and obtain the feedback from the communication process. During the first meeting the new working group agreed on a process where the members of different departments were invited to give feedback on the revised mission statement at a number of feedback meetings. It was agreed that visible leadership involvement and efficient face-to-face communication was a prerequisite for full understanding and support. It was also agreed that the previous process had been a valuable one, because the suggestions had increased a focus on the process and the result. It was also felt that the suggestions had increased understanding for the necessity of creating a motivating mission statement as a precondition for much-needed quality improvements.

Conclusion

This chapter has attempted to discuss the possibilities for improving the quality at educational institutions in a real-life situation. The European Model for Business Excellence was used as a framework for the discussion, and the case from the Aarhus Technical College was integrated. It was suggested that the European Model for Business Excellence could be used as a planning tool for a whole educational institution (a university, a business school, a technical college, etc.) to assure that the institution focuses on the right enablers (causes) when trying to achieve better results. It was also suggested that the model, with some modifications, could be used as a self-assessment tool to improve quality in the classroom.

To have success with such a process the institution needs strong leadership. This is not always the case at higher educational institutions, which are characterized by leadership in the style of different kingdoms (departments). The challenge, therefore, is to find out how to build a strong leadership in a way that all kingdoms move in the same direction. It was concluded that the traditional top-down strategic process might not be the right one to use in this situation. However, it was also concluded that there is a great need to establish a common overall mission with a long-term overall goal (a vision) related to and supporting the core values of the institutions. This is not an easy process, as illustrated in the last example given in this chapter. It is the authors' opinion that this is one of the most important areas that remains to be addressed in relation to leadership in educational institutions.

The second example referred to in this chapter illustrated the difficulties that may be faced in establishing an efficient tool for measuring students' satisfaction. There is always resistance from the teachers, caused by fear and misunderstanding. It was concluded that these resistances might have been avoided if the tool had been developed and implemented as part of a total process guided by an overall mission statement with necessary supporting core values.

The third example shows that a strategy based on partnership and students' involvement can be very effective in higher educational institutions. Small units can produce remarkable results if the people in those units have a proactive mind. It is interesting to compare the first draft (May 1998) of the new European Model for Business Excellence with this observation. In the draft model, one new enabler criteria and one new result criteria are included. Both of these criteria are focused on partnership. This is a good indication of how an important partnership is recognized by the members of the EFQM and the business community.

References

1. Dahlgaard, J. J., K. Kristensen, and G. K. Kanji, eds. Quality in Education. 1995. *Total Quality Management* 6(5 & 6). Special issue: *Total Quality in Education.*

2. Tribus, M. 1995. Total Quality Management in Schools of Business and Engineering. In *Academic Initiatives in Total Quality for Higher Education,* edited by H. V. Roberts. Milwaukee, WI: ASQC Quality Press. Tribus, M. 1998.

Quality management in education. Presentation to the 3rd World Congress on TQM, Sheffield.

3. Dahlgaard, J. J., K. Kristensen, and G. K. Kanji. 1998. *Fundamentals of Total Quality Management.* London: Chapman & Hall.

4. Dahlgaard, J. J., and Mi. Su. 1996. Experiences with a Japanese Training Package. Paper presented at the ICQ conference, JUSE, October, Yokohama.

5. Conti, T. 1997. *Organizational Self-Assessment.* London: Chapman & Hall.

6. Rybert, B. 1998. Evaluation of the Teaching at the Aarhus School of Business. In *Quality in Education—from Kindergarten to Post Graduate Education,* edited by J. J. Dahlgard and O. N. Madsen (in Danish). Aarhus: Centrum.

7. Kristensen, K., G. K. Kanji, and J. J. Dahlgaard. 1992. On Measurement of Customer Satisfaction. *Total Quality Management* 3(2):123–128.

Chapter 17

Managing the Quality of Management Training: An Overview of European Experience

AGNES H. ZALUDOVA

Introduction

The future economic and social development of the Czech Republic (CR) and the whole region of Europe is highly dependent on the maturity, competence, and performance of managerial personnel from the government level down to line managers in industrial enterprises. These desirable attributes of managers are partly inborn and partly induced by suitable education, training, and experience. Their promotion has become one of the key issues in the Czech Republic in connection with the transformation and recovery of the national economy with improving competitiveness on global markets, the ability to support adequate social and public services (for example, education and health), and on continually improving living standards, especially in connection with its prospective membership in the European Union.

In order to assist with promoting and upgrading the development of human resourccs in the Czech Republic in general and of managers as a key group in particular, a study has recently been undertaken about experiences with quality assessment and assurance and improvement of management training (hereafter abbreviated as QAMT), both on the level of commercial training institutions and on the national level. The study included an international comparison with the situation in countries of the European Union (EU) and recommendations for a suitable strategy and methods of application in the CR.[1]

Background and Objective of Study

According to the School of Management of St. Gallen University, management is understood to be the set of activities involved in the design, leadership, and development of the company with the objective of keeping it flexible and successful.[2,3]

Management training and development belong to the wider topics of adult education and lifelong learning. Management training forms a special part of further vocational training and is directed at enhancing the competence of managers, where *competence* is defined as *the set of knowledge, personality traits, values, attitudes, and skills needed for the effective execution of a particular managerial function.*[4] Management training is generally offered for different levels of management and takes a variety of forms, from formal training courses to a wide range of problem-oriented, practical methods and procedures of individual and team development of managers. A number of studies emphasize that it is not the training institutes, but enterprises and managers themselves that bear the prime responsibility for managerial development. In this respect the countries of central and eastern Europe are still lagging far behind their western neighbors. Their managers are often insufficiently aware of their training needs, and hence the actual demand for training does not correspond to the actual needs.

In view of the fact that management training is a service offered by training institutions to a wide circle of clients, it is necessary when assessing the quality of first training to specify the requirements as to content and form for different groups of clients (in the case of the present study, middle- and lower-level managers), and then to evaluate to what degree the acquired knowledge and skills of participants in the training program correspond to the specifications (requirements, expectations). Essentially there are two approaches to solving this problem. One approach consists of the creation of so-called management standards. This path was chosen by the managerial profession in the United Kingdom through the elaboration of a set of *management standards,* published by the organization Management Charter Initiative (MCI).[5] The other approach consists of leaving the content and form of the program to the mutual agreement of the client and the training institution.

In either case it seems useful to present a certain classification of managerial competencies (skills enhanced by basic knowledge and understanding) for middle managers, which corresponds on the one hand to the British MCI Standards and on the other to the syllabi of MBA studies common throughout the world. Such a classification can serve as a checklist when specifying training programs. As part of basic knowledge and understanding, we include knowledge about the international and European standards in the field of quality and the environment and about the requirements of the EU for equal opportunity and for the removal of technical barriers to trade and development. We recommend dividing the different subjects of management training into the following groups:

M.1 General Management: Basic management principles and methods, strategic management, marketing, business ethics, legal aspects, and others

M.2 Process and Operation Management: Purchasing, procurement, production, logistics, quality, quantity, costs, time, productivity, other processes and sector specializations, and regulatory domain, including environment, safety, health, liability, and so on

M.3 Financial Management and Accountancy: Principles, investment, banking, international finance, basics of accountancy, managerial accountancy, taxation, auditing, and other specializations

M.4 Human Resource Management: Recruiting and selection of personnel, team and individual development, self-development, planning, delegating responsibilities and evaluating work results, education and training, developing effective work relationships, and other specializations

M.5 Information Management: Communication, computers, information systems, and other specializations

M.6 Special Management Disciplines: Public sector management—central and local government, education, health, international business management, and others

Besides this content of training programs (for middle- and lower-level management), a special MCI standard for senior and top management (SMS) contains modules for the strategic functions of top management, their personal competencies, knowledge, and understanding, which together form performance standards for top managers. These performance standards are grouped into four areas which stem from the vision, mission, policy, and objectives of the enterprise. These areas are: understanding and influencing the environment; determining the strategy and mobilizing people; planning, implementing, and checking; and, finally, assessing and improving.

Figure 17.1 contains a graphical representation of an integrated management system based on the principles of the MCI standards. Into the upper part of the extreme left triangle, some of the functions of top management are noted. In the extreme right triangle there is a special group of activities belonging to the fields of process and operations management and relating to quantity, time, and productivity management, especially important for the current situation in central and eastern Europe. A detailed description of the content of activities in this area is given in the Prokopenko and North publication.[6]

The Training Process

The training process constitutes a special form of service provided by training institutions (the supplier) through the medium of internal and external (subcontracted) personnel (teachers, lecturers, trainers) in an interactive manner to participants (clients). The process, which has inputs and outputs, includes the creation of training aids (textual material, syllabi, case studies, solved problems, and so on) and the supplying of these aids to clients. Important inputs include information about clients' needs and actual trainer competencies. Active learning, problem solving in teams, and specific projects and their presentation all form important components of the provided service. The training service may be provided at the premises of the supplier or the client. The participants, some-

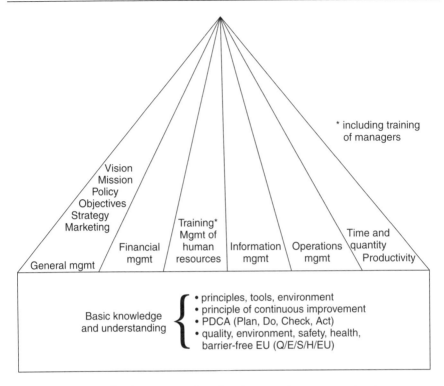

Figure 17.1.   Graphical representation of an integrated management system.

times called primary external customers, are persons who may be in different relationships to their organization (owners, employees, and so on). The end effect of the provided service manifests itself only when applied to the client's activities in his/her own organization.

Clear quality characteristics (measurable if possible) of the training process and its inputs and outputs must be defined (for example, content and duration of the training process, teaching methods, trainer competencies, incoming and outgoing competencies of participants, and so on).

Key processes connected with management training include:

1. Processes related to the organizational and administrative assurance of the training

2. Processes related to the analysis of training requirements, to proposed training programs, and their implementation and evaluation

3. Processes relating to the selection, preparation, and evaluation of lecturers, teachers, and trainers

4. Processes relating to research, development, and constancy activities

For all of these areas, the necessary activities should be described and verifiable quality characteristics specified which will be the subject of regular quality assessment, assurance, and improvement.

Quality Assessment and Quality Assurance

It may seem strange that the problem of quality assessment and assurance of management training had not been solved long ago. The main reasons why this area is still an open question are: its extreme complexity and multidimensionality, involving the wide discipline of management; the demanding activity of training, dependent on the interaction and competencies of student/participant and lecturer/trainer; the amorphous nature of *quality* in relation to management training; and the wide scope of the interdisciplinary science of *quality assessment and assurance.*

In the quality community, it is well known that the quality science has had its own history of development. Quality care developed from the simple inspection of product quality immediately subsequent to production (quality assessment), through documented preventive activities in the design production and usage phases (quality assurance), through applying statistical methods with the addition of feedback information and remedial action (quality control) to the modern overall activity of total quality management (TQM). During the early 1980s, the minimum requirements for a so-called quality assurance system were incorporated into the series of international ISO 9000 standards, with emphasis being placed on the possibility of demonstrating that such a system is implemented in the supplier's organization. ISO 9004-2 contains guidelines for implementing the ISO 9000 quality management system in a service-type organization, such as a consulting firm or training institution (see Figure 17.2 for representation of a quality management system for a training institution). At the present time, the second phase of revision of the ISO standards is taking place and a general model of the revised standards relative to a manufacturing organization is shown in Figure 17.3.

During the 1980s, the TQM concept became one of the leading principles for business excellence of any organization with these key attributes: leadership of top management, orientation to customer satisfaction, utilization of the creative abilities of employees, basing of decisions on objective measured data, and

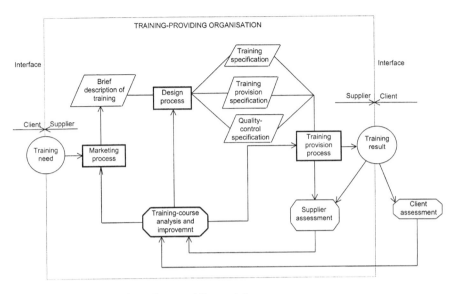

Figure 17.2. Quality loop for providing training.

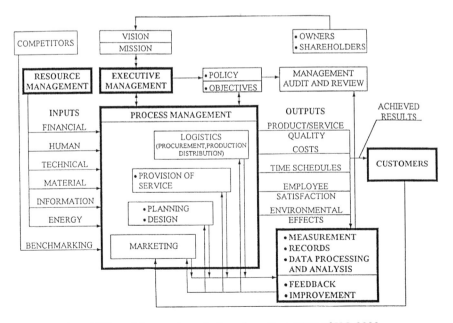

Figure 17.3. QMS model as envisaged after phase 2 revision of ISO 9000.

implementation of continuous improvement (see Figure 17.4) using the basic principles of the PDCA cycle (Plan-Do-Check-Act). TQM also became the basis of national and international quality awards in different parts of the world, including the European Quality Award, jointly sponsored by the European Foundation for Quality Management (EFQM); the European Organization for Quality (EOQ); and Directorate III of the European Union. The chief benefit of such awards accrues from the involvement of people in the process of analysis and self-assessment, which the preparation for the award entails.

Currently, the ISO 9000 and TQM approaches to quality management are widely applied both to the manufacturing of products and to the provision of services, and a combination of these two models was developed within the framework of the study for the quality assurance, assessment, and improvement of commercial management training institutions in the CR. At the same time, a number of other approaches were identified (discussed in the next section) and recommendations made for future benchmarking and eventual harmonization.

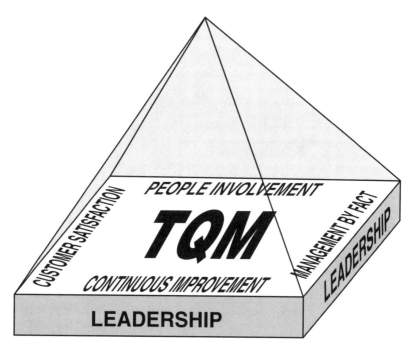

Figure 17.4.   Graphical representation of the TQM model.

In connection with the current needs of central and eastern Europe, it cannot be sufficiently stressed that the standardized quality system, combined with TQM is today considered to be among the most powerful strategic and competitive weapons of modern management. It is being incorporated as an essential element of so-called integrated management systems and as such must be an integral part of the syllabi of management training programs.

European Experiences with Different Approaches

Experiences with quality assessment and quality assurance of management training abroad, especially in European countries, show that there exists a general pattern of behavior of different stakeholders. For simplicity, the stakeholders are classified under the headings of

- Government and public authorities

- Industrial and commercial groupings

- Professional societies and associations with individual and collective memberships

- Management training institutes

- Other initiatives

The widest experience with systematic development of quality assessment and assurance of further education in general and of management training in particular appears to be in the United Kingdom, the Netherlands, and Denmark. The situations in these, some other European countries, the United States, and several structures of the European Union are now discussed under these categories of stakeholders.

Involvement of Government and Public Authorities

Many governments have proclaimed by law or by white paper (and are actively supporting) a policy of human resource development and restructuring of the education system in the direction of making higher education more valuable and more accessible to the population. In this sense they have established formal systems of quality assurance and assessments of training programs and institutions which are currently being validated and extended within the framework of various programs of the EU. Countries with strong government support and formal procedures for funding, assessing, and controlling at the national and regional levels include France, Holland, Portugal, and the United Kingdom. A further group of countries, including Denmark, Italy, Germany, Norway, Sweden, Switzerland, and the United States, have less formal systems, but support the quality-oriented initiatives and especially research projects involving industry and teaching establishments. The situation in individual countries with special reference to management training is now briefly commented upon and the main advantages and disadvantages of the different systems are summarized in Table 17.1.

Since 1990, the Employment Department in the United Kingdom, has been giving strong financial support to the national human resource development standard Investors in People (IIP), aimed at improving business results of British enterprises and ensuring the competitive advantage in world markets. IIP provides a planned approach to setting company goals and to training all levels of employees to achieve these goals in the interests of the whole organization. The standard is based on the principles of commitment, planning, action, and evaluation (CPAE). These principles are elaborated into 23 criteria, which can be audited so that organizations can become recognized by IIP.[7]

The Department of Trade and Industry in the United Kingdom plays a similar role in promoting the implementation in industry and public services (including health and education) of quality management systems with certification according to ISO 9000. It assists industry indirectly by providing limited financial support for consultants to advise companies on the introduction of a quality system according to the requirements and recommendations of ISO 9000.

The Department of Education and Employment in the United Kingdom has developed and is actively implementing the schemes of quality assurance and quality assessment:

- Higher Education Quality Council (HEQC)

- Higher Education Funding Council of England (HEFCE)

- Further Education Funding Council (FEFC)

- Further Education Development Agency (FEDA)

The HEQC and HEFCE schemes are aimed at evaluating and assuring quality of universities as a whole and their individual teaching programs. The FEFC/FEDA schemes perform the same functions for vocational training colleges.

No.	Approach	Advantages	Disadvantages
1	ISO 9000	After suitable interpretation of the criteria into the language of management training institutions, ISO 9001 or 9002 gives clear directions on installing a stable, documented, implemented quality management system. Included in QAMT model and guide-lines together with elements of model 2 (NQA).	The ISO 9000 requirements tend to be applied rather formally without the full involvement of staff and without much improvement activity or respect to the effectiveness of the system. This drawback may be offset by combining with the criteria of National Quality Awards. Tendency to apply only to admin. activities of training institutions.
2	National Quality Awards—NQA (e.g. MBNQA, EQA)	Experience with these models in industry and services (including small and medium enterprises) in Japan, USA and European countries is very positive. The Award model and criteria compel firms to assess their performance against best business practice, emphasize human resources, customer and employee satisfaction, continuous improvement and excellent business results. Included into QAMT model and guidelines.	Preparation for the Award is very time consuming, there is not much experience meantime with applications in education and management training. Pilot projects are running in some countries, including the USA, the Netherlands and Denmark.
3	Index of Client Satisfaction	Good potential tool for overall evaluation based on feedback from clients (firms) and participants. Used in CEDEO, NL and NTCI, UK. Currently used in Sweden and Germany. Recommended for QAMT.	Still little experience with use in management training institutions. Requires good computerized network in implementation.

(continued)

Table 17.1. Comparison of different approaches to quality management systems in training institutes.

No.	Approach	Advantages	Disadvantages
4	HEQC (Higher Education Quality Council), UK	Model of assuring quality in institutions of higher education in UK, based on self-assessment and peer evaluation. Used for management training institutions at MBA level. Transferred to other European countries through the EFMD and its EQUAL Program, recently improved by EQUIS Program to give it dynamic character.	Application of peer evaluation to commercially offered, competing management training institutions is problematic. Evaluation would have to be done by independent auditing center (see e.g. Strategic Audit Unit of EFMD).
5	HEFCE (Higher Education Funding Council, England), UK	Model for assessing quality of study programs. Using self assessment and peer reviews. Involves cooperation of teachers and students. Basis of approval of financial grants.	Lacks systems character. Concentrates on evaluation of staff development. Danger of only formal application. Not useful for commercially offered, competing programs of management training institutions, need for independent assessment body
6	EFMD/EQUAL/ EQUIS (European Foundation for Management Development)	Special criteria for management training institutions, developed in cooperation with professional organizations IM and IPD with special focus on MBA programs. Similar methodology to HEQC programs. EFMD operates Strategic Auditing Unit with broad criteria and aimed at stimulating self-evaluation. Recently developed quality improvement system EQUIS constitutes progress towards a dynamic quality system, intended as basis for international accreditation system. Could be useful for QAMT.	Comparison of assessment and accreditation practice in six countries shows existing big differences in scope and depth of quality system in management training institutions. Improved EQUIS criteria still lack an integrated systems approach.

Table 17.1—*continued.*

No.	Approach	Advantages	Disadvantages
7	FEFC/FEDA (Further Education Funding Council/Further Education Development Agency), UK	Self assessment and peer audit, applied in CR as EVOS program in Further Vocational Education by S@VS. Applied in UK to NVQs in management training. Cooperation with professional organizations IM, IPD and regional TECs and BL. Enables matching needs of industry with capabilities of training centers. Best set of audit criteria is Scottish SQMS, currently being verified in EU Leonardo Program. Further study recommended.	Implementation in UK in connection with NVQs very complicated, requiring Lead Body and Awarding Body approval, advisors, assessors, verifiers—internal and external, one to one assignment of student and advisor). Currently revised in UK to ensure better objectivity of external examiner. MCI management standards also revised to improve simplicity in practice. Whole area still in development.
8	EVOS (Evaluation of Higher Vocational Studies), CR	Program developed in CR with collaboration from NL. Model similar to that of FEFC/FEDA. Positive results of pilot audits in CR.	In the case of application to commercial management training institutions, need to avoid including in independent auditing committee professionals from competing institutions.
9	IIP (Investors in People), UK (Human Resource Development initiative)	Considered to be national standard aimed at systematic training and development of human resources. Contains 23 criteria, enjoys wide application in UK industry and public administration. Could be useful in other countries to raise the level of competence and accountability in all fields of activity.	Very complex system of implementation involving regional initiatives like TEC, BL, cooperation with NVQ structures and professional associations which act as Awarding Bodies. Current infrastructure in CR does not permit implementation. Need for wide training of consultants, facilitators and auditors.
10	CERTIKED, NL	Special interpretation of requirements of ISO 9000 for knowledge-intensive organizations, suitable for training institutes. Could be given a trial in other countries.	Need for special group to study and experiment with the CERTIKED criteria, their application and with certification auditing, need for training of consultants and auditors.

(continued)

Table 17.1—*continued.*

No.	Approach	Advantages	Disadvantages
11	CEDEO, NL	Useful, simple and transparent information system for clients and for management training centers on quality assessment of commercially offered management training programs and of their teachers/trainers.	Requires investment in operating an information system.
12	NTCI (National Training and Consultancy Index), UK	Similar characteristics to CEDEO, NL. Recommended for future development of QAMT in other countries.	Similar remarks to CEDEO.
13	SELECTassure, UK	Special portfolio type of professional certification/ registration of consultants and teachers/trainers, requiring demonstration of competencies. Suitable for developing in other countries in cooperation with professional associations.	Danger of formal approval of applicants and lowering of professional standards.
14	Personal certification by professional associations like IM, IPD, IQA, etc. in UK	Long practiced procedure in some fields in CR and abroad to uphold the standards of many professions, e.g. chartered accountants, quality managers and auditors. Recommended for QAMT (certification of managers, consultants and trainers) in CR	High demands on professional associations to maintain level of and administer examinations.

Table 17.1—*continued.*

No.	Approach	Advantages	Disadvantages
15	New Swiss Certificate for Training Institute Manager	Portfolio type application with final examination for human resource specialist in training. Recommended for future in CR	Requires financial resources at least for starting activity.
16	QS-9000 (Quality system of American automobile industry)—instructor certificate	QS-9000 requirements are extending to European suppliers. High demands on professional proficiency, practical experience, teaching ability, including demonstration teaching performance are made on external collaborators–certified instructors. Portfolio type assessment with demonstration. Continuing supervision and assessment of instructors demanded.	Strict conditions of work contract (e.g. ban on working for any other organization).
17	Personnel requirements of international certification bodies like BV, SGS, Lloyds, etc.	Relatively demanding qualifications, experience and examination of auditors for acceptance to the function of auditor/instructor or as external collaborator.	Strict conditions of work contract.

Table 17.1—*continued.*

In the field of management training at the university and MBA levels, the quality assessment and assurance methods of HEQC and HEFCE have been refined by two national bodies (the Association of Business Schools and the Association of MBAs), which require their member schools to run an accredited program of study. The requirements for accreditation are monitored by the European Foundation for Management Development (EFMD) and compared with similar procedures in operation in other European countries. The first analysis of activities of this type was described in 1994 in the publication[8] *Quality Assessment and Accreditation Systems for Management Education in Europe* (QAAS/EFMD) (for details see Appendix A).

A detailed survey of the published standards and criteria currently used by EFMD member bodies involved in the EQUAL (European Quality Link) project on evaluation of institutional or program quality as the basis of accreditation was published by EFMD in 1996.[9] A new direction of activity of EFMD since 1995 is the development of the system EQUIS (European Quality Improvement System), aimed at introducing a dynamic element of continuous improvement into the requirements for accreditation.[10] A summary of these two schemes is given in Appendix B. The EQUAL project is supported by the EU program SOCRATES. Several business schools from EU countries have already announced their interest to cooperate in the European Dynamic Model version of EQUIS project. They include: IMD (Switzerland), SDA Bocconi (Italy), Rotterdam School of Management (The Netherlands), Helsinki School of Economic and Business Administration (Finland), Ashridge Management College, and London Business School (United Kingdom). Voting among the EFMD member organizations shows that the majority of institutions are interested in innovating the present approach to assessment and accreditation of business schools and training centers (EQUAL) by introducing the criteria of the so-called dynamic model EQUIS.

It will be useful in the future to make a more detailed comparison of the proposed QAMT criteria (combination of ISO and National Quality Awards) with the assessment criteria of EQUAL/EQUIS so that the Czech quality system for training institutions is maximally compatible with the requirements of European structures.

In the field of further education and vocational training colleges, the FEFC/FEDA schemes are linked up to the awarding of National Vocational Qualifications[11] based on the requirements of the previously mentioned management standards, to a complicated network of activities of professional organizations (lead bodies, awarding bodies, institute of management, institute of personnel and development, regional bodies like technical and enterprise councils [TECs], business links [BL], local industrial companies, training institutes, and consultants).

Of special interest is the modification of the quality assurance system applied in further vocational education and training in Scotland. Special guidelines, entitled Scottish Quality Management System (SQMS)[12] have been prepared in cooperation between the Scottish Qualifications Authority and the Scottish Enterprise, which offers government support to small and medium-sized enterprises. This document serves as the harmonized framework for self-assessment in training institutes and for external audit. It is currently being verified within the EU LEONARDO program as a potentially useful document for the EU. In Scotland, it is the basis of a research project to harmonize the Scottish quality assurance systems for higher education.

In the United Kingdom, indirect government support is available to a number of semiprivate initiatives in the form of QUANGOs—quasigovernment organizations.

- Among such initiatives belongs the development of National Vocational Qualifications[11] and associated activities of the National Forum for Management Development and its executive arm, the Management Charter Initiative, responsible for the elaboration of British Management Standards.[5] In this connection the cooperating nongovernment organizations are the professional societies (for example, the Institute of Management, the Institute for Personnel and Development, the Confederation of British Industry, and others).

- Also falling into this category is support for the activities of regional technical and enterprise councils (TECs) and business links (BL), which assist with the implementation of NVQs and the principles of the IIP in firms all over the country.

- A further organization of the QUANGO type is SELECTassure[13] which certifies/registers competent consultants and trainers using a portfolio approval system with an interview and/or an examination if necessary. This activity is worthy of consideration in the future development of a QAMT network in the CR. More details about the conditions of SELECTassure are given in Appendix D. The advantages of this type of competence evaluation of consultants/managers/trainers is its comprehensive assessment of professional and pedagogical abilities and the effectiveness of performance in practice. The main disadvantage is the relatively high cost (fee of 275 GBP annually) and comparatively complicated administration.

In Holland the Ministry of Economics has supported a number of ventures, resulting in the formation and activities of the organizations CEDEO (providing information services to industry and training institutes in the field of management training)[14] and CERTIKED (providing certification service to knowledge-based service-type organizations like consultancies and training institutes[15]). The CERTIKED model has nine groups of activities and criteria, which have cross references to the requirements of ISO 9001. These criteria emphasize the project-like nature of knowledge-intensive operations and the role of research and development.

Strong support for the model of the European Quality Award (EQA) is given by the governments of practically all European countries at both national and regional levels. These awards have demonstrably stimulated private and public enterprises to strive for business excellence in their particular field and to provide role models for management in other companies. The implementation of the European Quality Award in the field of management training institutions is only in its infancy. Some Danish schools are beginning to prepare themselves for candidacy for the EQA. Information on the Danish situation is given by Dahlgaard.[16]

In the case of private management training colleges there is no compulsion to be subjected to any system of quality assessment and assurance, except that of self-interest. The quality issue is left to the market criterion of customer satisfaction (see the "Other Initiatives" section of this chapter). The most prestigious private business schools ensure their reputation by the quality of their teaching staff, course content, teaching methods, research activities, publications, and other services.

Involvement of Confederations of Industry, Chambers of Commerce, Trade Associations, and Other Employer Groupings

Large industrial corporations in the EU, such as Unilever, Phillips, ABB, BP, Volkswagen, 3M, ICL, IBM, Siemens, Renault, and so on are supporting the activities of the European Foundation for Management Development (EFMD) and its programs EQUAL/EQUIS. These programs are aimed at the unification of quality assessment and assurance of management training courses offered by universities and colleges at the MBA level, and also the unification of the European Foundation for Quality Management (EFQM) and its European Quality Award and other programs. In all of these efforts great emphasis is placed on regular self-assessment of the activities of the organization by its own staff, with the subsequent verification (audit) by an independent group of experts. This work at the level of the EU is based on the experience of training colleges and universities in member states, especially the United Kingdom and Holland. The articulated requirements of the national economy, industry, and the public services are a critical success factor in the implementation of these schemes. This area will require special attention in the future development of QAMT under current conditions of central and eastern European countries.

In many countries of the EU the Confederation of Industry and branch trade associations are offering training courses for NVQs, including the different areas of management knowledge and skills and the approach of TQM.

In the United Kingdom and many other countries of the EU (for example, Denmark, Holland, and Portugal), the Confederation of Industry is supporting government efforts to promote higher effectiveness and competitiveness in industry through the introduction of quality management systems and other programs of the nature of IIP.

Involvement of Professional Societies and Associations

As a general pattern in all countries, important stakeholders in the field of QAMT are professional associations (with individual and/or collective membership), such as the Association of Managers/Consultants (Association of Training Institutes, Union of Teachers, Society for Quality, and other professional societies). From the ranks of these organizations are recruited the key actors in management training; namely, the lecturers, consultants, and trainers. Research shows that the most evident involvement of these professional groups has been in the United Kingdom, Holland and Denmark.

In the United Kingdom, the Institute of Management, the Institute of Personnel and Development, the Institute of Quality Assurance, the Association of Business Schools, and many other organizations are deeply involved in implementing the scheme for awarding National Vocational Qualifications (NVQs) in various fields. Some of these professional organizations have been accredited nationally as lead bodies, responsible for the setting of NVQ competence standards, or as awarding bodies (in the different vocational areas) for approving assessment centers, which have authority to provide training for the granting of NVQs.[11] In the field of management training, the awarding bodies have a set of criteria which they apply to training and consulting organizations offering their services for NVQ management training. These criteria cover the aspects of strategic objectives of the applicant organization, marketing policy, management system (coordinators, advisors, assessors, internal and external verifiers), staff resources, programs offered, methods of assessing students' competencies (generally by personal portfolio), quality assurance (aimed especially at the management system, staff resources, programs, and assessment), physical resources, ethical issues, and candidate safeguards.

These criteria are essentially the same as those operated by the FEFC/FEDA, with special reference to management qualifications. Their simplest version seems to be the Scottish SQMS audit criteria.

In Holland, the formation of the organizations CEDEO and CERTIKED was instigated by professional societies and associations of consultants (OOA— individual membership and ROA—collective membership) and the association of training institutes (VETRON). These national professional organizations are vitally concerned about maintaining standards in their profession and are currently requiring that their member organizations (consultant firms, teaching colleges) operate a quality assurance system, for which special modifications of the ISO 9000 criteria and the EFQM model have been prepared by CERTIKED and CEDEO, respectively. Cooperation takes place with the quality training institute, KDI, and its certification arm, SKO.

Similar cooperation between different professional groups in Denmark to promote management development is demonstrated by the activities of the Danish Management Center, the Union of Danish Business Economists, the Danish Association for Economists and Lawyers and the Danish Association for Quality, with supporting activities of the universities and business schools.

A common feature of many western European countries is the requirement that professionals should hold some certificate as proof of their personal competencies (for example, a personal professional certification). Apart from university diplomas, many professional societies offer special courses and certificates of proficiency in special fields. Typical examples in the quality and management areas are the courses and examinations operated by the German and British Quality Associations (DGQ and IQA), various diplomas and certificates offered by the British Institute of Management and Institute of Personnel and Development, the requirements of the Dutch consultants' organization OOA, and so on.

A special aspect of professional certification in the case of teachers is the competence to impart knowledge and skills, which means having a second qualification in addition to their main field of specialization.

In Sweden, the situation is characterized by a large demand by industry for the services of professional consultants who will be able to conduct in-house courses, especially in QMS/TQM. Developments and cooperation are rather informal but are driven by the needs of industry. In Norway, the situation is similar to that in Sweden: less formal, but with positive development, driven by industrial needs. A significant change in professional relations is the recent fusion of the Norwegian Society for Scientific Management and the Norwegian Society for Quality to form the new Norwegian Society for Quality and Leadership. Such consolidation of professional expertise might be considered useful for future development of QAMT in other European countries.

In France, the quality professional organization Mouvement Francais pour la Qualité (MFQ), which was formed a few years ago by the fusion of several independent groups, offers a wide variety of services to French managers in industry. An especially successful experiment of the recent past is the organization of study trips of groups of French managers to the Center for Quality Management in Boston, Massachusetts. The groups take part in a special weekly course where the lecturers are CEOs from the foremost U.S. companies, and the tuition includes real problem solving and visits to U.S. companies.

Special features of the QAMT scene in the United States include the close cooperation of the quality and management professional organizations (American Society for Quality [ASQ] and American Assembly of Collegiate Schools of Business [AACSB]) with industry and government authorities. Currently this cooperation is manifested by jointly funded research projects under the title of Transformation to Quality Organizations (TQO). These projects are solved mainly by teams comprised of teachers and postgraduate students at universities or other teaching colleges in collaboration with members of industry and quality specialists. This collaborative effort is a very effective way of improving management training and should have a place in the QAMT solution for all countries. In particular, the whole area of modern teaching/training methods for the changing requirements of industrial companies (multidiscipline, flexible workforce and participative management systems) requires fundamental research and pilot verification.

Management Training Institutions

The situation in Europe can be characterized by two main factors pressuring management training centers to introduce a quality management system:

1. Pressure from education authorities as a condition of approval to provide educational and training services and/or receive government grants in connection with these services (for example, the United Kingdom, France, Portugal, and other countries involved in EFMD/EQUAL/EQUIS)

2. Pressure from industry, which requires a guarantee and recognition of quality of service of management training institutions in the form of an objective symbol of quality assessment and assurance

Some institutes are seeking straightforward ISO 9000 certification of the whole institution and are preparing to compete for the National or European Quality Award (for example, the Danish institute DIEU, for further vocational education). Some institutes (for example, in Holland) are satisfied with being assessed in CEDEO Information Bulletins without full certification audit, while others are going for certification by CERTIKED or other accredited certification bodics. Other renowned management training institutes like the de Baak Institute in Holland have attempted and given up the intention to gain certification by ISO 9000. They considered the amount of administrative effort to be too great. However, there is little doubt that they have their own internal QMS.

As mentioned, the commercial success of privately owned management training institutes depends only partly on the assurance given by a quality management system. To a large extent, the success depends on the inherent capabilities of the teaching staff, on flexible adaptation of the curricula to the requirements of the economy, on creative, innovative thinking and training methods, on developing partnerships with local industry and public services, and other initiatives.

Other Initiatives

At the worldwide level mention should be made of the activities of the International Association for Continuing Education and Training (IACET) in the field of continuing education units (CEUs). For several years further vocational education in the United States has been accompanied, for fields of study not granting credits for individual study modules, by a system of CEUs. This system enables persons who have not completed a university education to supplement their education and accumulate CEUs from various vocational programs.

One CEU is equal to 10 hours of participation in the education/training process. As with university credits, the CEU may be interpreted as a measure of quality assurance of the relevant training program, on the assumption that the institutions offering the programs have satisfied certain criteria. The organization IACET is currently carrying out an investigation on the desirability of extending the CEU system from the United States to other countries of the world, on the assumption that standard curricula for the individual subjects, standards of competence of the participants, and quality system standards for the training centers have been elaborated and approved. According to contemporary ideas, the quality system standards for training centers approved for CEUs should contain, on the one hand, program criteria and, on the other hand, administrative criteria.

The methodology of granting CEUs is a further private initiative aimed at unifying and demonstrating the quality of the education/training/learning process.

Another factor that contributes to improving the quality of private training institutions is an independent information service. In Europe there exists at least two such organizations for the area of managerial training. The first is the National Training and Consultancy Index (NTCI) from the United Kingdom. This private organization informs its members (over 500 enterprises) about future courses in the field of management training in the country, and also makes a systematic assessment of courses (internal and external) which have already taken place and makes this information, including an assessment of lecturers/trainers, available to its members.

A similar service is offered in Holland by the organization CEDEO, which operates a database on the quality assessment of managerial courses offered by about 500 training centers in Holland. Information is obtained on the basis of a questionnaire regarding the satisfaction of clients who have ordered courses. In addition, CEDEO offers an annual survey of all management courses, consultative services on the organization of in-house training courses for managers, and introduces quality systems in training institutions according to ISO 9000 or the principles of TQM and the European Quality Award.

In some countries there exists a special system of recognizing the competencies of consultants, lecturers and/or consultant and training institutions. One example is the SELECTassure system from the United Kingdom.[13] Applicants for registration/certification must present evidence about their professional qualifications and experience, undergo an oral examination, or demonstrate the passing of professional exams with one of the professional societies.

A new initiative in the area of professional examinations and certification for heads of training departments or centers has appeared recently in Switzerland.

The Swiss Federation of Organizations Offering Company Training (FSFE) has introduced (beginning in 1995) a special diploma for managers of training institutions/departments. This diploma is granted to candidates who pass a higher professional examination consisting of four parts: a diploma thesis, three written papers, an oral test, and a practical demonstration. Candidates are required to fulfill certain requirements before taking the examination: they must have a sound technical education, excellent general knowledge, four years of experience in the company or organization, and they must possess the federal qualification certificate. This initiative is inspiring for other countries and demonstrates that the solution via professional examinations is still implemented in Europe.

New Initiatives on the Level of the Graduate School of Management, SDA, Bocconi University, Italy

The graduate school of management, SDA, as a part of Bocconi University offers a variety of programs for executive management with different specializations, including public administration, and has an excellent reputation for the high quality of its services.[17] In the recent past, the SDA has introduced a number of new elements into its training programs, which have significantly enhanced the popularity of the school. They include partnerships with industrial firms; exchange visits with similar schools abroad; special research projects; innovation of standardized programs; consultancy and information services to clients; and cooperation with professional societies, trade associations, industrial companies, and organizations of public administration in creating tailor-made courses.[18]

All of these activities are implementable within the framework of a dynamic quality system for commercial training institutions in all countries.

Support from the European Union

Regarding the role played by the EU, much has been done from the position of the Directorate III for Industry and Directorate XXII for Education. Directorate III has recently published the European Quality Promotion Policy, which includes cooperation with the EOC and the EFQM on organizing seminars, conferences, the European Quality Award, and other initiatives (directed mainly at industry). Directorate XXII has been instrumental in promoting other projects to improve the quality of education and training within the framework of the programs PHARE, LEONARDO, TEMPUS, SOCRATES and so on.

According to the latest information, these two directorates are discussing future plans for closer cooperation, including the QAMT issues. This would involve better coordination of the efforts of EFMD/EQUAL/EQUIS on the side of business schools, the efforts of the European Federation of Engineering Consultants, and the efforts of the quality professionals EOC/EFQM. As a minimum requirement for management training institutes it is recommended that such institutes should have an academic council, which supervises regular self-assessment and external (peer or other independent forms) assessments of the institute and its programs. Top leadership of the EU is aware of the large potential for eliminating redundancies and for coordination and integration in the QAMT area.

According to sources in the EU, there is a growing awareness of the need for more knowledge and skills of TQM to be available in education and training systems. For example, in the United Kingdom, Spain, Denmark, France, Portugal, Norway, Sweden, and Germany TQM has been incorporated as a module into MBA courses and into other courses for managers and engineers at lower levels.

Conclusion

In view of the importance of management training for ensuring the competitiveness of individual European countries and the European Common Market as a whole, it seems useful to propose a general QAMT network linking the activities of the different stakeholders to a central independent coordinating body, which for expediency we call the National Grant Agency (NGA). Figure 17.5 contains 10 elements of such a network. The network was developed by the QAMT project team at two workshops with the participation of the Dutch organization CERTIKED. The elements are self-explanatory and follow logically from the information presented in this chapter. A key role will be played by the Council of Experts attached to the National Grant Agency. The main conclusions of the study, which led to the formulation of such a QAMT network, are summarized as follows:

1. For the government and central bodies it appears to be desirable to elaborate basic material for a prospective national policy for the development of human resources (including training of managers) and for the development of the economy (including aspects of quality, productivity, the environment, safety, and health). In view of its purpose, the National Grant Agency could initiate or assume this task.

2. To ensure coordination and harmonization with the activities of the EFMD and its programs EQUAL/EQUIS for quality assessment of training

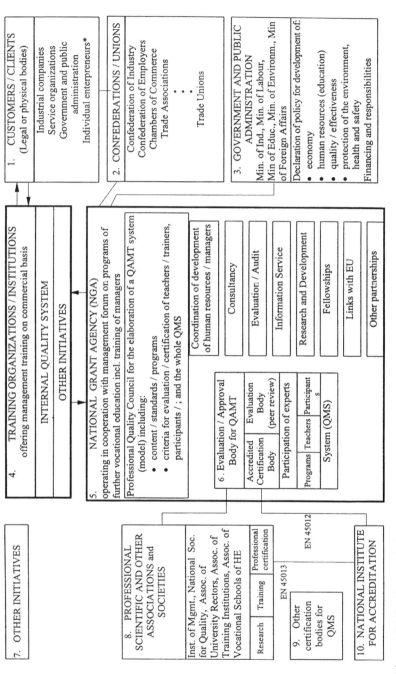

Figure 17.5. Proposal of a QAMT network at the national level.

institutions at the graduate and postgraduate MBA levels and also with similar activities pursued within the EU program LEONARDO relating to the secondary vocational school level, it will be useful for the further development of the QAMT/NGA system to compare the assessment criteria of all the different models currently applied in Europe, with the aim of improving the proposed QAMT/NGA model.

3. Experience with the quasigovernment organization SELECTassure could be used as an example of an accreditation/certification/registration body for professionals (consultants and lecturers/trainers of a portfolio type after demonstration of certain minimum professional and teaching requirements).

4. Confederations of industry, employers associations, chambers of commerce, and trade associations in individual countries could significantly influence the development of human resources and effectiveness in industry and trade by organizing training in new management tools, especially in quality assurance and improvement systems such as QMS/TQM, and by supporting efforts to compete for the National or European Quality Award.

5. Professional societies and associations with individual and collective membership (for the different areas of management, including quality) could contribute by offering personal professional qualification training and certification to their members. For lecturers/trainers in training institutions, this certification should incorporate both specialist professional competence and pedagogical (teaching) proficiency. It seems reasonable to organize a special three- to six-day pedagogical course for lecturers (professionals/specialists) in management training. This supplementary training could be offered either by one of the university pedagogical faculties or by some other institution.

6. According to the model of foreign national association of consultancy firms and training institutions, it is recommended that similar associations should advise their member organizations to introduce a quality assurance system (certified by an independent certification body or approved by the National Grant Agency). Full certification according to the ISO 9000 series of standards should remain voluntary. Certification according to the requirements of the NGA should be a condition for gaining financial support from the NGA.

7. The management professional organizations, including academic and educational training centers, should unite their forces in the form of a management forum with the aim of clarifying future ideas on the training of managers, the creation of qualification and competence standards for different levels of management, and the method of assuring quality of the whole training and learning process. The association most suitable for cooperating with the National Grant Fund in this direction seems to be the Association of Management Training Institutions.

8. An important task for the Management Forum in cooperation with the NGA will be the formulation, contracting, and monitoring of the solution of several research projects, aimed at the transformation of economic entities (companies) into learning organizations with continually improving quality and effectiveness. These projects should be solved by teams of professionals from teaching (academic) centers and from industrial and business practices.

9. Within the framework of individual private training institutions, it is recommended that (1) the institutions introduce a simple quality system according to the minimal requirements of the NGA, with assessment made by the NGA, or they introduce a full quality system according to ISO 9000 with an audit performed by an external certification body; and (2) the institutions introduce elements of continuous improvement of all activities, development of lecturers/trainers and other staff, and so on in the sense of TQM.

10. Within the framework of other initiatives, it is recommended that the NGA support, initiate, or advise training institutions to
   • Develop partnerships with industry and business
   • Arrange exchange visits with training centers abroad
   • Develop new teaching programs and methods
   • Link training and consultancy activity
   • Give priority to in-house "customized" training programs in collaboration with professional organizations.

References

1. Zaludova, A. H., et al. 1997. Quality Assessment and Quality Assurance of Management Training (Feasibility Study). Report on Project No. CZ 9305-01-01-03, December, National Training Fund, Prague.

2. Seghezzi, H. D. 1998. The Development of Integrated Quality Management—St. Gallen Concept. Chap. 2 in *The Best on Quality,* vol. 9, edited by M. N. Sinha. Milwaukee, WI: ASQ Quality Press.

3. Zaludova, A. H. 1993. Outline of Quality Management Systems Implementation in the Czech Republic. Proc. of CEI Conference, Quality Systems in SMEs, October, Prague.

4. Hoffmann, V., et al. 1996. *Czech Manager in Process of Transformation.* Prague: National Training Fund.

5. MCI Management Standards, 1995, London.

6. Prokopenko, J., and K. North. 1996. *Productivity and Quality Management—A Modular Programme.* ILO/APO.

7. British Standards Association. *Standards: Investors in People.* 1996, London.

8. British Standards Association. *Quality Assessment and Accreditation Systems for Management Education in Europe.* 1994. Brussels: EFMD.

9. British Standards Association. *A Comparative Framework of the Accreditation Standards Applied by Members of the European Quality Link (EQUAL).* 1996. Brussels: EFMD/EQUAL.

10. British Standards Association. *Guide to Self-Assessment: European Quality Improvement System.* 1997. Brussels: EFMD/EQUIS.

11. British Standards Association. *The ABC of NVQs.* 1995. United Kingdom: National Vocational Qualifications, Local Government Management Board.

12. SQMS. 1997. *Scottish Quality Management Systém.* Glasgow: Scottish Enterprise.

13. SELECTassure. 1997. *Application for Consultants and Their Practices.* United Kingdom.

14. CEDEO. 1993. *Towards Continuous Quality Improvement—A Method for Improving the Quality of Training Institutes in the Netherlands.*

15. CERTIKED. 1995. *Criteria for Quality Assurance.* The Netherlands: CERTIKED.

16. Madsen, O. N., and J. J. Dahlgaard. 1997. *The EFQM Model in Danish Public Sector Aspects of TQM, Aarhus School of Business Report,* November. Aarhus, Denmark.

17. Borgonovi E., M. Elefanti, and N. Pennarola. Market Driven Quality in Business Schools. Paper read at EFMD Conference, June, Prague.

18. Zaludova, A. H., et al. 1998. Managing the Quality of Management Training: The Role of the Index of Client Satisfaction. Proc. of World Congress on TQM, Sheffield.

Appendix A: Main Results of the "Quality Assessment and Accreditation Systems for Management Education in Europe" (QAAS/EFMD) Analysis, 1994

This document analyses the situation in several European countries in the field of quality assessment of management training programs and institutions of the university and commercial type. It records the results of a round table discussion of representatives of EFMD member organizations in 1993.

It was found that the majority of institutions operate an internal system of self-assessment, supplemented by external assessment in the form of peer reviews. For the assessment there exists certain rules, but the whole procedure is not standardized and is considered to be more of a tool for improving both the programs and the effectiveness of the institutions. The results of this discussion initiated research work by EFMD in this area.

The document presents the results from nine organizations in the United Kingdom, Spain, Italy, the Netherlands, the United States, and the special audit unit of EFMD. There is a need to harmonize the criteria and procedures for self-assessment and for external assessment (audit). EFMD is continuing with development in this area through its strategic audit unit. It offers courses for directors of training institutions. These courses are aimed at assessing the teaching institution from the following viewpoints.

1. Formulation of policy and mission

2. Resources (training staff and students)

3. Programs and other activities (for example, research)

4. Organization and processes

This initiative of EFMD is linked to some of the programs of the European Union (for example, ERASMUS and SOCRATES), within the framework of which there is an attempt to develop a system of mutual recognition of university credits for courses in different European countries (European Course Credit Transfer System).

Emphasis is placed on the idea that excellence of a training institution cannot be created by the accreditation process, but only by wise strategic leadership, which fosters maximum interaction of the values and potential of the institution with the needs and opportunities of the environment.

Appendix B: Results of the Reports EQUAL/EFMD (1996) and EQUIS/EFMD (1997)

In October of 1996 the EFMD published a document entitled, *A Comparative Framework of the Accreditation Standards applied by the members of the European Quality Link (EQUAL)*. This document presents information on published standards or rules used by the member bodies of EQUAL for quality assessment of their training programs and of the operation of the whole training center. The information is grouped according to the following categories.

Type: P criterion refers to program quality, *I* criterion refers to institution quality.

Area: A broad category description used to group the quality criteria. Key areas are assessment, delivery, entrance (student), marketing, policy, resources, results, and status.

Criterion: A brief phrase describing the criterion in question.

Description: A more detailed statement of the criterion in question.

Indicator: Symbolic notation of the institution in question with a number code relating to quality assessment (for example, number of full-time teaching staff).

The institutions providing information are the same as those contributing to the EFMD study of 1994 (see Appendix A), such as AACSB (the United States), ABS (the United Kingdom), AEEDE (Spain), AMBA (the United Kingdom), ASFOR (Italy), CEM (France), EFMF (Belgium), and the MVC (joint accreditation body of ABS and IM, closely linked with the NVQ system in the United Kingdom).

From the data provided it is clear that the majority of assessed programs and institutions are of a university type, linked to the educational system. The British organization MVC (Management Verification Consortium) deals with vocational schools offering training for National Vocational Qualifications (NVQs). The data are in a database and it is possible, according to category, to retrieve a brief characteristic of a situation in a given area.

Part of the document contains a survey of the criteria according to the individual assessed institutions. The most detailed information is contributed by the organizations AEEDE (Spain), AMBA (the United Kingdom) and CEM (France).

Work on the project is continuing since there are great differences in the situation in individual European countries. Common elements are, however, evident:

1. Accreditation of training programs and quality assessment of training centers is organized by the Association of Training Centers (Institutions). These centers may be universities, company training departments, private training and consulting firms, and so on.

2. Assessment (accreditation) of training centers is generally performed using self-assessment of the training institution in question, according to a set of criteria followed by an external audit by an evaluation committee of experts (peer review).

3. The documents of EFMD and/or of EQUAL make no reference at all to a third-party audit of the training center according to ISO 9000.

The most recent reports from EFMD contain information about a new EFMD initiative to approve the project EQUIS, the aim of which is the introduction of an award for management education institutions, the "European Quality Label." This project is to exist in addition to EQUAL, which will continue with the accreditation and assessment of institutions, with information exchange and with assessment of lecturers/trainers, and is supported by the EU program SOCRATES.

The EFMD unit for EQUIS will have its own board of directors with members from EFMD and EQUAL and including representation from universities and the business world. Within the framework of EQUIS it is anticipated that self-assessment and external assessment will be applied, based on the so-called European Dynamic Model (for continuous improvement).

Appendix C: Scottish Quality Management System

The SQMS manual recommends the following 14 criteria, of which the first 10 are basic management requirements and the last four are the core processes of a training institute.

1. Strategic management

2. Quality management

3. Marketing (customer requirements)

4. Staffing resources

5. Staff development

6. Equal opportunities

7. Health and safety

8. Premises and equipment

9. Communications and administration

10. Financial management

11. Guidance services

12. Program design

13. Program delivery (including teacher/trainer performance)

14. Assessment for certification

Cross references are given to the individual clauses of ISO 9001 and to the 23 criteria of the standard IIP. The manual also recommends some performance indicators:

Primary Performance Indicators

- Learner success
- Postprogram success
- Client satisfaction
- Learner satisfaction
- Quality of learning and teaching profile
- Unit cost profile

Secondary Performance Indicators

- Staff satisfaction
- Program cost
- Staff/learner ratio
- Learner progress
- Learner attendance
- Learner enrollment
- Average group size
- Utilization of accommodation
- Participation ratios for induction (of new staff)
- Participation ratios for staff development

Appendix D: Conditions of SELECTassure for Certification/Registration of Consultants/Managers/Trainers

The content of this standard is the following:

1. Qualifying criteria

2. Practical details about the applicant's consultancy or training institution

3. Practical details about the individual applicant (consultant, lecturer, trainer)

4. Fees

5. References

6. Code of practice

7. Conditions of application

8. Final checklist

The standard was introduced for the certification/registration/accreditation of consulting or training organizations or persons interested in cooperating on a regional level with technical and enterprise councils (TECs) and business links (BL) within the framework of the NVQ and IIP programs in the United Kingdom. Each applicant must go through a preliminary assessment according to certain qualifying criteria, with an oral interview to follow. The criteria include:

• Minimal length of practice

• Willingness to accept annual quality audits of the organization's quality system and plan of personal development of employees

• Demonstration of professional qualifications

• Membership in the Institute of Management and other professional associations

• Submission of the names of at least four references who will be requested by SELECTassure to give evidence of the applicant's competence by replying to a questionnaire

- Achievement of minimal value of Client's Satisfaction Index Rating (SIR)

- Annual affirmation of registration

- Adherence to SELECTassure Code of Practice

- Personal interview

The evaluation of the index SIR is performed by a special unit for Performance Audits, according to the replies of clients to the questionnaire.

Chapter 18

Case Studies of Quality Engineering Applications in India

BASANTA K. PAL

Introduction

Quality engineering is an optimization strategy developed by Dr. Genichi Taguchi. Taguchi formed a philosophy of marrying statistics and engineering methods to achieve rapid improvements in quality and costs by optimizing product and process designs.

As part of a national endeavor to improve basic infrastructure of telecommunication, the Japanese government appointed Dr. Genichi Taguchi to be in charge of promoting productivity of research and development (R&D) work at Electrical Communication Lab (ECL) during 1949. The number of people employed at ECL was one-fifth of Bell Telephone Laboratories in the United States at that time. For the final stage, many make-and-break performances were tested for the "relays" parts produced in both of the laboratories in Japan and Bell Lab. It was found that the parts produced from the former were better. A few years later, Western Electric Company stopped the production of cross-bar switching systems and started importing those from Japan for reasons of better quality.

Faced with the challenges of improving quality and productivity of R&D of telecommunications at the ECL during late 1940s, Dr. Taguchi developed standard *orthogonal array* tables, together with the associated concepts of linear graph. One of the major reasons for this success was known to be the extensive use of orthogonal array experimentation to expedite and improve the quality of the decision-making process. The journey toward quality engineering concepts and techniques began and continued through various revolutionary ideas and tools like *loss function, S/N ratios, parameter design, tolerance design, robust engineering, on-line quality control, robust technology development,* and so on. This article describes different quality engineering concepts and methods applied by the author in Indian industries.

Decision Making and Experimentation

Industrial organizations are constantly faced with the problem of decision making regarding product design, parts specifications, quality improvement, variability reduction, dominant factors affecting quality, cost reduction, import substitution, and so on, for economic prosperity or even for survival in an increasingly competitive market. One is confronted with several alternatives, which could be visualized from a technological background or by referring to available literature on the subject, with the problem being to choose out of these (possibly quite numerous or even infinite) alternatives, the one which satisfies the requirement at minimum cost. How then do we make the right decision?

The problem would have been simple to solve if sufficient research had already been carried out in the particular field, and the information gathered was made available in a form which could be readily utilized without recourse.

Experiences show, however, that the general situation is quite different, since the decision makers are not usually aware of the precise outcome associated with trying the various alternatives, at best only having some broad ideas about what is likely to happen. In most of the cases, even this much is not known.

An experiment has to be carried out either to discover something about a particular design or to compare the effect of several conditions on the phenomena under study. An experiment has been defined as a trial or special observation made to confirm or disprove something doubtful, especially one under conditions determined by the experimenter or an act of operation undertaken in order to discover some unknown principle of effect or to test, establish, or illustrate some suggested or known truth. In brief, the purpose of experimentation is to ensure that the experimenter obtains the data relevant to the task of decision making as economically as possible.

The Experimental Approach

As an example problem, to determine optimum moulding sand mix, we need to know:

1. Ratio of the return to fresh sand

2. Particle size of the fresh sand

3. Particle size of return sand

4. Gel-index of bentonite

5. Percentage of bentonite

6. Amount of coal dust

7. Percentage of water

In statistical terminology, the seven variables under study are called factors. For each factor, we may want to try out various alternatives (for example, we may try ratios of return to fresh sand at 1:1 and 2:1). Similarly, we may try bentonite at 5 percent and 7 percent. These alternatives for each factor are known as *levels of the factor for experimentation.* So, we then have the seven factors shown in Table 18.1, each at two levels, with which to experiment.

Choice of Factors

The first question that arises is how to choose the factors for experimentation. Choosing these factors is basically done through a cause-and-effect diagram. Here, our interest is to have a minimum permeability number of 100, a strength of 13 to 15 Kg/cm² and moisture in the mix between 3 percent to 4 percent. Obviously, some answers should be available either from published literature on the subject or the experience of the technical personnel about the factors, which are supposed to have an effect on the quality characteristics in which we are interested.

The criteria for deciding factors for experimentation are:

• The factor is assumed to affect the quality characteristics of interest

• There is a need to investigate the effect of such a factor

• The factor is controllable

Thus, the seven factors were chosen.

Choice of Levels

The choice of experimental zones for each of the factors has to be carefully done based on the available information about the likely optimum area. The number of levels is decided next. For example, if a straight line relationship can

	Level	
Factor	**1**	**2**
A. Return: Fresh	1:1	1:2
B. Particle size of fresh (AFS No.)	55	70
C. Particle size of return (AFS No.)	60	70
D. Gel. Index of bentonite	A	B
E. Percentage of bentonite	5	7
F. Percentage of coal dust	3	5
G. Percentage of water	4	5

Table 18.1.   Factors and levels for experimentation: sand mix.

be assumed, two levels may be sufficient; for a quadratic relationship, a minimum of three levels is required.

Designing the Experiment

Having decided on the factors and levels for experimentation for a specified objective, the remaining question is: How should we plan or design the experiment so that unambiguous results are obtained at a minimum cost? According to Dr. Gerald J Hahn:

> *Results of a well planned experiment are often evident from simple graphical analysis. However, the world's best statistical analysis cannot rescue a poorly planned experimental program.*

Classical Design

In the example of determining an optimum sand mix with seven experimental factors (each at two levels), one approach of experimentation, known as classical design, is normally used. An example is shown in Table 18.2.

The basic idea adopted in classical experimentation is to study one factor at a time, while all other factors are kept constant at their respective predetermined levels. Designing the classical experiment is done through an iterative process, requiring dynamic decisions about the next step based on the results of the previous steps. Here, experiments 1 and 2 are used to study factor A, which was found to be better at level 2. Thus, the third experiment is planned

Expt. No.	Factor						
	A	B	C	D	E	F	G
1	1	1	1	1	1	1	1
2	2	1	1	1	1	1	1
3	2	2	1	1	1	1	1
4	2	1	2	1	1	1	1
5	2	1	2	2	1	1	1
6	2	1	2	1	2	1	1
7	2	1	2	1	2	2	1
8	2	1	2	1	2	2	2

Table 18.2. Example of classical layout.

to compare factor B after fixing A at its better level. Experiments 2 and 3 are used to decide on B, and so on.

As an example, let us consider the quality characteristic of permeability. Assume that experiment 1 results in a permeability of 103, whereas experiment 2 results in 111. Therefore, we decide A is better at level 2. What is the reliability of this decision?

Two questions arise. While comparing A_1 and A_2, B, C . . . G are fixed at level 1 each; what happens if they are all fixed at level 2, or some at level 1 and others at level 2? Again, suppose experiments 1 and 2 are repeated under identical conditions; will the results be similar? If not, it is quite possible that a decision based on the first set of trials is going to be different from the one based on the second set.

Thus, though classical design is simple to conceive and easy to analyze, it suffers from poor reproducibility of results.

Factorial Experimentation

Another strategy of the experimental designs which may be applied here is factorial design. Seven factors each with two levels 2^7 means 128 different combinations. Factorial experimentation requires 128 trials, which give the information about the main effects of all seven factors and interactions between any two factors, between any three factors, and so on.

An estimate of the effect of a single factor obtained independently of the other factors involved in the experiment is called the main effect. If the effect of one factor is not the same at different levels of another factor, there exists what is known as interaction between the two factors.

Similarly, if there are 13 factors each of three levels, 1,594,323 experiments are necessary to arrive at the optimum combination through factorial experimentation. In fact, this number of experiments is astronomically high—it is neither practicable nor economically feasible. Also, when a set of trials are to be conducted with selected factors and levels, there are a host of other factors which are to be controlled at their respective desired ranges. This becomes practically impossible, thus increasing the error of the experimentation, which leads to low precision of the experimental results and a deleterious effect on the reproducibility of results. In fact, only if both the number of factors and their respective levels are small enough would factorial experimentation be a good strategy.

Orthogonal Array (OA) Design

For the same example of determining the optimum moulding sand mix, the OA layout (as shown in Table 18.3) is chosen.

There are eight experiments in Table 18.3, with each of the seven columns consisting of four 1s and four 2s. Consider factor C. We want to know which one of its two levels gives better permeability. This is done by comparing the average results of C_1 and C_2. It can be seen that half of the total experiments are tried for each of the two levels. Further, it can be seen that C is tried at level 1; A, B, D, E, F, and G are all tried twice at level 1 and twice at level 2, done also for the second level of C. Thus, the difference of the two levels C_1 and C_2 is determined as the average effect, which is independent of the condition of the other factors. This aspect of the layout is known as orthogonal property. Results of the OA experimentation are found to have better reproducibility as compared to those of classical design because of the following.

1. Effect of factor is determined while the conditions of other factors vary; average results are compared, as against individual results in the classical design.

2. The number of experiments is comparatively much lower compared to that of factorial and, at times, is the barest minimum. A well-planned experiment is often tailor-made to meet specific objectives and to satisfy practical constraints. Orthogonal array (OA) is a method of experimental design developed by Dr. C. R. Rao during 1947. Dr. Taguchi developed linear graphs and interaction tables and made it possible for the engineers

Expt. No.	Factor Col.	A 1	B 2	C 3	D 4	E 5	F 6	G 7	Permeability
1		1	1	1	1	1	1	1	103
2		1	1	1	2	2	2	2	111
3		1	2	2	1	1	2	2	92
4		1	1	2	2	2	1	1	98
5		2	1	2	1	2	1	2	132
6		2	1	2	2	1	2	1	78
7		2	2	1	1	2	2	1	92
8		2	2	1	2	1	1	2	113

Table 18.3. Orthogonal array L_8.

and scientists to apply OA design without understanding the complicated theory behind the construction of the OA design matrix. During the mid-1970s and early 1980s there were numerous applications in many Indian industries, mainly for solving problems of industries.

Historically, the bulk of our product and process designs are from foreign collaborators. Even where the products and processes are indigenously designed, sufficient engineering exercises have not been carried out. As a result, there are numerous problems of reproducibility, leading to high quality losses as well as problems of reliability resulting in nonfulfillment of customer satisfaction. Taguchi methods of orthogonal arrays addressed these problems effectively in many Indian companies during the mid-1970s and 1980s. A few case studies are discussed to illustrate the wide range of their applicability and the vast scope of realizing benefits through such application.

Case Studies

Case Study 1: Reduction of Gas Porosity in Malleable Iron Castings

Problem Definition

This study relates to the reduction of gas porosity in a type of casting. The overall rejection of this foundry was around 37 percent. Analysis revealed that rejections due to gas porosity of a particular type had reached an alarming figure of 52 percent and only 18 percent of production conformed to required specifications at the time of the study.

Initial discussions showed that there would be as many as 30 factors which could contribute to the occurrence of gas porosity. Also, no precise knowledge of the extent of effect of these factors, either individually or in combination, was available. Hence, there was no alternative but to take the approach of actual experimentation to analyze the problem.

Objectives of Experimentation

The experimentation was done in two phases—first in the laboratory and then in the plant. The objectives were framed as:

1. To standardize the percentage of ingredients of facing sand mixture, with the objective of optimizing permeability and green strength, from laboratory trials

Code	Factor	Level		
		1	2	3
A	Returns: Fresh Sand (Wt)	100:00	75:25	50:50
B	Bentonite (Wt)	4%	5%	6%
C	Coal Dust (Wt)	4%	6%	8%
D	Water (Wt)	4%	5%	

Table 18.4. Factors and levels: Lab-scale experimentation.

2. To carry out a plant-scale trial based on the optimum factor combination to avoid gas porosity defects

Design (Laboratory Scale)

The factors and levels decided on for experimentation in the laboratory are shown in Table 18.4.

The total number of experiments for the above would come to $3^3 \times 2^1 = 54$. As this was considered too large, the OA design of L_{27} (3^{13}) was chosen, which called for only 27 experiments. Interactions $A \times B$ and $B \times D$ were considered likely to be present.

For each sand mixture combination, four samples were taken and compression strength permeability and moisture were recorded.

Results (Laboratory Scale)

Data obtained on 27 experiments were subjected to statistical analysis, and the results were:

1. The higher the percentage of fresh sand addition, the better the permeability and the lower the compressive strength. It was advisable to use 25 percent to 40 percent fresh sand to achieve the required permeability and strength.

2. The effect of bentonite on permeability was negligible, whereas 4 percent lead to low strength compared to 5 percent and 6 percent.

3. Coal dust drastically lowered the permeability, whereas it had no effect on strength.

4. Moisture between 4 percent and 5 percent was found to have no effect.

Based on results of laboratory experiments and other technical considerations, the factors and their levels for experimentation at the plant scale were chosen, as shown in Table 18.5. All factors were considered at two levels only.

The experiment of 10 factors each with two levels was planned through an L_{16} (2^{15}) experiment. It involved four metal preparations. Twenty castings were poured for each of the 16 combinations and were examined for gas porosity and other defects. Data were analyzed and the factors contributing to gas porosity were identified and presented in order of their importance:

D	Return: fresh in moulding sand
K	Vent diameter of core
H	MR percentage in core sand
F	Coal dust percentage
B	Pouring temperature
A	Scrap quality

Sl. No.	Stage	Factor Code	Description	Level 1	Level 2	Unit
1	Metal	A	Scrap Quality	Non-Rusty	Rusty	—
		B	Temperature of pouring	1400 – 1450	1350 – 1400	°C
2	Moulding sand	C	AFS of sand	65	55	AFS
		D	Returns: Fresh sand	3:1	2:1	÷
		E	Bentonite	5%	6%	Wt
		F	Coal dust	3%	5%	Wt
3	Moulding Practice	G	No. of vents per pattern	28	12	—
4	Core sand	H	Moisture of sand	1.5 – 2.5 %	<1%	Wt
		J	AFS of sand	65	55	AFS
5	Core practice	K	Vent diameter of core	6	16	mm

Table 18.5.   Factors and levels (plant-scale experimentation).

An optimum combination of the important factors was worked out and the expected rejection for this combination was estimated at 5 percent. Confirmatory trials indicated the actual rejections were around 5 percent, compared to the earlier level of 52 percent.

Case Study 2: Breakthrough Application

This case study related to an oil circuit breaker. Analysis of customer complaints revealed that leakage of the upper insulators in the installed oil circuit breakers was a recurring problem. Upper insulators were replaced free of cost at the consumer end and several alterations and modifications that were tried proved futile. When this problem was suggested to be taken up for experimentation, the sharp reply from technologists was that this was purely an engineering problem. It took considerable efforts to convince the plant management that such problems really called for technostatistical studies. This problem was then studied.

Leakage of the insulator assembly is understood to occur if the stresses developed in the field due to tripping of circuit breakers exceeds the strength of the joint of the insulator assembly.

This problem can be tackled either by controlling the stresses in the field or by improving the strength of the joint of the assembly. Obviously the latter was chosen because this was something that could be done in the industry. After many deliberations with the technical personnel, and after observing the process of manufacture, factors and levels were chosen for experimentation as shown in Table 18.6.

Table 18.6 shows there are several ways of processing the insulator assembly. Which method will prevent leakage in the field, as well as prove cost-effective? The search was to find out the best combination amongst many possibilities. This is carried out objectively and efficiently through statistically designed experiments. In this case of $2^9 \times 2^2$, or 4608 factor combinations were tried in 16 experiments using an L_{16} (2^{15}) orthogonal array. Insulators were assembled according to the 16 treatment combinations and tested until failure, and pressure was noted. The data were analyzed and an optimum combination was discovered, which resulted in a strength 725 psi, as opposed to the standard 250 psi. This was tried and later implemented to the satisfaction of both the plant and its customers.

Case Study 3: Restoring a Product Line

Solid core porcelain insulators manufactured by an industry faced high rejection, the major cause of rejection being a widely fluctuating and a low average

Factor		Levels		
Code	**Description**	**1**	**2**	**3**
A	Flange (Step of Gasket)	2.0 mm	4.0 mm	
B	Gasket Thickness	3.0 mm	4.0 mm	
C	Hardness of Gasket	55° shore	65° shore	
D	Fixing of Asbestos Rope	Ramming	Loose	
E	Compression Pressure	1 Ton	1.5 Ton	2 Ton
F	Lead	Usual	Type	
G	Method of Heating	Direct	Indirect	
H	Pre-heating Temperature	90° C	100° C	110° C
I	Time Lag Between Puring & Pre-heating	20 min	15 min	
J	Caulking Round	2	4	
K	Araldite Sealing	Without	With	

Table 18.6.   Factors and levels: Oil circuit breaker.

value of the tensile failing load (5.4 to 14.5 T, against a minimum of 9.9 T), and a high incidence of porosity and erratic recovery (fired and green) from 12 percent to 55 percent. Several efforts to improve the situation, like change in the raw material composition, process control parameters, and so on, yielded little or marginal benefits. These reasons were strong deterrents to continue further production on economic grounds.

Factors and Their Levels

The problem was discussed with concerned technical personnel, past data and available literature were referred, and various factors and levels to be experimented were identified. These are illustrated in Table 18.7.

Apart from the 10 factors mentioned in Table 18.7, three more factors were included to study the effect on recovery, failing load, and so on, because of positioning of insulators inside the kiln (see Table 18.8).

Experimental Layout

Ten factors each at three levels (3^{10}) conventionally call for 59,049 experimental combinations to be tried. In addition, the effect of three outside fac-

Factor	Code	Levels 1	2	3	Unit
Mineral-I	A	200	180	160	Kg/Charge
Mineral-II	B	High	Low	Medium	Kg/Charge
Clay Group	C	C1-I	C1-2	C1-3	Kg/Charge
Grinding Hours	D	High	Medium	Low	Hours
Model Drying	E	ED*	ND-2**	ND-3**	Days
Rate of Drying	F	4	6	8	Hours
Glare Sp. Gravity	G	1.59	1.61	1.57	gm/cc
Rate of Heating	H	Slow	Fast	Medium	°C/hour
Crown Temperature	J	Std.	Std – 10	Std+10	°C
Rate of Cooling	K	Medium	Slow	Fast	°C/hour

* Electrical drying   ** Natural drying

Table 18.7.   Factors and levels (solid case insulator).

Factor	Code	Levels 1	2	3
Block	X	Left	Center	Right
Row	Y	Top	Center	Bottom
Column	Z	Front	Center	Rear

Table 18.8.   Factors and levels (kiln).

tors in the kiln also had to be examined. The suitable OA design for this situation, $L_{27}(3^{13})$, was used to design the experiment, which calls for only 27 experiments.

Optimum Process Parameters

Optimum process parameters are to be determined by taking into consideration the combined results of tensile failing load, nonporosity, green recovery, and fired recovery. ANOVA was carried out on these four characteristics. The level which gave the overall better recovery, taking all the four characteristics together, was chosen as the optimum one.

Overall optimum thus obtained was $A_3\,B_2\,C_2\,D_1\,E_3\,F_2\,G_2\,H_3\,K_2\,K_1$.

The optimum combination was tried on a pilot scale. Encouraged with the results, a separate production line was installed for production of this group of items in large scale. As a result of this exercise, the overall recoveries have improved from 12 percent to 55 percent to around 80 percent; also, product quality was found to be consistently better with regard to both tensile failing load and nonporosity. Sustained and better performance in production of this group of insulators yielded an additional annual revenue of Rs. 20 million per annum for several years.

This case study presents an approach for planned production experiments designed to investigate process parameters in ceramic manufacture. The results show that it improved the confidence of the engineers and managers of the plant in solving problems of design and development without referring to the collaborators. Further significant financial gains were also achieved by the company year after year.

Loss Function

Taguchi defines *quality* as the loss a product causes to society after being shipped, other than any losses caused by its intrinsic functions. An article with good quality performs its intended functions without variability and causes little loss through harmful side effects, including the cost of using it.

A *product* or *process* performs the best when all the characteristics of the product or process are at their respective nominals or target values

$$L = K.E(Y - m)^2, \text{where m is the target}$$

$$= K.E(Y - \mu + \mu - m)^2, \text{where } \mu \text{ is the population mean}$$

$$= K.[E(Y - \mu)^2 + E(\mu - m)^2]$$

$$= K(\gamma^2 + \sigma^2); \text{where } K = A/\Delta^2, \text{where } \gamma = \mu - m$$

A = Average cost of failure

Δ = Tolerance

Example: Time rating of watch: 0 ± 2 seconds

Factory A	Factory B
+2	0
+1	+1
−2	0
−1	0
+2	−1
$E(Y - m)^2 = 14/5 = 2.8$	$2/5 = 0.4$
$L = 25 \times 2.8 = 70$	$25 \times 0.4 = 6.25$

Where A = Rs. 100/− and Δ = 2 Seconds; K = Rs. 100. ÷ 4 = Rs. 25.

Factory A was observed to lose shares of the market at the cost of factory B. The traditional method of evaluation of quality (percentage of conformance to design specifications) indicated 100 percent conformance for both A and B. However, quality evaluation through loss function indicated a big opportunity for improvement in the case of factory A. It can be easily demonstrated that the loss function reduces with the reduction of variability as well as deviation from the target. Thus, a continuous quality improvement program includes a reduction in the variation of the product performance characteristic about their target values.

Online QC Application

Case Study 4: Control of Metal Composition

Control of metal composition is one of the prerequisites for controlling defects and improving the mechanical properties of malleable cast iron. Both carbon and silicon contents were found to vary beyond their specified limits. Carbon percentage was observed to vary from 2.37 percent to 2.88 percent. Less than 50 percent of the observations were found to conform to the specifications (2.55 percent to 2.65 percent). The status of silicon percentage was not much different. A study was therefore initiated to devise procedures for achieving better consistencies in the composition of metals, especially with regard to carbon.

Prevailing Practices

The procedure for metal preparation was observed in order to learn the present practices, the controllability, and the practical constraints that have to be taken care of while evolving control procedures.

A charge mix consisting of different scraps, foundry returns, pig iron, and so on, is fed into the furnace. After meltdown, other additives like ferro-silicon and petroleum coke are added to adjust for carbon/silicon. Thereafter, a sample is taken for a chill test and a sample is sent to the laboratory for carbon determination. The chill test indicates the level of carbon and silicon, and ferro-silicon is added for adjustments. Mild steel is used to reduce the carbon or silicon percentage.

Salient points arising out of the observations are: (1) the controllability of carbon percentage in the heat can be improved if the decision about the amount of additives can be made on an objective basis, and (2) the adjustability of silicon is based on the chill test, which is not a sophisticated one. However, objective decisions regarding the amount of ferro-silicon would help; these are typical occasions where additives are weighed crudely.

One constraint is that carbon and silicon cannot be precisely estimated in the charge mix. Since the quality of scrap, a major ingredient of the charge, is unpredictable, adjustments are to be made at the earliest opportunity based on the results of a single observation only.

β—Correction Factor

The following procedure was adopted:

Let: μ_c be the aimed-at average (2.60 percent in our case);
$\hat{U}$ be the estimate (the test result of carbon percentage) before correction;
μ be the population parameter (the actual carbon percentage in the melt, which is unknown);
deviation from the target value is $(\hat{U} - \mu_o)$.

Now, we have to decide when to correct and, if correction is necessary, what adjustments are to be made in order to achieve the target value.

Let β be the correction factor, which is assumed to be non-negative. Therefore, the amount of correction made is $-\beta(\hat{U} - \mu_c)$.

Thus, μ becomes $\mu - \beta(\hat{U} - \mu_o)$ after correction, which is supposed to be close to the target value (μ_o).

Thus, β is determined, which minimizes

$$E\,[\mu - \beta(\hat{U} - \mu_o) - \mu_o]^2$$

By differentiating this function with respect to β and equating to zero, the estimate of β is found to be

$$= 1 - 1/F \text{ when } F = (\hat{U} - \mu_o)^2/\sigma^2$$

$$= 0 \text{ if } F \leq 1$$

Estimation of Prediction Error

Data on the carbon percentage were obtained for three days, two heats/day, three ladles/heat, and two tests per ladle.

Analysis of variance was carried out to evaluate the components of variance. A prediction error standard deviation was estimated.

Application

A control scheme using correction factors requires estimates of β on every occasion. Estimation of β further requires deviation from the target value as well as standard deviation for prediction. Calculation of β on the shop floor and converting the mathematical formulae to physical quantities of petroleum coke or mild steel is a time-consuming as well as mistake-prone operation. Preparation of suitable ready reckoners to deal with different shop floor situations like varied melt quantity, initial carbon content, and pick-up percentage of the additives would help melters to implement this procedure without any difficulty.

Ready reckoners were prepared for the amount of petroleum coke to be added to increase the carbon percentage and for the addition of pig iron for reduction of the carbon percentage.

Implementation

The control scheme that evolved was implemented. This helped to achieve a consistent carbon percentage around the target value. The success of this scheme depended on the ability to transform the mathematical exercise to simple shop floor procedures in the form of ready reckoner or nomograms, which the melters can understand and operate by themselves.

Robust Design

Recognize that the choice of the target level (nominal) of product and process parameters at times has a spectacular effect on the reduction of variability. Thus, the design exercise carried out to decide the nominals of product/process parameters is known as *parameter design*.

The goal of parameter design is to determine how to synthesize levels for product or process parameters to achieve robustness at least cost. The concept of design of experiments is a method that can be used to identify the effect of different parameters on performance.

Parameter design studies typically involve at least two types of factors: *control* and *noise* factors. Control factors are those that the engineer can specify, set, and maintain. Noise factors are factors that are not controllable, either from a practical or cost standpoint.

The inclusion of these two types of factors is required so that their interaction can be evaluated. It is through this evaluation that the state of robustness is achieved. The measure used to evaluate the effect of this interaction, with regard to robustness, is the *signal-to-noise (S/N) ratio*.

Case Study 5: Robust Process Development for Ceramic Tiles

This case study relates to a process of manufacturing ceramic tiles used as liner in a material handling system, where abrasive and corrosive material is continuously used. Bulk density was one important quality characteristic. The existing process was incapable of meeting the specification of bulk density of 3.40 percent to 3.60 percent, as the process capability index was about 0.5 percent.

The process of manufacture includes mixing, weighment, pressing, drying, and firing. Position variation in the kiln was found to be the main cause of high variation. The traditional approach would be to look for a better designed kiln, which is a costly solution.

The task was to carry out a search for the best combination of controllable factors, which would be immune to location variations within the kiln. Accordingly, four design factors such as weight (three levels), water percentage (three levels), temperature (two levels), and soaking time (three levels) were chosen for study. Temperature and soaking time were known to interact.

$L_{18}(2^1 \times 3^7)$ orthogonal array was chosen for fixing the four design parameters in the inner array. Noise (the uncontrollable factor) was the position within the kiln. Considering the design of the furnace as well as past observations, six locations within the kiln were identified to represent both extreme and average conditions.

Tiles produced under each of the 18 treatment combinations were placed in each of the six positions in the kiln. The signal-to-noise ratio 10 log [$(S_m - V_e)/n V_e$] where $S_m = (\Sigma y_i)^2 /n$ and $V_i = [\Sigma(y_i - m)^2]/(n - 1)$; (m = 3.50), was calculated for each treatment combination. Analysis of variance revealed that weight and interaction between temperature and soaking time were significant. The best combination was identified, and it was found that the process standard deviation within a kiln could be reduced to 0.028 as opposed to 0.067. The process capability index was improved to approximately 1.2 from the existing level of 0.5. A better process was objectively determined and the problem was solved from within, thus avoiding the need for capital investment and long lead time.

This example uses a nondynamic S/N ratio to desensitize the manufacturing process by exploiting the interaction between control and noise factors.

Case Study 6: Robust Fiber Process

Improvement of fiber quality with respect to physical and visual characteristics like spinning faults, tenacity, elongation, and so on, up to the level of benchmarking, was sought. The present control procedure consisted of monitoring the quality of direct and indirect raw material, machine parameters, and process parameters against their respective norms in each of the multistage operations. A close look at the results on any day revealed that a number of the process parameters were beyond their respective norms. It was further communicated that unless quality of raw material was improved and processes and machines in specific areas modernized, all process parameters could not be controlled. The following questions were considered necessary to be addressed:

Are all the factors equally important? If not, which ones are dominant?

How are the dominant factors objectively determined?

What are the levels and tolerances of the dominant factors?

Can the number of dominant factors be reduced by robust process design?

Normally, application of experimental design is recommended to arrive at an objective determination of robust levels. However, in this case of multistage chemical process, conduct of plant scale experimentation was ruled out. Also, there existed no suitable pilot plant. The question arose as to whether the use of production and laboratory data to seek answers was possible. Different models of multiple correlation were tried but with no success. Application of the robust process design concept was applied in this case. Important process parameters were short-listed through collective wisdom of concerned personnel and analysis of available data. A set of 100 multivariate data on the selected process parameters and corresponding quality characteristics was compiled from production and test reports. Factors were classified as control factors and noise factors, depending on their controllability. Two-way stratification was done for each combination of noise and control factors to examine the existence of their interaction. Figure 18.1 shows a pictorial presentation of one noise factor (ball fall) and one control factor (CS_2). It is known that ball fall in the range of 50 to 60 is best suited for minimizing spinning faults. However, maintaining ball fall in a specific narrow range was not found to be feasible with

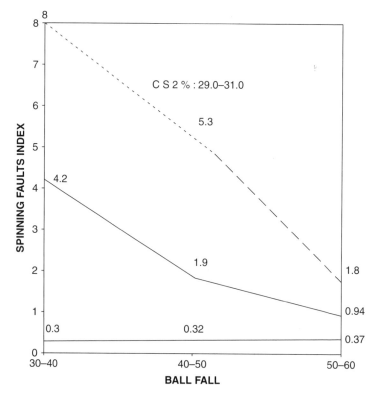

Figure 18.1. Average response curves. SPG, FLTS VS BF at different levels of CS2%.

the existing facilities and raw material. Since ball fall and CS_2 were found to interact, it is possible to choose a level of CS_2, about 33 percent, which desensitizes the effect of ball fall. Thus, CS_2 above 33 percent is the robust level.

This method was applied to objectively arrive at the list of dominant factors and their robust levels. Noise factors were not required to be controlled, which helped the company avoid large capital investments. The quality of product improved, cost reduced, and the confidence of engineers and managers improved.

Exploitation of Nonlinearity

Case Study 7: Robust Process: OPU

This case study discusses how the overall variability of a process was reduced and a target achieved by exploiting the nonlinear relationship between the control factors and responses. Four factors were investigated, each at three levels, using fractional factorial experimentation. All the factors were found to be statistically significant. Relationships were established and it was observed that two of them were nonlinearly related. This was exploited to reduce variability, whereas two other factors, which were found to be near-linear in the range of experimentation, were used to set the target. Figure 18.2 shows the pictorial presentation of one of the nonlinear relations.

OPU is desired at 0.28, which means a circulation rate of 11.32 would result in an average OPU of 0.28. However, this would mean a control of circulation rate at a narrow range would be essential and in spite of this product variability will be high. A choice of 13.14 will ensure minimum variability and the need for stricter control is eliminated. Thus, this methodology helped to achieve quality at cheaper prices.

Case Study 8: Wet Grinding Process Improvement through Dynamic S/N Ratio

In a wet grinding operation, the search was to determine the robust levels of (A) water percentage, (B) clay type, (C) clay percentage, and (D) quantity of river pebbles in order to achieve a specified particle-size target consistently at minimum possible grinding hours.

The range of experimentation of each of the three quantitative control factors was identified, and three levels were chosen for A, C, and D, whereas two levels were chosen for clay type (B).

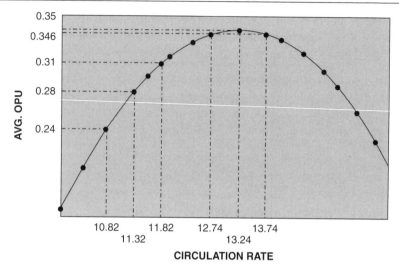

Figure 18.2.   Exploitation of nonlinearity.

In this example of wet grinding, the grinding media and new set of river pebbles once fixed are to be used for a number of cycles, though their conditions change. Discharge of ground material, known as *slip*, was not completely possible within the time frame. Some quantity is always left over. All these are known to have an effect on particle size but are not precisely controllable. Thus, three noise factors were chosen:

Left-over slip in kg.	(X)	120 ± 10	180 ± 10	240 ± 10
Grinding media	(Y)	New	Medium	Old
River pebbles condition	(Z)	Fresh	Medium	Old

Control factors are to be assigned to a suitable design matrix, called *inner array,* and the noise factors to another design matrix, called *outer array,* Thus, the minimum number of experiments needed was 81 (9 × 9) . This approach was found normally infeasible in a plant-scale experimentation. Taguchi's method was modified to suit the practical situation.

All the control factors and noise factors were assigned to the same design matrix. (L_{18} OA) (see Table 18.9)

Since grinding hours was a signal factor, each of the 18 treatment combination samples were observed after 15 hours, 18 hours and 21 hours for each after-treatment combination.

There was no interest in knowing the best levels of X, Y, and Z, since they are not controllable. The best operating levels of A, B, C, and D were to be determined, while X, Y, and Z would be varying in their respective ranges. Eighteen experiments were conducted and samples were taken at three levels of signal factors. Thus, a set of 54 (18 × 3) test results was available. Level analysis was carried out for each of the four control factors. A dynamic S/N ratio was calculated for each of the levels of the control factors using the formula ($10 \log \beta^2/\sigma^2$) and robust levels were determined. Figure 18.3 shows a graphical presentation with respect to factor A.

Which is the best level? Average, variability, as well as the slope (β) from 15 hours and 21 hours are to be considered. A higher slope means a higher rate of reduction in particle size. Higher slopes, lower variability, and lower target will be the best level. A_3 has the highest variability and almost no grinding action over time. A_1 has grinding action but higher variability. A_2 has the best grinding action (highest slope as well as lowest variability); thus A_2 is the best level. This can also be obtained by using an appropriate S/N ratio ($10 \log \beta^2/\sigma^2$) for different levels.

Col. No.	1	2	3	4	5	6	7
Factor	B	A	C	D	X	Y	Z
Sl. No.							
1	1	1	1	1	1	1	1
2	1	1	2	2	2	2	2
.	.	.	.	.	.	.	.
.	.	.	.	.	.	.	.
.	.	.	.	.	.	.	.
17	2	3	2	1	3	1	2
18	2	3	3	2	1	2	3

Table 18.9. Experimental plan: Wetgrinding process.

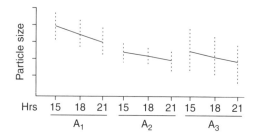

Figure 18.3. Graphical presentation of control factors.

This case example demonstrated how the concept of a dynamic S/N ratio helped to arrive at robust process design, which resulted in the desired particle size at 15 hours of grinding as against the practice of 21 hours.

Evolution of Robust Technology Development

In the manufacturing industry, the process through which a product as process design is developed is very crucial for a company's competitiveness. There are two stages in a design process:

1. Synthesis

2. Analysis

Synthesis is further divided into the following stages.

a. Selection of system (concept)

b. Determination of the center value of parameter

The former (system design) requires the creativity of the designer. It is important to carry out sufficient market research and design research to create a new system based on a new design concept to satisfy the customer. If it is a new system, it can be protected by patents. The latter (parameter design) is in the field of quality engineering. One is not sure that a new system will be competitive or not unless parameter design exercises are carried out. Therefore, it is extremely important to efficiently complete parameter design on the selected system in a short period of time. For the design of a large system, it is important to divide the total system into modules such as subsystem, component parts, elements on material parts, then simultaneously conduct developments for these modules.

In parameter design, the focus is on evaluating the interactions between control and noise factors. This is evaluated through the use of nondynamic S/N ratios. In recent years, Dr. Taguchi has focused on the dynamic system.

In quality engineering, it is important to improve the quality in the market through the use of far-upstream quality. Quality is classified as belonging to four stages.

Downstream quality: Quality characteristics useful to the customers (for example, fuel consumption in motor vehicles, noise in a generator, picture clarity in a color TV, and so on).

Midstream quality: Quality characteristic during production like dimensions in machine operation, physical properties in heat treatment operation, and so on. Both of these problems have been tackled effectively through orthogonal array experimentation.

Upstream quality: Quality characteristics during product development such as smaller the better, larger the better, nominal the best. Parameter design using orthogonal array and nondynamic signal-to-noise ratio have been used to tackle such robust product and process quality designs.

Far-upstream quality: Quality characteristics for technology development. Nondynamic S/N ratios are used to measure how a function is close to the ideal. In technology development, it is important to develop a technology that can be applied to a wide range of products, instead of designing or producing a particularly defined product. Application of technology development brings many advantages, such as flexibility, reproducibility, and faster development. Engineers in product design and production engineering areas must develop robust technology at the R&D stage so that technology can be easily transferred to new products. Therefore, there is no specific product target in technology development and the technology thus developed has flexibility. In the case of production engineering, instead of trying to produce the products from one drawing, it is important to establish flexible technology that enables one to easily produce products from any drawings within a certain range.

Conclusion

Quality engineering concepts have been accepted all over the world. In fact, Dr. Taguchi has often stated that, "The adoption and continued utilization of the

Dynamic approach represents the path that virtually all world class organizations will take to establish themselves as leaders in their industries, irrespective of their geographical location."

Suggested References

1. Pal, B. K., and R. A. Rao. 1986. Increasing Profitability through Experimental Approach. Paper presented at the National Conference on Foundry, India.

2. Pal, B. K. 1989. Taguchi Methods in Indian Industries—An Experience. International Conference on Quality Control Proceedings, Buenos Aires, Argentina.

3. Pal, B. K. 1987. Process Capability Improvement through Taguchi Methods. ICQC Proceedings, Tokyo.

4. Pal, B. K. 1993. A Collection of Quality Engineering Applications—Indian Industries. ISI, Bangalore.

5. Pal, B. K., and J. Roshan. 1996. Developing Objective Strategies for Monitoring Multi Input/Single Output Chemical Process. In *Quality Improvement through Statistical Methods.* Bovas Abraham, Birkhauser.

6. Taguchi, G. 1981. *Online Quality Control During Production.* Japanese Standards Association.

7. Pal, B. K. 1998. Quality Improvement through Statistical Methods. ICQI Conference, Lahore, Pakistan.

8. Taguchi, G. *Quality Engineering for Technology Development: How to Reduce Product Development Cycle Time.* Trans. by Yuin Wu. Japanese Standards Association, Tokyo, 1988.

9. Wilkins, J. 1994. *Introduction to Quality Engineering & Robust Design. Case Studies & Tutorial.* American Supplier Institute. Detroit.

Chapter 19

TQM in the Twenty-First Century: The Japanese Approach

KENZO SASAOKA

Introduction

The new approach to integrating quality management into business management responding to the name change from total quality control (TQC) to total quality management (TQM) in Japan is described in this chapter.

The activity was initiated by the TQM committee of the Japanese Union of Scientists and Engineers (JUSE), which produced three publications: (1) *TQM Manifesto* in January 1997, (2) *Total Quality Management in the 21st Century*, a report in June 1998, and (3) *Viewpoint of Examination for Deming Application Prize*, by Y. Iizuka, in July 1998. All three publications are in Japanese.

The author has translated the second document into English as an early source of information for readers of the IAQ books as his contribution to one of the ongoing projects of the International Academy for Quality (IAQ), with permission from Professor Yoshinori Iizuka, Chairman of the TQM Committee, JUSE.

Progress of Reformation Activities

April 1996

JUSE decided to change the traditional term *TQC* to *TQM*, which was already being used widely in the world. This name change opened an opportunity to rebuild the TQC in Japan to meet the challenges of the global business environment.

July 1996

The TQM committee was founded in JUSE by eight new leaders from IAQ in Japan, chaired by Professor Yoshinori Iizuka of the University of Tokyo. Their roles were:

- To clarify the significance of the name change from TQC to TQM
- To clarify the concepts of the renamed TQM
- To develop a master plan to promote understanding and implementation of TQM as the new TQC

January 1997

A summary of study and discussion in the committee was published as a booklet, *TQM Manifesto*, from JUSE on its fiftieth anniversary (Japanese language only).

June 1998

The Deming Prize committee revised the examination criteria according to the change from TQC to TQM, and released the "Viewpoint of Examination," replacing the former checklist for the Deming Prize (1994) and which will be applied starting in 1999.

June 1998

The first book on the Japanese TQM, including basic concepts and examples in real businesses, was published by the expanded TQM committee with seven additional members from industry, entitled *Total Quality Management in the 21st Century.*

Basic Perception on Japanese TQM

We recognized TQM as a philosophy and methodology to pursue superior quality in business and other operations by means of qualitative improvement of the management systems.

Quality is a most intrinsic attribute of any object considered. It is more essential than other attributes like quantity, cost, delivery, or efficiency. Based on this intrinsic universality of the concept of quality, we believe we can generate a centripetal force to mobilize an entire organization to the ultimate goal of the company by focusing on quality.

Viewed in this way, TQM expands its objective from the traditional "product and service quality" to a much wider "whole management quality."

Thus, TQM should be a management science, with tools and practices to contribute to improving performance of an organization through better quality of its management systems. A conceptual model of Japanese TQM is illustrated in Figure 19.1. The author strongly wishes to see the reform of Japanese industry philosophy in the era of global economy of competition and coexistence by concentrating all efforts of organizations under the new concept of quality.

Explanation of the Structural Model

Purpose of TQM

TQM is a management science and systematic tool to help organizations to become a respectable existence in society. *Respectable existence* means:

CONTRIBUTE WITH SYSTEMATIC APPROACH TO ACHIEVING ENTERPRISE OBJECTIVES

Enterprise Objective
Become Respectable Existence in Society

- Attain mission of organization
- Ensure appropriate profit
- Establish co-delighting relationship with all stakeholders (customers, suppliers, employees, shareholders, society)

By providing high customer satisfaction products and services
    On customer's view points/through quest for quality
Based on the enhanced organizational ability
    Core technology/Speed/Vitality

[USE SYSTEMATIC APPROACH TO MANAGE ENTIRE ORGANIZATION EFFECTIVELY AND EFFECIENTLY]

1. Top Management Leadership – Vision and Strategy
2. Execution of Management Systems
    - Maintain/Improve/Innovate
    - Breakthrough plan/Daily operation/Cross-functional operation
2.1 Management systems for products and services quality (throughout the product cycle)
2.2 Management Systems for other management elements (cost, delivery, productivity, safety)
3. Enrich Fundamental Resource of operation
3.1 Development of human resources
3.2 Effective use of information
4. Basic concept and Methodology of TQM
4.1 Scientific tools and measures
4.2 Philosophy of TQM

Figure 19.1.   Holistic structure of Japanese TQM.

- To reliably attain the mission of an organization.

- To fairly earn appropriate profit.

- To consistently establish positive relationships with all stakeholders, customers, suppliers, employees, shareholders, and society.

- By providing high customer-satisfaction products and services, based on the customer's viewpoint and quest for quality.

This should be consistently achieved by enhancing key abilities of an organization, such as core technology, speed, and vitality.

Framework of TQM

TQM is a systematic approach to managing entire organizations effectively and efficiently. It should contribute to the systematic improvement of quality of management processes and management resources. Management processes include vision, strategy, planning, design, development, procurement, production, sales, support and service. Management resources include: people, organization structure, information, knowledge, technology, equipment, and location.

This is further explained in outline form.

1. Top Management Leadership – Vision and Strategy

    a. In order to respond to the structural change of today's business environment, long-range vision and strategy for the future by top management leadership are required. TQM intends to contribute a rational approach to this top management role.

    b. Strategic HOSHIN management is a new methodology to help design and implement business strategy effectively.

2. Execution of Management Systems

TQM aims for:

—The reliable maintenance of established processes.

—Continual improvement of individual processes.

—Breakthrough innovation of process combination through systematic approaches, utilizing any effective tools.

The planning process and plan-do-check-act cycle in implementations are essential steps for TQM. Three types of management operations are:

—Breakthrough HOSHIN planning and its implementation.

—Daily management of each departmental operation as business fundamentals.

—Cross-functional company-wide operations to optimize a specific management element (cost, delivery, and so on) are the core of TQM.

    2.1. Management Systems Focusing on Product-and-Service Quality

        Product-and-service quality is a most essential part of TQM and directly relates to competitiveness. We inherit the historic achievement of TQC in this subject. Product-and-service quality is realized and assured as an integrated result of all relevant management systems through product planning, R and D, manufacturing, procurement, quality assurance, marketing, sales, support, and service.

a. Quality should be evaluated by customer satisfaction.

b. There are two aspects of quality. One is a quality of what the design intends to offer, and the other is a quality of conformation to the designed specification. The former is a strategic issue and the latter is an implementation issue.

c. Effective coexistence or positive integration with ISO 9000 is a valuable subject for TQM.

d. The scope of Quality is expanded from quality of goods to quality of works, processes, and resources.

e. Through the evolution from TQC to TQM, our target on quality further expands to quality of management and organization.

2.2 Management Systems of other Business Performance Factors

TQM's methodology can be applied to other factors of business operation, such as cost, quantity, delivery, safety, and so on beyond the narrower meaning of product-and-service quality.

3. Enriching Fundamental Resources of Operation

3.1 Human Resource Management

TQM can help enhance quality of human resources in organizations. Examples of implementation are:

—Training and education programs.

—Communication and shared beliefs.

—Evaluation and promotion systems.

—Employee satisfaction programs.

Teamwork is effective for the development of human resources. QC circle is a symbolic activity of employee participation and mutual development of people in TQM.

3.2 Information Management

Advanced information and networking technology opened an opportunity for:

—High-speed operation on a global scale.

—Knowledge base on a global scale.

Information technology becomes a powerful and essential tool to fundamentally innovate business processes and achieve total optimization, as shown by today's business process reengineering.

4. Basic Concept and Methodology of TQM

4.1 Scientific Tools and Measures

Because of the wide definition of *quality* in TQM, various management tools or templates can be applied in its implementation. For example:

—QC/TQC tools: QC 7Tools/statistical tools/New QC 7Tools/New Product Planning 7Tools/Strategy Planning 7Tools/QFD/QC-Story steps for problem solving, and so on.

—Tools from reliability engineering: Reliability estimation/FMEA/ FTA/DR.

—Tools from other management sciences: OR, IE, VE, IT, and so on.

4.2 Philosophy

Quality

1. Quality is evaluated by how the customer is satisfied with a product or service.

Customer's impression and value.

2. Requirements and conformance to them. (narrower)

3. Quality of works, processes, and management. (Integrated Quality)

Management

1. Management is an integrated activity of planning, adjustment, and supporting to achieve a goal of an organization efficiently; not a control.

2. Management cycle: Plan-Do-Check-Act.

3. Process management (routine process, project process), management by fact.

4. Improvement, innovation: foresight/forecast/prevent (for the future).

Humanity

1. Personal growth through active working.

2. A thinking worker performs better.

3. Total participation, teamwork, (for example, the QC circle).

4. Respect for individuals and their creativity.

Chapter 20

Quality in Developing Countries

LENNART SANDHOLM

Introduction

Countries are often classified as *developing* or *developed.* This terminology is misleading, as countries that are classified as developing could in many respects be more advanced than some so-called developed countries (for example, when such facets of human life as morale, culture, social relations, democratic rights, and equal opportunities are taken into consideration).

A clearer grouping would be into *industrialized* versus *less-industrialized* countries or, alternatively, into *economically developed* versus *less economically developed* countries. This is, in fact, what is meant by the developed versus developing classification.

Neither developing nor developed countries can be regarded as forming a homogeneous group; they show differences in terms of industrial development, natural resources, size, economic strength, access to markets, national policy, human resources, and so on.

Factors Impeding Quality Improvement

Developing countries face several problems with regard to quality. The nature of these problems differs depending on the country's current phase of development. Consequently, the solutions to the problems also differ.

An increasing number of developing countries are liberalizing their economies and adopting export-oriented policies. These changes lead to an increased awareness of the importance of quality.

Discussions that the author has had with many representatives of developing countries show that there are several factors impeding improvement of quality in developing countries, of which the major ones seem to be:

> *Low purchasing power:* The vast majority of people are poor. Their purchase decisions are based on price considerations only. The manufacturers consequently aim at low prices, using cheap and low-quality materials.

> *Shortage of goods and absence of competition:* The shortage of goods provides some guarantee to the manufacturers that everything produced will be sold; as a result, they show very little interest in quality. Restrictions on the importation of goods, along with high custom barriers, protect locally produced goods against competition from goods produced in more industrialized countries.

Foreign exchange constraints: Most developing countries have a shortage of foreign exchange, and the industrial sector of the economy has to compete with other sectors for the insufficient amount available. This leads to obsolete technology, inadequate machinery, and poor material, all of which have an adverse effect on quality.

Incomplete infrastructure: The infrastructure is not satisfactory. In most developing countries there are shortcomings in areas such as power supply, transport, communication, and education. In addition, specific services in areas important to quality development (for example, standardization, testing, training, and consulting), are not adequate for the needs of the enterprises.

Inadequate leadership: There is a short-term view on the business, which leads to a quantity-oriented management culture. Business leaders rely on a few key members of personnel. The need for an overall coordination of activities is overlooked. Quality is regarded as a technical issue only, managed by technicians. There is no proper awareness of the strategic importance of quality to the enterprise among owners and top managers.

Inadequate knowledge: The managerial as well as technical knowledge of personnel in industry is generally limited. In some developing countries the problem of limited knowledge is compounded by the transient nature of the work force. (It is not uncommon to find that 20 to 50 percent of the work force is replaced within three to six months.) Under these circumstances, it is difficult to achieve a skilled workforce. The high illiteracy rate in many developing countries adds to the problem.

National Efforts for Quality

The problems related to quality in developing countries are of such a nature that they cannot be solved on a company level only. In fact, efforts on a national level are necessary, and these depend largely on the national policy of the country. In some countries, the government is ahead in developing means for an effective quality program. National efforts include:

Standardization: Preparation of national standards covering terminology, sampling methods, testing methods, specifications, quality management systems, and codes of practice

Certification: To attest that products comply with standards, as well as to attest that quality-related activities are carried out in accordance with certain standards on quality management systems

Export inspection: Ensuring the quality of certain products for export through preshipment inspection

Legislation: Enforcement of standardization, certification, accreditation, export inspection, and so on through acts of parliament and legislature

National promotion: National programs to promote a general awareness of quality

Education and training: Development of the necessary knowledge and skills, as well as exertion of influence on attitudes

External assistance: Assistance from international organizations, bilateral aid programs, transnational corporations, and so on to short-cut the development process

Institutional infrastructure: Services offered by institutions in the areas of standardization, certification, accreditation, testing, metrology, quality consulting, and training

Professional societies: To develop the competence of quality professionals and practitioners

The steps to be taken on a national level are determined mainly by the governments of the respective developing countries. The way this is done depends on the policy of the government. In some developing countries there is a centrally planned economy, and in these we will often find a strong reliance on governmental institutions and legislation. In other countries only some basic needs (for example, standardization, education) are met by the government. There is a growing trend among developing countries toward less government intervention and more deregulation.

Standardization

Standardization plays a major role in promoting the industrial and economic development of a country. Many developing countries have realized this and as a consequence set up national institutions to handle the standardization activities.

National Standardization

Standardization activities on a national level are dealt with by a national standards body. This institution, carrying full government recognition (in many developing countries through legislation), is responsible for the development and publication of national standards, as well as for keeping them up-to-date. In preparing standards, the national standards body calls upon the knowledge and experience of manufacturers, users, government departments, universities, and so on. This is normally done by setting up technical committees with wide representation.

Regional Standardization

Developing countries in the same region have similarities in climate, culture, governmental policies, consumption, industrial production, and so on. Therefore, there might be a need for common standards. In order to deal with these regional issues in the field of standardization, regional standards organizations have been formed.

Such regional standards organizations exist in Africa (African Regional Organization for Standardization [ARSO]), in Arab Countries (Arab Organization for Standardization and Metrology [ASMO]), in the Caribbean (Caribbean Common Market Standards Council [CARICOM]), and in Latin America (Comisión Panamericana de Normas Técnicas [COPANT]).

International Standardization

International standards are an important means of communication in international business and trade. With the globalizing of trade, the need for international standardization increases.

There are three international standardization bodies that are most important to developing countries: the International Organization for Standardization (ISO), the International Electrotechnical Commission (IEC), and the Codex Alimentarius Commission (CAC).

Developing countries can gain by adopting or adapting international standards as national standards, as the process of standards development is time-consuming and costly. Many developing countries do not have the professional resources necessary to prepare standards in certain areas.

As international standards are providing the key to international markets, it is important to developing countries to be able to see such standards internationally established for products that are vital to their national economies. In addition, they are concerned for the safety and the health of their citizens.

Certification

Certification means to verify conformance with certain requirements. This can take many forms: from a simple statement by the manufacturer that the product conforms to the specification, to a third-party certification in which an independent body verifies that the manufacturer operates in accordance with a recognized standard on quality management systems.

Certification on a national level is very often combined with standardization. This means that national standards bodies in developing countries use a third-party certification program to operate.

Product Certification

This involves checking and certifying that products comply with the standards.

The purpose of a product certification program is to give the buyer confidence that the product is of a certain quality or that it meets quality requirements. Such certification goes beyond the seller's assurances that the product conforms to the requirements and beyond the buyer's own verification; instead, systems operated by impartial bodies are used (third-party certification). The impartial certification body can be a governmental or nongovernmental organization. In developing countries the national standards body normally assumes this responsibility.

In developing countries there are various reasons for having a third-party certification program. One is to upgrade quality in the domestic market. Owing to shortage of goods and the absence of competition, which very often prevail in developing economies, product quality is likely to be poor, and a mandatory certification system can provide a minimum quality level. A second reason is to promote exports. A certification system can be an important factor in enabling developing countries to secure access to foreign markets. A third reason is to prevent importation of products of inferior quality. Some developing countries have had the misfortune to be used as dumping grounds for unscrupulous foreign manufacturers.

System Certification

There is a trend to move from product certification to system certification. This means that the supplier's credibility is demonstrated by the assessment and registration of his or her quality system.

The assessment of the supplier's quality system is carried out by an independent certification body against an applicable quality system standard in order to establish whether or not the system conforms to the standard. Standards usually referred to are the international standards on quality management systems ISO 9001 and ISO 9002 (or the equivalent national standards).

In some developing countries, the national standards body has been assigned the quality system certification task. As soon as the auditing capability of the staff is developed and the necessary management structure is set up, quality system certification will be one of the major tasks of the national standard bodies in developing countries.

As there is a great demand for quality system certification, many foreign (mainly European) certification agencies are operating in developing countries on a commercial basis. The certification has also become a business opportunity for local consultants. The less scrupulous ones form two organizations: one to set up the quality systems and to write the quality manuals for their clients, and one to certify that these quality systems and manuals conform to the quality system standards ISO 9001 or ISO 9002. The certification organization might have achieved accreditation by a body in Europe on rather loose ground.

There are doubts about the validity of quality system certification, as this mainly relies on documentation in the form of quality manuals, work procedures, instructions, and records generated during the operation of the quality system. Product quality, as well as the customers' perception of quality, are not considered. Such doubts are more valid in developing countries compared to industrialized countries. In developing countries top management more often only pays lip service to quality. They see the ISO 9000 certification as "some kind of magic key," which will open doors to export markets for their products. For them it is most important to obtain the formal certificate. There will be no basic change in the quality culture of the enterprise, nor will any real product quality improvements take place. The limited experience in quality management among assessors and auditors in developing countries will also create doubts about the validity of the certification.

Export Inspection

In assuring foreign buyers goods of an acceptable quality, plans for preshipment testing and inspection of products for export are used. Some developing countries have legislation dealing with export inspection. The legislation generally applies to specific commodities that are of key importance for the national economy (coconut, coffee, cocoa, fruit, jute, rice, rubber, and so on).

As a consequence of the deregulation of the markets, the trend is to get away from compulsory systems for export inspection enforced by law. Instead, the export inspection is a matter for the market forces, which means that the trading partners (the exporters and the importers) set up and agree on how to ensure the quality of the deliveries. Third-party certification is then increasingly applied.

Legislation

National standards bodies in developing countries have been established by acts of parliament or legislature. Such acts, normally called *standards acts,* stipulate the role of the national standards institute in promoting standardization throughout the country. Provisions related to the enforcement of standards are sometimes incorporated into some of these laws, (for example, foods acts or certification mark acts).

The standards act may also deal with weights and measures. In some countries such standards are covered by a separate weights and measures act, which also deals with the testing of weighing and measuring equipment to ensure that it is fit for use in trade.

There may also be legislation on export inspection, which is the case for certain items in some developing countries.

National Promotion

In an increasing number of developing countries, national programs for promoting a general awareness of quality have been launched with the involvement of government agencies and trade and consumer organizations. The national programs usually have the following components.

High-level recognition: Support from ministries and important national organizations is granted. Even the head of state may be involved.

Publicity: Public media such as newspapers, magazines, radio, and television are used.

Conferences, seminars, and other meetings: Speeches are given by political leaders, industrialists, quality professionals, and so on.

Slogans: Slogans such as *Quality first* are disseminated through posters, pamphlets, stickers, badges, and so on.

Logotype: The campaign has a common emblem displayed on posters, flags, pamphlets, and so on.

Awards: Deserving companies and individuals are recognized through awards, which are presented with great publicity.

Quality month: The promotional activities may be concentrated in a particular month.

National Quality Awards

Promoting quality among enterprises by means of a national quality award program has in recent years become an important factor to improve the competitiveness of the industrial sector in many industrialized countries. Experience shows that these programs stimulate improvements of quality and productivity to an extent that goes beyond the effects of ISO 9000. The awards criteria have become a yardstick for enterprises, which allows them to assess their own situation and to guide their improvement efforts.

National quality awards have also been launched in some developing countries (for example, Argentina, Brazil, Colombia, India, Republic of Korea, Malaysia, Philippines). In most cases, either the Malcolm Baldrige National Quality Award or the European Quality Award has served as a model in the development of the set up and the awards criteria.

The responsibility for the national quality award is in some developing countries assumed by a governmental organization, and in others by a foundation financially supported by the private sector. The latter is the case in Argentina and Brazil. The National Quality Award in Argentina was established by legislation passed by the Argentinean parliament. The administration of the award is delegated to a private foundation (National Quality Award Foundation [FUNDAPRE]), funded by member companies and by the government.

Education and Training

A key to quality upgrading is education and training, which involves developing necessary knowledge and skills as well as influencing attitudes. In developing countries, it is necessary to direct activities of this kind not only toward manufacturers and service providers but also toward consumers; consequently, the activities are very far-reaching. The difficulties are aggravated by the normally high illiteracy rate in these countries.

National Level

Education and training in the quality field can be dealt with in different ways within a developing country.

Educational Institutions

Quality management topics are to an increasing extent included in the curricula of engineering universities and institutes, particularly in the more industrialized developing countries. The courses offered deal mainly with more trendy tools, such as statistical process control, quality function deployment, benchmarking, and ISO 9000. Topics related to top management are rare. The courses are usually taught by professors who have limited experience in industrial work and management. There is a limited supply of locally developed textbooks.

Courses and Seminars Offered by Associations, Institutes, and Other Organizations

In countries that have reached a higher level of industrialization, courses and seminars are offered by national institutions for standardization, productivity, and so on and by professional associations (manufacturers' associations, national quality societies), as well as by consultants. Some countries are active in inviting foreign lecturers. As a consequence of the great interest in ISO 9000 certification, the majority of courses offered are in this field (for example, the implementation of ISO 9000, preparation for ISO 9000 certification, quality system auditing). International consulting and registration firms (mainly European-based) offer lead assessor training that can lead to registration by the International Register of Certified Assessors (IRCA).

Meetings and Conferences

An important activity of a national quality organization is to hold meetings and conferences at which practitioners can exchange ideas and experiences. Countries with a more developed industrial sector generally have a quality association that is active in this way. Such organizations are the Chilean Association for Quality (ASCAL), the China Quality Control Association, and the Philippine Society for Quality Control.

Self-Instruction

Independent study of books and journals can provide considerable knowledge in the quality management field, particularly for managers and engineers. In many developing countries there is, however, a shortage of such literature, owing to the lack of foreign exchange, a national language with limited readership, and so on. Some national quality organizations publish a journal or newsletter as a means of promoting the professional development of their members.

In-House Training Programs

Successful enterprises in industrialized countries have adopted a strategy that includes a massive in-house training program with the objectives of changing everyone's attitudes and giving new skills and knowledge. In these enterprises training in quality is provided for everyone regardless of function and level. Such training starts with top management and then works its way down the organization, level by level. This kind of massive training is rare in developing countries. In some larger enterprises, training in various narrow concepts and tools is provided.

On-the-Job Training

On-the-job training is the principal method of training workers and inspectors, even in developing countries. Instructions are given by the supervisor or a more experienced inspector. The result depends on both the technical ability and the ability of the instructor to instruct and motivate. In general, these abilities vary more in countries that have a limited industrial tradition.

International Level

Developing countries also have opportunities for training on the international level by sending trainees to more industrialized countries. International organizations such as the United Nations Industrial Development Organization (UNIDO), the International Organization for Standardization (ISO), and the Asian Productivity Organization (APO) organize quality training programs for developing countries.

UNIDO, in cooperation with the government of Japan (Ministry of International Trade and Industry [MITI]) and the Japanese Association for Overseas Technical Scholarships (AOTS) organizes a five-week training program on quality improvement of industrial products every two years. The program, intended for quality managers and production managers, focuses on problem solving.

Since 1973, the government of Sweden has been sponsoring training programs in the field of quality for developing countries. The training programs in Sweden have been attended by quality professionals and managers from 80 countries in Africa, Asia, Europe, Latin America, and the Caribbean. The author is responsible for these programs.

External Assistance

External assistance plays a significant part in the industrial and economic growth of developing countries by making it possible to shorten the process of development. There are various forms of assistance.

Assistance from International Organizations

There are international organizations providing assistance to developing countries in the field of quality. Some of them work worldwide (mainly within the United Nations system) and others work on a regional basis. Significant organizations of this kind are the European Union (EU), Food and Agriculture Organization of the United Nations (FAO), International Organization for Standardization (ISO), International Trade Centre UNCTAD/WTO (ITC), United Nations Development Programme (UNDP), United Nations Industrial Development Organization (UNIDO), World Bank, and World Health Organization (WHO).

Bilateral Assistance

A great deal of the external assistance to developing countries is through bilateral aid from industrialized countries. In this way, quality experts have assisted in various developing and training programs.

Assistance from Transnational Companies

External assistance may also take the form of collaboration with foreign manufacturers to obtain benefits such as technical know-how in joint ventures, import of plants and equipment, or consultant service. This kind of assistance is vital to developing countries.

Institutional Infrastructure

Industrial enterprises require access to an infrastructure of institutions able to render a wide range of services (for instance, in the areas of standardization, certification, accreditation, testing, metrology, quality consulting, and training). Developing countries that are in the process of industrializing must also provide for development of such an institutional infrastructure.

National Standards Body

In most developing countries, a national standards body is in operation primarily to provide services in standardization, certification, testing, and metrology. Unlike standards bodies in the West, national standards bodies in developing countries are usually governmental agencies established by law and funded by their respective governments. Due to the importance of standardization to both the public and private sector, some developing countries restructure their national standards bodies as joint public/private sector bodies. In the early stages of industrial development some form of government support is needed. A balanced representation of all groups interested in standardization should be considered: industry, trade, consumers, professional associations, the government.

The national standards bodies have not traditionally provided any services to industry in the fields of quality consulting and training. In consequence of the great interest for ISO 9000 certification and registration, an increasing number of national standards bodies in developing countries have started offering training in areas related to ISO 9000, such as quality systems implementation and auditing.

In most countries the standards bodies are governed by a council responsible for working out policy guidelines, as well as for approving standards. The drafting of standards is supervised by technical committees representing manufacturers, users, university-affiliated institutions, research centers, and so on. Usually, there are technical committees in particular fields, such as electrical, mechanical and civil engineering chemicals, and textiles.

The staff of a national standards body is headed by a chief executive officer or director, who is usually in charge of departments for standardization, certification (sometimes called quality control or quality assurance), metrology, laboratory services, information, and administration.

National Quality Council

With the increasing awareness of the fact that quality is an important element behind the economic growth of a country, the necessity of having a national institutional infrastructure for the following activities is becoming more and more apparent.

- Creating awareness about quality and its economic benefits, including administering the national quality award
- Promoting new concepts in quality management
- Training in quality-related subjects
- Accreditation of certification bodies
- Registration of certified auditors for quality systems

These activities should not be assigned to governmental agencies only, although governments have to take a major initiative in these areas. They should be autonomous, free from bureaucratic control, and set up in close cooperation with the private sector.

Professional Societies

A national quality society can play an important role in promoting quality nationwide, both in developing and in more industrially developed countries. Quality societies or associations are being formed in an increasing number of countries. Some of the national societies offer individual membership only and some offer institutional membership only, but most offer both.

Some societies are very active, for example, the Argentine Institute of Quality Control (IACC), the Brazilian Association of Quality Control (ABCQ), the Chilean Association for Quality (ASCAL), the China Quality Control Association, the Institute of Quality Control Malaysia, and the Philippine Society for Quality Control (PSQC). These societies organize conferences and seminars, conduct training programs, and distribute information (newsletters, journals, and so on).

Conclusion

Developing countries face several problems with regard to quality. The nature of these problems differ considerably depending on the country's existing situation for the phase of development. The liberalization of their economics and adoption of export-oriented policies however, are changing the quality awareness. Quality certifications, registration of certified auditors, implementation of quality program standards are beginning to show real improvements for meeting the competition in an extraordinary way.

Chapter 21

Stages of Quality Practice in Developing Countries of the Asia Pacific Region

Miflora M. Gatchalian

Introduction

For more than two decades of quality promotions, training, consultancies, and practical work experiences mostly in food industries in developing countries, the author experienced a myriad of differing quality practices used by companies. Based on no less than 1000 companies of different types and of various sizes, many commonalties were noted. When analyzed, groupings into a finite stage of quality practices were made possible. This confirmed the author's thesis that companies in developing countries could be practicing quality control (QC) measures at different degrees of sophistication. The extent of the use of quality tools and techniques could also be related to size of company and to the nature of products manufactured.

The presentation in this chapter is not a result of any scientific research undertaking. It is merely a sharing of the author's experiences and observations cumulated over the years. In what follows, the author is sharing her findings that she has already shared in various local and international conferences, symposiums, forums, lectures, and workshops in the Asia Pacific region. She obtained a consensus among participants relative to major characteristics of the different stages of quality practice. Several participants even identified their own companies as having the features of at least one of the stages discussed in this chapter, while others requested assistance on how they could move to the next-highest stage. It is the author's earnest hope that constructive criticisms will be applied to this presentation to allow for further refinements. Only major similarities and differences have been presented in this chapter.

Based on similarities of prevailing practices, the five groupings captioned as *stages in quality practice* include:

Stage I	Quality awareness
Stage II	Quality control (QC)
Stage III	Total quality control (TQC)
Stage IV	Total quality management (TQM)
Stage V	Company-wide quality improvement (CQI)

Each of these stages, with their respective general descriptions, are shown in Figures 21.1 to 21.5. It is possible that some companies may find themselves actually having characteristics that could span through two to three quality development stages without possessing all the characteristics of the lower stage.

Stage I: Quality Awareness

Many of the "cottage" type, small-scale companies (with less than 20 employees and factories without automation) in developing countries are still at the quality awareness level (Stage I). Figure 21.1 shows the list of major distinguishing characteristics at this stage. There are four levels:

- *Management realizes the importance of quality control (QC) practice:* However, at this beginning level, the appreciation of management is limited by the lack of knowledge and/or understanding of modern quality concepts and tools. Besides, the companies being too small, they do not pay much attention to the many intricacies that are necessary to follow "modern" quality practices. Nevertheless, attempts at utilizing some measures to "control" raw materials, in-process activities, and finished products are made.

- *Workers are simply told of the management desire for quality:* This happens without necessarily knowing whether their quality perceptions are the same. Documentation is not a usual practice, which could result in inconsistent process implementation. Since most small-scale companies are generally family-owned and operated, specifications are usually kept in

---

LEVEL I - QUALITY AWARENESS

1. Management knows the importance of quality.

2. Workers are told of management's desire for quality.

3. Both management and workers rely on routine manufacturing operations and on inspection.

4. Participation in quality education and training seldom happens

---

Figure 21.1. Distinguishing characteristics of companies at Level I in the stages of quality practice.

the mental memory of the manager/owner who is normally the father/mother or the eldest or most enterprising son or daughter. "Trade secrets" are zealously guarded and, as such, workers are not generally made aware of quality requirements. At this level, recording and reporting systems are not yet in place. What is hammered into the minds of the employees is the need to pay close attention to the process to meet the minimum requirement for acceptability of the finished products.

• *Both management and workers rely on routine manufacturing operations and on inspection:* This is the only means utilized to prevent release of defective products or the use of defective raw materials. Few, if any, quality testing instruments are available in the company. Products with either critical and major defects are sorted out, if seen by the inspector. The major objective remains to sell as much of the outputs as fast as possible. For as long as profit is realized, the operations tend to continue. It is no wonder that survival rates of small companies are generally known to be low (less than 50 percent of those who start remain in business after three years).

• *Participation in quality education and training seldom happens:* Some of the companies may send participants to public quality training programs, which are offered free or at very low costs. Since these companies have limited capital, neither paid in-service training nor consultancy services are availed of by the companies. Quality improvement progress is generally slow, except for some cases where the manager/owner has started to appreciate modern quality practices.

Stage II: Quality Control (QC)

• *Compartmentalization of quality responsibilities* is a major characteristic of companies at this stage (see Figure 21.2). If a QC department is a part of the organizational structure, then the responsibility for quality is assigned mainly to them. Others in the production line simply follow what is dictated to them as "company standards or specifications," which could be in the form of written specifications focused on product or the processes. Some raw material control system may also exist to a limited extent. There is a prevailing belief that with close attention to raw material and process controls, the finished product will have minimal defects/defectives.

LEVEL II: QUALITY CONTROL (QC)
(Conformance)

1. Compartmentalization of quality responsibility as basis for conformance.

2. Quality Control Department is given the responsibility for quality.

3. Top management is given the prerogative to make "go or no go" decision.

4. Only technical personnel are sent to public seminars.

Figure 21.2. Distinguishing characteristics of companies at Level II in the stages of quality practice.

- *Quality control department is given the responsibility for quality:* There is the prevailing belief in the company that controls set are being guarded by the QC department. Inspection is done in practically all stages of the operations (raw material, in-process and finished product assessments). If problems occur, the QC personnel are expected to react for immediate redress. Action is generally reactive rather than proactive or preventive. However, use of tools for quality measurement are generally in place.

- *Top management is given the prerogative to make a "go" or "no go" decision:* The result is that serious conflicts regarding product quality between the QC and production departmental heads are encountered and expected to be referred to the top management for final action. The latter is given the prerogative to make the final decision on whether or not to hold or release a questionable production. Because of the observed inspection and reporting practices, especially on-line, the QC staff are sometimes labeled as "policemen" or "Gestapo" by people from the production department. In many instances, conflicts arise between the two departments and remain a major problem for the company. At this stage of quality practice, the QC personnel's main objective is to guard product quality at all costs. On the other hand, production people believe they have the responsibility to meet the targeted production volume set by marketing staff.

• *Only technical personnel or trainees are sent to public seminars or training programs:* At this stage, it is very unlikely that top management or QC department heads would attend quality seminars or training programs, no matter how high the level of expertise available from the invited speaker. There is a general belief that the training will only be a waste of time for the busy executives. To date, however, with increasing globalization and urgency of need for new knowledge, this practice is fast changing.

• *Quality management programs conducted by expatriates:* These programs are found attractive by local executives at this stage of quality practice. However, difficulties are generally met because of their inability to connect their low level of quality practice understanding to the highly sophisticated language of the invited speaker. On various occasions, the author has observed that expensive public "quality management" programs conducted by foreigners invariably draw a sizable crowd of business executives. But, whether these participants are there to really learn advances in quality or simply to socialize with other participants from prestigious companies, or both, is hard to fully ascertain. A premium price is paid for imported technology, even if it can hardly be applied to the local situation in the developing country. This especially poses a problem when the international resource speaker could not bring down the level of language to that of the general participants.

Stage III: Total Quality Control (TQC)

The training and consultancy visits of many Japanese and other international experts to developing countries in the Asia Pacific region, plus the readily available promotional materials on TQC have generated much interest on this topic. In the last two decades, the search for a right approach to TQC has been a major concern in companies of many developing countries. Financially speaking, many stable foreign-owned large companies have spent enormous sums of money for international consultants to either introduce, implement, or sustain TQC practices in their organization. In exceptional cases, some medium-scale companies, who have undergone Stages I and II, believe they are ready for Stage III, which is TQC (Figure 21.3).

LEVEL III: TOTAL QUALITY CONTROL (TQC)

1. Everyone is involved in sustained and successful application of quality control.

2. Everyone has mastered the approaches to PPM (Planning, Prevention and Monitoring).

3. Effective applications of the 3Ps of quality (Performance, Pricing and Punctuality).

Figure 21.3. Distinguishing characteristics of companies at Level III in the stages of quality practice.

- *Everyone is involved in a sustained and successful application of quality control in practically all aspects of the operations:* Successful and sustained TQC at this stage is characterized by extensive use of quality tools and techniques. Invariably, the practice of statistical quality control is understood and utilized by everyone where necessary. Quality control education and training becomes a must for everyone, both for updating and skills upgrading purposes.

- *Everyone has mastered the approaches to planning, prevention, and monitoring pertaining to quality functions:* There is the acceptance of the individual role to perform expected quality functions. This, in turn, is derived from a supportive group of management that has declared its "quality policy" in support of the company's quality mission and vision. Quality leadership is, therefore, an accepted practice by management.

- *There is an effective and meaningful application of quality practices associated with performance, pricing, and punctuality ("3Ps" of quality):* Everyone in the organization is expected to know and understand their contributions toward the attainment of the desired product performance. Likewise, pricing, which is associated with profitability, becomes a serious responsibility of the employees since they are focused on controlling costs of production with a consequent goal of waste reduction, while delivery of promised goods on time or as promised spells punctuality. Therefore, everyone, in this context, implies that all employees of the company are fully aware of their individual responsibility for quality, regardless of their job functions or level or status in the organization.

The TQC situation in companies may seem too ideal to actually happen. Yet, this is found to exist in many successful companies, some of which are small- to medium-scale operations. Some of these companies may think of applying for certification to the ISO 9000 standards. The many approaches to TQC installation and sustenance for these companies are readily available from the right sources. One of these sources of information is contributions of members of the prestigious International Academy for Quality, the Quality Press of American Society for Quality, the European Organization for Quality, and the Asia Pacific Quality Organization. Locally, the Philippine Society for Quality (PSQ) has also shown some capabilities to provide assistance in the form of training or consultancy.

Stage IV: Total Quality Management (TQM)

If TQC would seem to be close to an ideal company situation, there is still a higher stage that companies can aim for. In fact, some Japanese companies already report having arrived at this stage. Some large multinationals and a few local companies believe they already have a successful TQM practice. Their success stories (known to be only between 20 percent to 35 percent of those who started) and concrete status relative to their competitors tend to support the contention. During most of the author's public "quality" seminars and training programs, the author has observed that large-scale companies readily proclaim to being in Stage IV (see Fig. 21.4). Yet, during the in-service training in some of these companies, where discussions on the different stages are done amongst them, participants from the same company do not always agree with each other relative to their prevailing quality practices. Management tends to vocalize their belief that they are at a fully matured TQM stage. But, as one goes down the hierarchy, less and less staff members share the same belief.

- *There is extensive applications of statistical quality control:* Where the TQM is the adopted philosophy and practice, all useful quality tools and techniques, including statistical quality control applications, are expected to be in place. Education and training for the whole company in this stage are so generally aligned that they would contribute to the realization of company goals and directions. An implemented training program results in

---

LEVEL IV: TOTAL QUALITY MANAGEMENT (TQM)

1. Extensive use of SQC and problem solving techniques and sustained company-wide quality education and training.

2. Very good labor-management relations and communications.

3. Profits from increasing productivity are shared.

Figure 21.4. Distinguishing characteristics of companies at Level IV in the stages of quality practice.

improvement in each person's quality practice. At this stage, the company most likely gets certified as meeting the ISO 9000 quality management system standards. Some can be on the planning stages for a possible measure of TQM success based on the Malcolm Baldrige National Quality Award criteria (or the adapted version of Philippine Quality Award). Under the PQA criteria, these companies could probably obtain a score of 500 points or more (with the highest score being 1000 points).

• *Good labor-management relations and communications are easily observed:* Although many quality professionals may disagree on the difference between TQC and TQM, the author wishes to share her own experience and observations. Perhaps the greatest difference between the two is the contrast between the words *control* and *management.* From the author's point of view, control simply implies the ability to prevent the occurrence of defects or defectives through strict conformance to specifications. On the other hand, management includes control as well as the resiliency to meet any unexpected occurrences to enable one to always maintain the desired quality level. TQM, therefore, implies a great dependence on the human contributions to quality maintenance. Knowledge, skills, practices, and attitudes relative to the right quality practices are modeled by the company leadership. Continuous quality updating and skills development are major expectations.

Therefore, careful personnel recruitment and constant mainstreaming of quality ideas and directions become prerequisite.

- *Profits from increased productivity are shared:* Particularly for developing nations, the practice of profit sharing greatly increases positive management attitudes and improved employee relationships. Employees are committed to their responsibilities to make sure that the company remains viable and that they share in the company's growth and development. A growing profitability picture becomes a result of the continuous quality improvement practices employed company-wide. Hence, sharing of profits in one way or another easily becomes a part of the overall management plan and strategy.

Stage V: Company-wide Quality Improvement (CWQI)

This stage refers to a long climb to success. The search for continuous quality improvement is shared by everyone in the company as a lifelong dream. For instance, after undergoing Stages I to IV, it should be terribly discouraging for a company to allow backsliding. The taste of triumph, after having hurdled the difficult climb to Stage V, deserves to be sustained. The structure that enables the continuous climb to company-wide quality improvement (CWQI) is not supposed to be toppled down. Company leadership at this stage holds the responsibility to provide for the stimulus for a sustained elevation of the planning, prevention, and monitoring practices. A statistically based monitoring system becomes necessary for proper planning toward a higher level of quality practice, which will assure prevention of errors in the practice of TQM. Profits are shared company-wide (see Figure 21.5).

CWQI normally becomes a company slogan. At this stage, everyone in the company is seen as a "quality person" charged with the responsibility of continuously seeking quality improvement opportunities, not only for his/her particular job, but also for the whole company and the community. Successful transfer of quality knowledge, skills, good practice, and attitudes becomes everyone's responsibility. Well-planned training programs, geared toward continuous personnel upgrading, become the lifeblood for sustaining CWQI.

Conclusion

The consulting experience of the author based on work with many small, medium and large size companies in the Asia Pacific Region show that there are

---

LEVEL V: COMPANY-WIDE QUALITY IMPROVEMENT

1. Updated Quality Education and Training for everyone is the company's concern.

2. Recognizing that being "better than the best" is everyone's concern; full awareness of competitor's performance.

3. Well-developed quality improvement program (with quality evaluation and training components)

4. Profits from increasing productivity are shared.

Figure 21.5. Distinguishing characteristics of companies at Level V in the stages of quality practice.

five distinct stages of quality practice: quality awareness, quality control, total quality control, total quality management, and company-wide quality improvement. Each of these stages are discussed with underlying characteristics and degrees of sophistication involved in their practices.

Acknowledgments

The author gratefully acknowledges the help received from: participants of training programs conducted by QCI, Inc, since 1985; the articles from *Quality Progress,* a monthly journal published by the American Society for Quality (ASQ) and from its Annual Quality Congress Proceedings; selected articles in 1994 proceedings printed by the Philippine Society for Quality (PSQ); proceedings from the Annual Latin American Congress sponsored by the Instituto Mexicano de Control de Calidad (IMECCA) in Mexico; proceedings from the Asia Pacific Quality conferences (APQO) since 1985 .

Chapter 22

New Roles of a Manager in the Twenty-First Century

H. James Harrington

Introduction

Too many managers expect their employees to correct the problems that are created by management. They cannot. Management must solve 80 percent of the problems that face most organizations. With this conviction in mind, this chapter begins by stating that management's role must change. It must remove the major roadblocks that have been put in the way of the employees before the employees' zest can be unleashed. A good rule of thumb is that the management team should solve 50 percent of its problems before the employees attack the 10 percent to 20 percent that they can control. Ron Hutchinson of Harley Davidson said, "If we really want to communicate a change in direction and a change in approach, what we need to do as senior managers is to demonstrate that we are going to live by a new set of rules and play by these rules."

Several years ago, when I was conducting a focus group meeting at a Canadian cookie manufacturing company, we discussed what was needed to be done to improve the quality within the organization. A gray-haired woman in her early fifties spoke up, "The white hats [management wore white hard hats when they walked out into the manufacturing floor] don't really care about this company. They are all college graduates and they can go out and get a job any place within a matter of months if this factory closes down. But I have worked here all my life. The only thing I know is how to make cookies. If this place closed down, I'd never be able to get a job. We care about what we do. We want to do a good job. Management doesn't care."

Frank Squires, a leading management consultant in the United States, has stated, "Management is not against quality. Quantity just has higher priority. Management's order of importance has always been quantity, cost, and quality." In the 1980s, management loudly proclaimed that quality was the top priority. But in reality, the priorities never changed. Management empowered employees, and then cut back on the work force as productivity improved. As a result, management lost employees' trust and loyalty. You can buy people's time, you can buy their physical presence, you can even buy their mental effort, but you cannot buy their loyalty, their trust, and their enthusiasm. These key requirements for any improvement process have to be earned by management. It is hard for management to:

- Admit it makes mistakes

- Apologize

- Shoulder the blame

- Take time to explain

- Be honest

- Admit it does not know all

- Share information

- Take advice

- Not change the rules when it is to the advantage

- Alter management styles to meet different employees' needs

Yes, it is hard to do all of this, but it pays big dividends and it is what managers must do if they are going to succeed in the twenty-first century. Our professors and management consultants make this all sound easy. They talk about empowerment, employee involvement, participation, and motivation, along with a neat little package of how all of this fits together in a simple formula. But I assure you, there is nothing like a little experience to tear apart the theoretical.

Why Start with Management First?

A good production worker consistently performs at the parts-per-million error level. Most managers perform at the errors-per-hundred level. Why do we live with these gross management errors? We set low expectations for our managers. We just do not expect management to perform at the parts-per-million level. We have grown to accept mediocrity in superior management performance. The biggest opportunities for improvement in business today are in management performance.

If you look at what the major roadblocks are to improvement within most organizations, they are:

- Lack of employee trust

- Lack of delegation

- Lack of management credibility

- Untimely decision making

- Lack of training

- Misdirected measurement systems

- Poor communications

- Lack of employee loyalty

- Fear of risk taking

- Lack of continuity

Each of these roadblocks can only be broken down by management. Without the removal of these roadblocks, the organization cannot make major progress.

Management action over the past decade has certainly dampened the employees' spirits and increased their distrust of management's loyalty to them. You cannot pick up a newspaper without seeing articles about employee layoffs, government cutbacks, and organizations requesting that their employees put forth additional effort with less and less resources. Too many managers today believe that loyalty is dead. In reality, loyalty and trust are down because management has driven them down. It reflects the frustration the employees have with managers who have not bothered to truly take a keen interest in developing a close personal relationship with and personal responsibility for their employees.

Management has destroyed their credibility, often without knowing or understanding why. Typical mistakes that management makes which destroy credibility are the following:

- Hiding bad news from the employees

- Half-truths and outright lying

- Missions, values, and visions that are not lived up to

- Not taking action on poor performers

- Decision dodging

Caught in the Middle

Let's be honest with ourselves. Middle and first-line managers have been caught up in a pressure cooker as the country presses for flatter organizations, and programs like self-managed work teams become a way of life. In the 1980s, managers made up 10 percent of the U.S. industrial work force. Organizations like AT&T had more than 100 layers of management. Certainly, they were prime candidates for job elimination. Management guru Peter F. Drucker stated, "The cynicism out there is frightening. Middle managers have become insecure, and they feel unbelievably hurt. They feel like slaves on an auction block." Organizations like IBM, General Motors, Westinghouse, General Electric, Mobil, Ford, and DuPont have slashed their management ranks. Management jobs have been combined, creating what we originally thought would be more meaningful and challenging work. Instead, we have created an atmosphere where managers feel overburdened and underappreciated.

The middle and first-level managers are very unsure of their status in most organizations today. The probability of being let go is much higher than the probability of promotion. Their futures have been put on hold and their life savings are in jeopardy. It is absolutely imperative that we do not skip over them and go directly to our employees, or we will lose their support. The early retirement programs that most organizations have implemented in the late 1980s and early 1990s have allowed the most talented and most knowledgeable managers to escape the organization. We cannot further alienate the managers we have.

Managers Are Ultimately Held Accountable

When all is said and done, the management teams are the ones who are held responsible for the organization's performance. How well the managers perform is directly reflected in their promotions, salaries, and longevity with the organization. In the United States, management's exposures are limited to reduced salary or loss of position. In China, poor performance is dealt with in a much more hostile manner. For example, a Chinese newspaper reported that "Eighteen factory managers were executed for poor quality at Chien Bien Refrigerator Factory on the outskirts of Beijing." The managers, 12 men and six women, were taken to a rice paddy outside the factory and unceremoniously shot to death while 500 plant workers looked on. A spokesman for the Ministry of Economic Reform, Xi Ten Huan, said, "It is understandable that our citizens would express shock and outrage when managers are careless in their attitudes toward the welfare of others."

China is not the only country that holds its managers accountable in its own way. Russians feel the same way. The *Pravda* newspaper, in 1985, reported that three female factory managers were sentenced to two years in a labor camp and fined $14,000 for producing poor quality clothes at a government factory. In addition, they were fined 20 percent of all future salaries.

It is not the intention here to recommend these types of stern actions on the U.S. government's part, but it is time that management take the responsibility to improve the quality and productivity of our organizations.

If our management team is going to be held accountable for improvement, then they must be involved in the implementation of any improvement process. This involvement must extend far beyond knowledge of its existence. The management team must become the leaders of the movement. They must be the shakers, the movers, and the teachers. If our employees are to excel, then our management must excel. As someone once said, "We are what we repeatedly do. Excellence, then, is not an act. It is a habit."

In order to improve their personal performance, top managers need to define what they do, and not things like "motivate employees" or "manage a department." These are their assignments. Examples of what management do are:

- Attend meetings

- Read and answer mail

- Answer telephone calls

- Delegate work

- Chair meetings

They should then select a maximum of eight of these behavioral patterns they want to improve. Each selected pattern should be recorded on a small card that can be easily carried in a purse or coat pocket. Each time the manager does not behave as defined, he or she has made an error, and a check mark should be placed on the appropriate card. Once a week, the total number of errors should be counted and plotted on a run chart. We recommend that each manager set an improvement target of 10 percent of the first month's error rate. When this target is reached, it is time to add eight more behavioral patterns to the list and start again. Each manager should post his or her performance charts in a visible place in the office. Sharing these personal values can have a major positive influence on the individual as well as on the organization. Eventually, this approach will be used by all managers and employees to measure their personal improvement.

Why Managers First?

Why do we have to start with managers first? The answer is simple if we look at their areas of responsibility. Managers are responsible for:

- Allocating resources

- Establishing the organization's structure

- Selecting the leaders

- Developing the processes

- Setting performance standards

- Making job assignments

- Preparing the job description

- Providing the measurement and reward systems

- Setting priorities

- Selecting and training employees

Considering management's responsibilities, it is obvious that these responsibilities should be executed in a superior manner in order to succeed in the improvement process. Only when management executes their responsibilities can the enthusiasm and pent-up creativity that exists in our employees be released.

Why Is Management the Problem?

Dr. Joseph M. Juran has long stated that 80 percent to 85 percent of all problems are caused by management. Donald Stratton, Manager of Quality at AT&T Network Systems, reported the following findings in a *Quality Progress* article:

- Eighty-two percent of the problems analyzed were classified as common cause. These are process problems owned by management.

- Eighteen percent of the problems analyzed were special cause. These are problems that were caused by people, machinery, or tools. Only a small portion of these problems can be solved by employee teams.

Of the 82 percent of problems that are management-controlled:

- Sixty percent of the corrections could be implemented by first- and second-level management.

- Twenty percent could be implemented by middle management.

- Twenty percent could only be implemented by top management.

It is easy to see that the major problems within organizations are the processes that management are responsible for modifying and controlling. Unfortunately, all the talk in the world and the desire to do something good does not get it done. The employees cannot correct the problems that management has created. Only management's personal involvement in the improvement process will bring about the required changes.

Management's New Role

It is often heard that quality should be first among equals (quality, cost, and schedule). But today's golden triangle of quality, cost, and schedule requires that management ensure that all three are met at the same time. It is easy to get one at the sacrifice of the other two. For example, we can get schedule with poor quality and high cost, or we can get high quality at high cost and long schedules. But today's customers demand all three at the same time. Managers that meet these demands will grow and prosper, and those that do not will be out of work.

Management's role is changing. The survival of a manager rests in his or her ability to keep pace with this changing environment and to be a role model for the employees. There are two types of managers working today:

Old Management Style	New Management Style
• Gives orders	• Gets agreement on objectives
• Holds back data	• Openly exchanges information
• Expects employees to work long hours	• Requires results
• Stresses individual performance	• Stresses team performance
• Gains approval decisions from above	• Makes decisions after discussions with the affected employees
• Primary job is to get the assignment completed	• Primary job is to enable the employee to complete the assignment
• Takes credit for employees' work	• Gives credit to the employees
• Tells how to do it	• Explains why it needs to be done
• Works within the organization's structure	• Changes the organization's structure to meet the activities' needs
• Chief reward is self-promotion	• Chief reward is growing employee capabilities
• Thinks of him-/herself as boss	• Thinks of him-/herself as a manager of human development
• Follows the chain of command	• Works with anyone necessary to get the task completed

• Thinks of him-/herself as a manager of a discipline	• Thinks of him-/herself as a manager of processes
• Sets schedules	• Stresses urgency of the job, approves schedules set by employees
• Dodges unpleasant tasks	• Takes immediate action on unpleasant tasks
• Delegates unimportant, uninteresting jobs	• Makes job assignments based on individual capabilities and skills
• Gives the best worker more assignments	• Keeps a balance of work expectations between both good and bad performers
• Pay is based on time on job	• Pay is based on knowledge and contribution
• Stays aloof from the employees	• Employee and management share outside activities
• Feels minorities and women have to be specially treated	• Treats everybody in a special manner
• Worries about employees who could replace him/her	• Develops a backup for themselves
• Manages all employees the same way	• Adjusts management style to meet the employee's personality and task assignment
• Checks to be sure employee never fails	• Allows employees to learn from failure, as long as the impact is not too detrimental to the organization

Basic Principles

Sophisticated management methods rely on some basic principles that must be mastered before these methods can be applied. Managers who have not mastered these basic principles are vulnerable to be left out in the cold during the next restructuring cycle. These basic principles are:

- *Delegation:* Management must be able to accomplish assignments by delegating work to their direct reports. Management must be able to free themselves to do planning, break down barriers, teach, measure, and network.

- *Appraisal:* Management must be able to develop individual performance goals in cooperation with the employees and provide honest, continuous feedback on performance compared to these goals.

- *Disagreements:* Disagreement between management and employees can be healthy. Management needs to understand both sides of the situation to make the very best decision. "Yes" men or women are not helpful.

- *Decisiveness:* Management cannot be reluctant to make a decision. Often, "gut feeling" is an extremely important part of managing the organization.

- *Positive attitude:* If the manager conveys a feeling of failure, the department is doomed to defeat.

- *Five-way communication system:* Management must establish excellent upward, downward, sideways, supplier and customer communication systems. It must be willing to share information with employees. Information is power. Every year, Robert Crandall, CEO of American Airlines, conducts 20 to 30 president's conferences in his 165-city route system, ensuring he maintains open communication with all of his employees.

- *Investment in people:* Management should invest heavily in employees, provide them with training, and help them grow and mature. This is one of the best investments an organization can make. Art Wegner, CEO of Pratt Whitney Turbo Manufacturing, sent his design engineers into the plant to spend six months on assignment as general foremen. Certainly, this is a major investment in their future, but it has paid off in improved manufacturability of new products designed by these engineers.

Conclusion

The improvement process must be embraced by management before the employees are exposed to it. Managers are the only ones who can correct 80 percent of the problems most organizations face today. With so much of the improvement opportunities resting in management's hands, there is no need to involve the employees until many of these major problems have been attacked and solved. The management team must demonstrate that they are willing and able to change before they ask the employees to change. Management has a beautiful bald eagle boxed into a 4×4 cage. Encouraging that eagle to soar produces little results and soon becomes discouraging to everyone unless management breaks down the bars that imprison the eagle. The key to successful management is simple. It is getting back to basics:

- Treating employees as you would like to be treated
- Setting a positive work ethic example

- Encouraging those who fail and praising those who succeed

- Providing honest evaluation of an individual's efforts

- Stepping up to the unpleasant situations

- Being friendly and having a smile on your face

- Freely giving credit to the people who do the job

- Portraying a sense of urgency and importance regarding the work that is being performed

As the famous Notre Dame head football coach, Knute Rockne, said, "The trouble in American life today, in business as well as in sports, is that too many people are afraid of competition. The result is that in some circles people have come to sneer at success if it costs hard work and training, and sacrifice." No manager can be successful without a great deal of hard work, training and sacrifice. If we are not willing to give all our concentration to do the job, then management is not the right career path for us.

Suggested Reference

1. Harrington, H. J. 1995. *Total Improvement Management.* New York: McGraw-Hill.

About the Contributors

Ove Hartz is Professor at the Department of Industrial Management and Engineering, Technical University of Denmark, where he teaches in the area of quality management and conducts research specializing in strategy and model development for total improvement. Professor Hartz has been Academician of the International Academy for Quality (IAQ) since 1979. He is Vice President for external affairs, Danish Society for Quality (DFK), Past President of the European Organisation for Quality (EOQ), and Past President of DFK. He has published more than 150 books, reports, and articles and given presentations at international conferences in more than 20 countries.

Gopal K. Kanji is Professor of Applied Statistics and Director of Management Sciences Research Centre at the Sheffield Hallam University, Sheffield, United Kingdom. He has published more than 60 research papers and eight books on statistics and total quality management (TQM). He is the founder/editor of *Journal of Applied Statistics* and *Total Quality Management*. Professor Kanji has been a consultant to many companies in the United Kingdom and Asia, and as chairman of the committee he helped develop a European Master's program on TQM under the umbrella of the European Foundation for Quality Management (EFQM). He is an Academician of the IAQ and has organized four World Congresses for Total Quality at Sheffield Hallam University.

Abdul Malek bin A. Tambi is Lecturer of Business and Management at MARA Institute of Technology, Malaysia, and presently a Ph.D. student at the Sheffield Hallam University. He has written several papers in the areas of operations research and management science and presented his research findings in many world congresses.

John D. Hromi is Professor Emeritus and founder of the John D. Hromi Center for Quality and Applied Statistics, Rochester Institute of Technology, Rochester,

New York. An Academician of IAQ and former editor of Academy's *The Best on Quality* book series, Dr. Hromi has been the Fredrick H. Minett Distinguished Professor at RIT. He is an ASQ Fellow, and former President and Chairman of the Board of American Society for Quality (ASQ). He has received ASQ's Automotive Division's C. C. Craig Award, ASQ's E. L. Grant Award, Lancaster Award, and Edwards Medal for his numerous outstanding contributions and work in modern quality management. He is a judge for the RIT/*USA TODAY* Quality Cup Award and for the New York State Excelsior Award.

Tito Conti, formerly Vice President of Corporate Quality with the Olivetti Group and former CEO of one of the companies of the Group, is now an independent consultant in management, organization, and quality. A Past President of the European Organisation for Quality (EOQ), Dr. Conti has served, from 1987 to 1992, as President of UNINFO, the Italian Standardisation Body in the area of information technology and was a visiting professor of total quality management at the Padua University (1992–1994), Bologna University (1995), and Pisa University (since 1992) in Italy. Apart from his two recently published books, *Building Total Quality* and *Organisational Self-Assessment,* (London: Chapman & Hall, 1993, 1997), Dr. Conti has written numerous papers and reports, and was the assistant editor of Dr. J. Juran's book, *The History of Managing for Quality* (Milwaukee: ASQC Quality Press, 1995). He is currently the Vice President of the Italian Association for Quality and a Vice President of the International Academy for Quality.

Alain-Michel Chauvel, a pioneer of the quality movement in France, has been active as a professor, author, consultant, and organizer of quality associations for over two decades. His books include *Gestion de la Production et des Operations* (1980), *Administration de la Production* (1984), and *Gestion de la Qualite dans Construction* (1985). He has also coauthored three other books and contributed more than 50 articles to various international quality magazines. A much sought-after speaker, Mr. Chauvel has presented papers and lectured internationally in the United Kingdom, France, Portugal, Spain, Italy, Austria, Czechoslovakia, the former Soviet Union, Belgium, Singapore, Japan, Brazil, Morocco, Mexico, and Chile.

Timothy E. Weddle is a management consultant in organizational improvement, information systems, product development, and technical support operations. He has over 20 years of professional and managerial experience as a director and consultant. His professional memberships include organizations such as American Society for Quality (ASQ), Institute for Industrial Engineers, Association for Health Services Research, American Sociological Association, and Healthcare Information and Management Systems Society. He specializes in mapping out social mechanisms that initiate and revitalize TQM in organizations.

William A. Golomski is president of W. A. Golomski & Associates, a technical and quality management consulting firm based near Wisconsin. A leader in communicating quality concepts, principles, and methodology and author of 10 books and over 300 papers and speeches, he has promoted the subject of quality control and allied arts and sciences in companies and organizations throughout the world. He is an elected Fellow of Royal Society of Health, Institute of Industrial Engineers, New York Academy of Sciences, and the World Association of Productivity Sciences. He and Timothy Weddle have collaborated on many research topics, including work values, organizational sciences, health care, and quality management. Mr. Golomski is a Vice President of the International Academy for Quality and an honorary member of American Society for Quality.

Geoffrey H. Bawden is Executive Director of the Workplace Safety and Health Division in the Labour Department of Manitoba government, Winnipeg, Canada. In his varied career with the provincial departments of Environment and Labour for over 26 years, Mr. Bawden has led the successful completion of a host of change-management projects and initiatives. A past chairman of the Canadian Association of Administrators of Labour legislation—Occupational Safety and Health Committee, he is chairman of the Board of Governors of the Hazardous Materials Information Review Council, a member of the Institute of Public Administration of Canada (IPAC), and a member of Intergovernmental Working Group on Occupational Safety and Health Harmonisation.

Gregory H. Watson is President and Managing Partner of Business Systems Solutions Inc., based in Florida. He has authored five books and over 70 articles related to total quality management, benchmarking processes, business systems, and management of technology. An Academician of IAQ, he is a Vice President of ASQ, where he participated in "The ASQ Future Study" and developed the ASQ Technology Master Plan and Research Plan. Mr. Watson served as a judge for the Texas, Florida, and New York State Quality Awards.

Barrie G. Dale is the United Utilities Professor of Quality Management and Head of the Operations Management Group at the Manchester School of Management, UMIST, United Kingdom, and Director of the Trafford Park Forum. During 17 years of continuous research into quality management, Professor Dale has produced 10 books and some 300 papers on the subject. During this time he has obtained funding of over 3M sterling to pursue a range of projects in total quality management. He is coeditor of the *International Journal of Quality and Reliability Management* and editor of the McGraw-Hill *Quality in Action* book series. Professor Dale is an Academician of IAQ.

Rune M. Moen is a Consulting Engineer and Researcher at the Norwegian Institute of Wood Technology in Norway. A holder of a Ph.D. in total quality management from the Norwegian University of Science and Technology, Dr. Moen has done extensive research in the area of quality management and has published more than a dozen papers in many international journals and conference proceedings.

Asbjørn Aune is Professor of Quality Management at the Norwegian University of Science and Technology and scientific advisor to the Foundation for Scientific and Industrial Research (SINTEF), Norway. He has carried out research and published 12 texts and over 50 papers on quality sciences and quality management technology in journals internationally. An Academician of IAQ, Professor Aune has taught quality-related courses at the Narvik Institute of Technology and coordinated many continuing education seminars for quality leaders and facilitators. He is an Honorary Member of the Norwegian Association for Quality and Leadership and a member of the Swedish Society for Quality, American Society for Quality, Association for Quality and Participation, and the Danish Society for Quality.

Thong Ngee Goh is Professor of Industrial and Systems Engineering at the National University of Singapore, and a member of the International Advisory Board of Graduate Program in Engineering Manufacturing and Management of the University of Washington, Seattle. Specializing in application of statistical methodologies for excellence in quality and productivity, he serves on the editorial boards of *Quality and Reliability Engineering International, International Journal of Production Economics, International Journal of Reliability and Safety Engineering, The TQM Magazine,* and *Asia Pacific Journal of Quality Management.* Professor Goh is an Academician of IAQ.

Kenneth S. Stephens is Professor of Industrial Engineering Technology at the Southern College of Technology, Marietta, Georgia. He has carried out research and lectured extensively throughout the world on quality control, quality assurance, TQM, and related world economy, and has the unique and extensive experience of acting as UNIDO advisor to many governments in developing and underdeveloped nations in Asia, Africa, and Latin and South America on setting up export-related quality initiatives and agenda. He is the coauthor of the textbook *Modern Methods for Quality Control and Improvement* (New York: John

Wiley, 1986), and author and coauthor of many other books and research papers and reports. An Academician of IAQ, Professor Stephens is the associate editor of *The Best on Quality;* and winner of ASQ's E. L. Grant Award and Lancaster Award.

Hitoshi Kume is Professor at Chuo University, Faculty of Science and Engineering and Professor Emeritus of the University of Tokyo, Japan, where he served as Professor for 18 years succeeding the chair of Professor Kaoru Ishikawa. He is the recipient of the famous 1989 Deming Prize of Japan, for his extensive research and publications in the field of TQM. Professor Kume is a member of the Science Council of Japan, a member of the Deming Prize Committee, and a member of the Japanese delegate with ISO TC 176 committee responsible for ISO 9000 quality management standard development. An Academician of IAQ, he is a course leader of the executive seminars on TQM with the Japanese Society for Scientists and Engineers (JUSE).

Dietmar Mangelsdorf is Senior Director in the Information and Communication Network Group of Siemens AG, Germany, and responsible for Corporate Quality and Environmental Management Systems with its Institute for Quality Engineering, Testing and Approvals. He has carried out research and published extensively on topics of test technology, quality engineering, quality management, and systems and product certification. Mr. Mangelsdorf is an Academician of IAQ, and serves as a member of the German National Advisory Committee for Standardisation for Quality Management, Certification and Accreditation of Competent Bodies & Laboratories (DIN NQSZ), the Technical Advisory Group of the German Electrical and Electronic Manufacturer's Association (ZVEI), and the German Society for Quality (DGQ).

Jens J. Dahlgaard is Professor of Quality Management at the Aarhus School of Business, Aarhus, Denmark. He was one of the founders of the European Masters Program in Total Quality Management and chairman of its Academic Board, and the Danish Quality Award. He was awarded the Chinese Friendship Award by the Aviation Industries of China for his contributions to education and research in China and for arranging the first international conference on Quality Management and Economic Development held in Zhengzhou, China, in 1997. An Academician of IAQ, Professor Dahlgaard is advisor to several companies embarking on the quality journey.

Ole N. Madsen is Administrator at the National Danish School of Social Work, Aarhus, Denmark, and works on several projects related to public sector quality management. He was formerly an Associate Professor of Public Quality

Management at the Aarhus School of Business. He has published several books and articles on subjects within the field of total quality management in public sectors.

Agnes H. Zaludova is CEO of QDS Associates, a consulting company for quality, dependability, and statistical methods. She has served as a university lecturer (1941–1945), research scientist, and consultant in applied mathematics at the National Research Institute for Machine Design, Prague (1946–1980) and in research laboratories of the CKD Engineering Corporation (1980–1990). She is the Honorary President of Czech Society for Quality and Honorary Member of European Organisation for Quality (EOQ). An Academician of the IAQ, she is also a member of the Royal Statistical Society (London), The Statistical Institute (The Hague), ASQ, and is serving as a representative of the Czech Republic in ISO TC 176 Technical Committee responsible for ISO 9000 standards, and the IEC TC 56 Technical Committee.

Basanta K. Pal is Honorary Visiting Scientist and Director of the Ascent Quality Services at the Indian Statistical Institute, Bangalore, India, where he was Head of the Institute and its Statistical Quality Control and Operations Research Division. He has been a teacher, consultant, and researcher for over 35 years in the field of statistical quality control and total quality management. His special interests include research into Taguchi methods and the statistical methods of problem-solving techniques. An Academician of IAQ, he is a Life Member of the National Institution for Quality and Reliability (India) and member, Indian Statistical Institute, Karnataka Branch, India.

Kenzo Sasaoka is Executive Advisor to Yokogawa-Hewlett-Packard (YHP) Limited, Japan, where he served previously as its President and Chairman of the Board before retiring. Under his leadership, YHP, Japan, won the Deming Application Prize for quality improvement in 1982, and the Ishikawa Prize for product development innovation in 1988. An Academician of IAQ, Mr. Sasaoka is past president of Japanese Society for Quality Control. He was awarded the famous Deming Prize for individual in 1996 for his valuable contributions in the field of quality control.

Lennart Sandholm is a management consultant and President of Sandholm Associates, a consulting and training institute in Sweden. He was for 10 years Corporate Quality Manager of Electrolux. He served as Adjunct Professor at the Royal Institute of Technology, Stockholm, Sweden, from 1989 to 1995. He has conducted seminars in over 40 countries and published many books and papers. An Academician of the IAQ, Dr. Sandholm is an elected Fellow of ASQ,

Honorary Advisor to the China Quality Control Association, Honorary Member of the Philippine Society for Quality Control, and Past President of the Swedish Association for Quality. He is the recipient of ASQ's E. L. Grant Award and Lancaster Award.

Miflora M. Gatchalian is founder and president of Quality Consultants International Inc., a Philippine-based quality management consulting company. Dr. Gatchalian's major research interests are in the areas of food supply quality control, statistical methods, sensory evaluation techniques, customer satisfaction measurements, and total quality management. She is Secretary General of the Asia Pacific Quality Organisation, a past president of both the Federation of Institutes of Food Science and Technology in ASEAN and the Philippine Society for Quality Control. Previously a United Nations consultant on quality, she is founding President of Philippine Association of Food Technologists and an Academician of IAQ.

H. James Harrington is a principal with Ernst & Young LLP and serves as their International Quality Advisor. He is also the Chairman of Emergence Technology Ltd., a high-tech software and hardware manufacturer and developer. Dr. Harrington has authored 10 books on various topics on quality, including *The Improvement Process, Poor-Quality Cost, Excellence—The IBM Way, The Quality/Profit Connection, Total Improvement Management* and *High Performance Benchmarking.* He is the former president and Chairman of the Board of ASQ and IAQ. The Harrington/Ishikawa Medal was named after him in recognition of his support to developing nations in implementing quality systems. He is an elected honorary member of seven quality professional societies and has received numerous awards and medals for his work in the field of quality management.

Table of Contents of Volumes 1 to 9
The Best on Quality Book Series

Volume 1
(1988)

Academician Hermann J. Zeller, Editor of Volumes 1 to 4
Published by Carl Hanser Verlag Publisher, P.O. Box. 86 04 20
8000 Munchen 86, Federal Republic of Germany

Chapter 1: Keynote at the Helm

- "Quality from the Viewpoint of the Chief Executive Officer," by Armand V. Feigenbaum

Chapter 2: Future Tasks on Quality

- "New Quality Technologies and Methodologies Required to Meet the Social and Industrial Needs of the 90s," by Dr. Walter Masing

- "Education for Quality Recommendations for a System of Integration of Quality in Education," by Jean-Marie Gogue

Chapter 3: National Activities on Quality

- "National Activities on Quality—The Example of the United Kingdom," by Norman Burgess and Roy Knowles

Chapter 4: Challenges of Today

- "Quality from the Very First, a Prerequisite for Competitiveness," by Hermann Zeller

Chapter 5: Excellent Experiences of the Past

Chapter 6: The International Academy for Quality (IAQ)

- "Middle Management Training—A Way to Improve Business Efficiency," by Alain-Michel Chauvel

Chapter 8: The Unforgotten Past

- "Quality Control—A Top Aid to Top Management," by Leslie E. Simon and Charles A. Bicking

- "Critical Analysis of Some Standardised Sampling Inspection Procedures," by Agnes H. Zaludova and Jan Havelka

Chapter 9: The International Academy for Quality (IAQ)

- Constitution (Updated April 1990)

- History

- The IAQ Quality Award

- Addresses

- Regional Distribution of IAQ Members (status January 1991)

Volume 5
(1995)

Academician John D. Hromi, Editor of Volumes 5 to 8
Published by Quality Press, American Society for Quality
611 East Wisconsin Ave, Milwaukee, Wisconsin 53202 USA

Section I: IAQ Project Papers

Chapter 1:   "The Deming Prize," by Yoshio Kondo, Hitoshi Kume, and Schoichi Schimizu

Chapter 2:   "American Quality Awards: Profiles in Excellence," by Raymond Wachniak

Chapter 3:   "The Malcolm Baldrige National Quality Award: Seven Years of Progress, 7000 Lessons Learned," by A. Blanton Godfrey

Chapter 4:   "Federal Quality Institute Awards for Federal Government Groups and Employees," by William A. J. Golomski

Chapter 5:   "NASA Excellence Award for Quality and Productivity," by Raymond Wachniak

Section II: Other Papers Dealing with Quality Awards

Section III: Localized Quality Awards

Volume 7
(1996)

Volume 8
(1997)

Volume 9
(1998)

Academician Madhav N. Sinha, Editor of Volumes 9 to 12
Published by Quality Press, American Society for Quality
611 East Wisconsin Ave, Milwaukee, Wisconsin 53202 USA

Index

Index